Effective Communication for Managers

Getting Your Message Across

CHRIS SIMONS AND BELINDA NAYLOR-STABLES

CASSELL

Cassell

Wellington House   PO Box 605
125 Strand   Herndon
London WC2R 0BB   VA 20172

© Chris Simons and Belinda Naylor-Stables 1997

British Library Cataloguing-in-Publication Data
A catalogue record for this book is available from the British Library.

ISBN   0-304-33120-1 (hardback)
                 0-304-33125-2 (paperback)

Typeset by The Bill Gregory Partnership, Polegate, East Sussex
Printed and bound in Great Britain by Redwood Books, Trowbridge, Wiltshire

Contents

About the Authors

Chris Simons MSc (Management), BEd, FRSA, FIPD, MIMgt

Chris Simons, Managing Consultant, founded the human resource consultancy organization Growth Through Training Group in 1985, her previous career having spanned thirty years of administration, marketing, personnel management, and lecturing in higher education.

Chris is involved in all aspects of management development training and consultancy, but she is particularly known for her work in the area of behavioural and interpersonal skills. Chris is an assessor and accredited consultant advisor for the Investors in People award, and is an associate consultant for HDL Training & Development Ltd for their Investors in People programmes, also tutoring and assessing their management development programmes which are accredited by Henley Management College.

She is the author of four computer training manuals published by Macmillan.

Belinda Naylor-Stables BEd, DipSofDoc, Cert ITD (Software)

Belinda Naylor-Stables, Training Consultant, has nearly twenty years' experience in project management and training.

After graduating from London University Belinda joined Pirelli Ltd in a management capacity. From there she joined the National Computing Centre where she was a Training Consultant for three years. For the last fifteen years her work has involved developing software training and management training for a wide range of organizations from small businesses to major international blue chip companies. She has also been involved in the development and use of Telecottages in the South West. Recently she has managed and co-ordinated the introduction of multimedia for the North London Consortium of Colleges.

She is the author of *Typesetting for Microcomputers* published by Quorum Technical Services.

Foreword

In the last 20 years we have had a plethora of books on all aspects of communication, many by people whose powers of *oral* transmission are very limited or those whose powers of communication depend on the skill of those who have programmed the computers.

Technology goes on extending the network of communication round the world and into space but in the beginning and in the end individual men and women must ensure that the human spirit, the human imagination is not strangled by this infinitely stranded network.

Of the many tutors, trainers and teachers I have seen at work with adults, Chris Simons stands out as one who combines the magnetism of the professional oral communicator with the skills of office and business management. She has her finger on the human pulse yet can use all her other fingers precisely on the equipment necessary for smooth and productive organisation.

Above all she realises that success in life – especially in the realms of leadership and management – depends on the inter-relationship of people: getting the best out of all types of individuals; creating the right attitude; picking up the cue – whether verbal or physical using time efficiently and economically; making the most of resources (remembering always that the greatest resources are *people*) and, through it all, remaining calm and optimistic.

The three parts of this book, *'How we communicate the message through: our behaviour; the written word; information technology'* demonstrates the range and versatility of Chris Simon's experience. How fortunate the men and women are who have the stimulus of her clear insight; her breadth of human understanding; her common and uncommon sense and her ability to judge strengths and weaknesses in organisers and organisations and to point the way to maximum efficiency.

I recommend this book to all who need a tonic injected into the nervous system of their business organisations, especially for managers at various levels whose success depends on securing the co-operation of those whom they guide and lead and the appreciation of those by whom they are engaged.

George Bernard Shaw in his typically ruthless style said:

> There are only two qualities in the world: efficiency and inefficiency; and only two sorts of people: the efficient and the inefficient.

If we believe it to be true (and this is a competitive world in which we live) then any student who takes this book, not just to a desk but to heart, will not only be efficient but warmly so.

Christabel Burniston M.B.E.
President of the English Speaking Board

Acknowledgements

I would like to thank Belinda Naylor-Stables for joining me in this project and contributing the final part of the book concerning the use of information technology in effective communication.

My grateful thanks are also due to Rosemary Helyar who has been a great inspiration and encouragement and has made many valuable suggestions which I have been able to incorporate into this book.

Chris Simons
1997

Introduction

'Why yet another book on communication skills?' I asked, when this book was suggested. Yet of some hundreds of supervisors and first line managers surveyed, a large majority said the book they would value most in this series would be on the subject of communication skills.

Perhaps it is not so surprising when you think about it, because making ourselves understood and understanding others is what has made the world go round since Adam and Eve. Most organizations would probably agree that communication needs to be improved. Misunderstandings and ambiguities appear to be much easier to communicate than the message we actually mean the receiver to receive!

What, then, is this business of communication? The first thing to say is that it is an art rather than an exact science. It is extremely creative and can be anything that the communicator wants it to be. The second thing is that it is a skill. Everyone is capable of it, just as we are all capable of singing or drawing. Some are better than others, however, and – as with any skill – we can always improve with training and practice. There is no optimum level for the skill of effective communication.

Notice the word 'effective' here – it is the key to good communication. It may seem easy to impart our explanation, information, instruction or whatever, but it is only **effective** when our message is received by the person or people we are addressing **and understood in accordance with our intended meaning**. More about this in part one of the book.

From the beginning of time, the human and animal kingdoms have made themselves understood. While on holiday in Greece a couple of years ago, I was watching a group of cats playing outside the dining room window of the hotel. I was fascinated by the ways in which they communicated with each other. The threatening stare with tails erect, the submissive closing of the eyes with lowered head, the furtive crouch with raised paw ready to pounce on a potential prey, the confident and trusting roll on the back . . .

The communication process can be summed up in one word – **behaviour.** We communicate by two main kinds of behaviour:

1 Verbal – that is, oral communication;
2 Non-verbal – the use of body language and other communication tools at our disposal, from the pen to the sophisticated equipment such as the word processor.

This book seeks to look at the way we communicate through behaviour. It is divided into three parts.

The first part considers **oral presentation** and includes:

- verbal communication and body language;
- telephone techniques;
- questioning techniques;
- communication in meetings;
- interviewing skills;
- speaking in public;
- preparing and giving formal presentations.

The second part involves **written** communication and includes:

- business letters
- internal memoranda
- reports
- written requirements for meetings
- business documents
- the presentation of information in graphical form
- personnel issues for line managers
- material for publication

The third part is an overview of business communication through **information technology** and includes:

- telephone systems
- pagers
- mobile telephones
- fax machines
- telex services
- video conferencing
- business television
- microfiche
- video
- computers and their applications
- CD-ROM
- computer networks
- Email
- Internet
- teleworking

My co-author, Belinda Naylor-Stables and I hope you will enjoy the book. We have tried to write it in such a way that you can dip into it wherever and whenever you choose, rather than reading it from cover-to-cover in one go. More than anything, we hope you will be a better communicator for having read it.

Chris Simons

PART ONE

HOW WE COMMUNICATE THE MESSAGE THROUGH OUR BEHAVIOUR

CHAPTER ONE

The Message – Spoken and Unspoken

IN THIS CHAPTER WE WILL LOOK AT THE FOLLOWING AREAS:

- communicating verbally;
- communicating through body language;
- listening;
- barriers to effective communication taking place;
- the behavioural psychology of communication.

Communicating verbally

As a supervisor, you are in a position of management. That means that your role is to get tasks done through people. How then, can your staff achieve success in the task you set them unless you clearly and unambiguously communicate your message in a way they can fully understand?

Someone once said:

75 per cent of oral communication is

IMMEDIATELY

lost/ignored/misunderstood.

The remaining 25 per cent is forgotten within weeks

A sobering thought!

Consider the following statement. Do you agree that it is a suitable definition of the word 'communication'?

> Communication
> is the process of conveying the wishes, ideas and feelings
> of one person to another.

Do you feel that there is something missing from this definition? You are right if you do, because I could happily speak to you in a foreign language which you did not understand, attempting to convey my wishes, ideas and feelings to you, but we would not get very far because you would not understand what I was talking about. Therefore, communication would not have taken place.

Communication must always be a two-way process. The 'receiver' must be prepared to listen and must understand the message in the way it was meant. A better definition might be:

> Communication
> is the process of conveying the wishes, ideas and feelings
> of one person to another
> and
> having them received in the way in which they were meant.

Some years ago, I taught business studies to young people in a further education college. It was the punk era and many of the students had hair all colours of the rainbow, with safety pins in various parts of their anatomy. Their interest in business studies was minimal most of the time and although they all dutifully looked at me and **appeared** to be taking in what I said, I am quite sure from the blank expressions that many of them were miles away from business studies in their thoughts. They were no doubt aware of my voice droning on but were they actually listening and receiving my pearls of wisdom? I doubt it!

My mother is profoundly deaf. If I were to speak to her without first getting her attention she would not hear me. She would not **receive** my communication. Therefore, I have to touch her or find some way of making her look at me so that she can make sure her hearing aid is switched on and/or be prepared to lip-read my communication. It is sometimes quite funny in our family because if my mother is watching television and someone wants to get her attention from the other side of the room, they wave an arm across her line of vision to communicate their need to speak to her. It occasionally resembles some kind of fantasy forest of prehistoric arm waving Simonssauruses.

The point about all this is that unless the person you are trying to communicate with is listening and prepared to receive your communication, you may as well not bother. The responsibility for the effectiveness of communication is that of the **sender**, who has a duty to check with the receiver that the message has been correctly heard and understood.

So often we take for granted that we are communicating effectively and when things go wrong we blame the receiver of our communication. Yet, when you think about the following 'six steps to dialogue' it is amazing that effective communication ever takes place at all:

Supposing I speak to you. We have –

1   What I think I say;
2   What I say in fact;
3   What you think I say.

(None of these are necessarily the same thing, of course, and already there are three chances for the communication to break down.)

As a result of what you hear (or think you hear) of my message, you then reply to me. We have –

4   What you think you say;
5   What you say in fact;
6   What I think you say.

If you think about this, it is amazing that effective communication ever takes place at all! Let me give you an example.

Recently, a local radio reporter telephoned me to say she would like to do a radio interview with me. I agreed and we arranged the date and time. She asked if it was possible to walk to my office from the station. I replied that it would take her about 10 minutes and proceeded to give her directions. When I had finished, there was a prolonged pause and she said uncertainly, 'You do mean the **radio** station don't you?' I had assumed she meant the **railway** station! (Never assume, by the way – I am sure you know the old adage 'To assume makes an ASS (of) U (and) ME'!)

We can analyze the above incident to see how the six steps to dialogue fit here:

Firstly, the reporter's request for directions to my office:

1   What she thought she said;
    The Reporter **thought** she had implied that she would be travelling from the radio station;

2   What she said in fact;
    She **actually** said could she walk to my office from 'the station';

3   What I thought she said;
    I **assumed** she meant the railway station;

Then my reply:

4   What **I thought** I said;
    As a result of my interpretation, I thought I gave her accurate directions from the station;

5   What **I said** in fact;
    I gave her directions from the railway station (but did not actually mention the word 'railway');

6   What **she thought** I said;
    The reporter thought I was trying to give her directions from the radio station!

Let us look a little more closely at the way in which dialogue takes place. We can analyze this into a cyclical flow diagram:

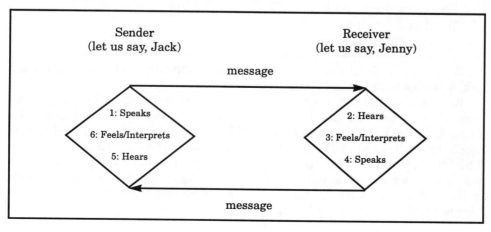

The above 'flow of dialogue' works like this:

Step 1 – Firstly, the sender (Jack) must ensure that the person receiving (Jenny) is 'switched on' and listening. Remember my mother mentioned earlier, who wears a hearing aid – she cannot 'hear' unless she is 'switched on'. The person to whom you wish to speak needs to be tuned in and giving full attention to what you are about to say. Jack therefore needs to give thought to getting Jenny's attention. He could, of course, say 'Heh you. . .' or something similar. He could speak to the air in the room, hoping the right person will tune in, but it is probably more successful to address Jenny by her name. He will also need to use an appropriate tone of voice and body language – we will look at that later.

Having got Jenny's attention, Jack now speaks to convey his message.

Step 2 – Jenny listens to and (providing she is prepared to do so) hears the message.

Step 3 – Whatever communication we receive, we feel something about it and we interpret its meaning.

Spend a little time pondering this point. Think about any kind of communication you receive: from a conversation, a letter, television or radio, newspapers and magazines. . .

Whatever message we take in, we feel something about it – happy, sad, upset, angry, satisfied, dissatisfied and so on. We also interpret the meaning of the message, often in the light of our own attitudes and prejudices if we are honest, or sometimes based on our previous experiences about the situation or the source of the message. At this point, too, the six steps to dialogue discussed earlier come into play because we may not 'feel' and 'interpret' in the way the communication was meant. For example, what I think you say may be quite different to what you meant, but I get the 'wrong end of the stick' and therefore **feel** something quite inappropriate. Hence, misunderstandings and ambiguities arise.

Step 4 – In the light of her own specific interpretation, Jenny may feel it necessary to reply to Jack. However, Jenny – who is now to become the sender of the communication – cannot assume that Jack is still 'switched on and receiving'. It may be necessary, therefore, to check on this before sending the reply message.

Step 5 – Jack, now the receiver himself, listens to and (providing he is prepared to do so) hears the reply.

Step 6 – He then feels and interprets something about the reply message. He may be amazed that his original message was interpreted in the way it was! Or, he may be pleased that the message was received in the way it was. Who knows!

As a result of Step 6, the cyclical flow of dialogue may be continued step-by-step into a full blown conversation (or argument!).

What a complicated business this subject of communication is, you are probably thinking. Exactly so! The fact that so much communication breaks down and is ineffective bears out this fact. That is why the skill of communication has not only to be understood in theory, but practised, practised and practised, again and again to get it right.

What do I mean by a skill? A skill can be defined as something we need to practise in order to learn it. We cannot acquire a skill merely by being told how to do it. Knowledge is different. I can tell you that the Battle of Hastings took place in 1066 (knowledge), but I cannot tell you how to ride a bike or swim. You have to take action yourself to practise the skill of riding a bike – theory is not enough. Likewise with communication skills. You can understand all the theory, but this does not mean that you are a good communicator and communication is one of the most important, basic management skills.

There is a fundamental need for clarity, simplicity and appropriateness of the message.

The most important thing to remember if you are the person originating the communication is that it is likely to go wrong!

Recognize that misunderstanding is a strong possibility and be alert for evidence of it.

It is up to you to check, check and check again that your message has:

- been received (not just listened to, but really heard);
- been understood;
- been interpreted in the way you meant it;
- been 'filed' in the receiver's mind in the 'right file' and any action required noted by them.

It is also up to you, the sender of the message, to ask whether any clarification is needed, further information required, and so on. The listener should feel they can test understanding of a message: 'You mean that. . .?' As a manager, it is sometimes frustrating that subordinates seem to need a great deal of explanation and clarification, but if you become impatient or make people feel humiliated by such aggressive remarks as 'Surely you understand that' (implying: 'you twit'!), they will just close up and try to undertake the task (or whatever result the communication requires) without the full facts and probably do it wrong anyway. This will ultimately be more frustrating for you and de-motivating for them.

But over and above all that we have said in this chapter so far, there are still further facts to be considered in oral communication. Not only are we concerned with the words we use, but two other important factors need to be considered:

- The way we say the words (tone of voice, emphasis and so on); and
- Our body language.

'IT'S NOT WHAT YOU SAY, IT'S THE WAY THAT YOU SAY IT'

Only a very small percentage of the impression you make on other people stems from purely verbal communication – that is, from the words you use. A much greater impact comes from your non-verbal messages, the most significant features of which are your voice and your body language.

Activity

To establish the significance of non-verbal communication, you are asked to estimate the percentage proportions used in an effective communication of:

- the actual words used;
- the way the words are spoken (voice pitch, tone, emphasis, volume etc);
- the body language used (stance, facial expression, gestures etc)

and complete the pie chart below.

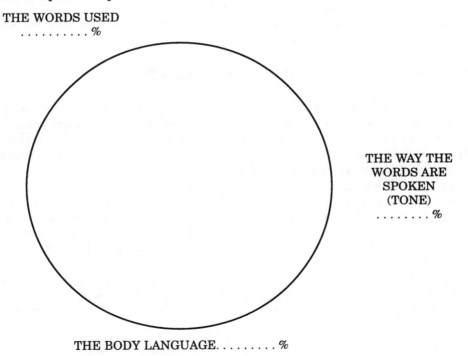

THE WORDS USED
. . . . %

THE WAY THE
WORDS ARE
SPOKEN
(TONE)
. . . . %

THE BODY LANGUAGE. . . . . %

(The researched answers to this exercise may be found at the end of this chapter on page 43).

Very often, we put the major percentage of importance on words (and indeed in written communication it is right to do so, but in this chapter we are concerned with oral skills). However, we should not minimize the importance of the way we say things (especially on the telephone, where – at least until we have video 'phones readily available – we are unable to use any body language to clarify our message). And just think how a change of emphasis can totally change the meaning of words:

> 'Will you come down **here** and have your breakfast?'
>
> or
>
> '**Will** you come down here and have your breakfast!'

We all have different voices – some attractive, some less so; some with regional or 'class' accents, some without. As long as we can be understood, these will probably not prevent effective communication. However, as Christabel Burniston puts it:[1] 'If you mumble, through embarrassment; put an edge to your voice, through tension; talk too much, through not considering your listener, your voice immediately makes other people tense and communication becomes much more difficult.'

More will be said about voice in chapter two when we discuss effective presentation.

Communicating through body language

There are numerous books on body language and its use in communication cannot be doubted. Some of the work that follows on body language is familiar in training programmes and has been used, with variations, by many trainers. I regret, however, that I have been unable to trace the original source and therefore cannot directly acknowledge the author. There are a number of different meanings and specific characteristics in the body language of different nationalities and cultures. In certain areas in India, for example, a nod of the head may mean 'No' rather than 'Yes'. In some countries, it is quite common and acceptable that men who are good friends can walk hand-in-hand. In other countries this is only accepted for women and mixed couples.

Body language falls into two categories: conscious and unconscious. Of conscious body language, perhaps the most obvious is the hand gesture.

Examples of conscious hand gestures:

- **a wagging, pointing finger:** accusing, threatening;
- **a raised, clenched fist:** angry, threatening;
- **a finger raised to the mouth:** Sssh;
- **a hand behind the ear:** I cannot hear you.

A further example of body language is posture. This is an interesting one because posture can display two signals. Where the person's words and thoughts tally, the body stance will tend to be in a straight line from head to toe. This is a 'clear signal'.

Where a person's thoughts and words are not in agreement, the body line between head and foot will in some way be broken or bent – a 'double signal'.

TYPES OF 'CLEAR SIGNAL'

Figure 1.1

This demonstrates adult, assertive behaviour with no hidden messages, manipulation or 'games' in the communication. It indicates that the person is feeling confident and happy about what they are doing or saying.

Figure 1.2

This person takes an forward sloping stance, wanting to dominate others or being emphatic in what they say, often using an aggressive hand gesture as above, or with arms 'akimbo'.

Figure 1.3

A person leaning backwards says they are not happy with their situation. They may be feeling defensive or submissive and are generally saying they do not want to be there!

TYPES OF 'UNCLEAR' SIGNALS

Figure 1.4

This bent position is saying 'I am saying this but I don't really mean it'. A salesperson giving exaggerated attention to a customer. Someone saying 'No' but not really meaning it until they say it using the posture of Figure 1.1.

Figure 1.5

The characteristic stooping posture of a person who is self-conscious about their height or figure. It is a mixed message because the person could 'stand tall' (Figure 1.1) in the sense that they are perfectly capable and intelligent people.

Figure 1.6

Some short or small people would like to appear bigger than they are. They unconsciously try to inflate themselves to feel important. (You also sometimes see this stance in managers who wish others to be aware of their status!)

EXAMPLES OF OTHER UNCONSCIOUS BODY LANGUAGE:

* **the eyes:** did you know that your pupils may dilate when your interest is aroused? Conversely they may contract to signify distrust, hostility and so on;

- **the shoulders:** raised shoulders illustrate tension, lowered shoulders indicate a relaxed attitude;
- **the head:** we tend to tilt the head to one side when we are interested or curious, raise it when we feel in control and confident, and lower it when we feel fearful, defeated and insecure.
- **the arms:** are they crossed in protection?
- **the legs:** people tend to cross their legs at the knee with the calf of the upper leg pointing away from the threatening scenario
- **the hands:** nervous movements, hands gripping the furniture, 'thumb clutching' clenched hands all communicate a person's true feelings, sometimes despite what they are saying

WHAT DO THESE FACES TELL YOU ?

Our faces are usually our most expressive feature. Even without muscular expression, you can tell something from the following drawings – the shape of the mouth and angle of the eyebrows are significant signs of moods and feelings such as anger, happiness, sadness etc.

Activity

The following activity is not original but the source is unknown. Write below each drawing below the feeling or mood you think best describes its expression. (Suggested answers at the end of this chapter on page 43)

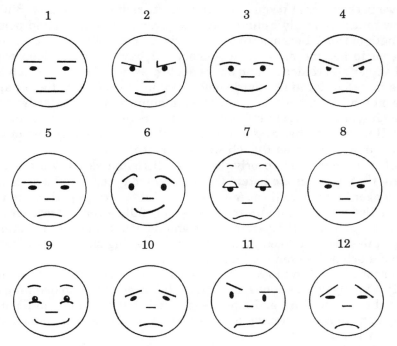

Figure 1.7:   *Moods shown by the face*

It is, of course, silly to interpret one body language sign in isolation. For example, crossed arms may merely indicate that a person is cold! If a person touches their nose, partly covering their mouth as they speak, it could be an indication that they are feeling anxious about what they are about to say, or it could be they have an itchy nose!

The whole body needs to be taken into account in order to assess a person's non-verbal communication. At least three or four signals need to be in place to read something significant and then within the situational context.

Listening

So far we have tended to concentrate on the skills of the person sending the message, but the person or people receiving the communication must also carry responsibility for the message getting across effectively. As we have said before, two people are involved in dialogue: the person speaking and the person listening. Therefore, we should be aware of the skills involved in listening. It should not be a passive thing but a participative activity. It is sometimes difficult to concentrate if we are not actually speaking, especially if we have a lot on our minds and on the whole, we are very bad at listening.

People often do not think of listening being a skill, but it is (look again at the description of a skill on page 18). Managers need to be good listeners, but most managers are so busy talking they do not always see their role as a listening one.

We probably take for granted the fact that we listen all the time. We may think we listen to what people say; we listen to radio or television. But I wonder how much we really **hear** ? Have you ever been with a blind person for any length of time? Because they are deprived of one of the major senses, the rest seem to become more acute somehow. I have a blind friend who is a gospel singer and composer and she is acutely aware of sounds which I merely take in as background – bird songs, running water, a rustle of paper, an indrawn breath, a cat gliding past. The communication that Marilyn takes in from such sounds, however minute, is a whole realm which I miss out on altogether. Her ears are her eyes and she has almost total awareness of what is going on around her even though she cannot see.

Most of us have very poorly developed listening skills. We are so busy **looking** that we forget to listen. Our society today tends to be a visual one. We no longer listen to radio as much as we used to (except perhaps in the car, when we listen with 'half an ear' as we – hopefully – concentrate on our driving). Some of us might listen to music and no doubt it is very meaningful to us, but unless we are keen musicians, our listening skills are probably not taxed as much as listening to language.

The spoken word on tape or CD is not as popular as music and I sometimes think it is partly because one has to give full concentration to listening **all** the time to the spoken word and most people find that extremely difficult to do. When you have been listening to the spoken word on tape or radio, have you experienced the sudden awareness that you have 'missed a bit' because your mind drifted off somewhere else? Then you have the annoyance of having to rewind the tape to a place that you recognize, or, if you are listening to radio, being reconciled to having lost part of the story. There is also, of course, the quality of the communication. Where the voice of the speaker is particularly soporific or indistinct, it is very difficult to maintain one's concentration.

Television, computers, videos, newspapers, magazines – so many **visual** communicators these days (and very good they are because we certainly take in more by watching **and** listening than by just listening). The down side to this, however, is that, while our eyes might be somewhat squarer, our ears seem to have shrunk!

It worries me that young people spend so much time taking in visual communication from television, computer and video games. Very few listen to non-visual broadcasts (except perhaps music which often is a general input of sound and does not require a discerning ear). Reading aloud to children seems to have declined in popularity which I think is a great pity, both from the reader's point of view and that of the child. You will probably think I am a real fuddy-duddy by now, but – as Gertrude Stein used to say – 'there it is'!

Another cause of our failure to listen properly is, I think, the stresses and pressures we face daily, particularly time pressures. So many of us seem to spend every day trying to fit 26 hours into 24. We are all rushing about madly, juggling all kinds of balls in the air at once in order to get through our 'To do' lists for the day. We find ourselves sitting in meetings thinking about what to have for dinner, or whether the car will start after work as we forgot to get the battery charged, or whether our secretary will still be in the office after the meeting because we forgot that letter we really **must** get out tonight.

Because most managers are stressed and hassled, they fail to listen properly most of the time. They are also being asked constantly to make decisions, sometimes quickly and without considered thought. This leads to them starting to formulate a reply to a message almost as soon as they start to receive it.

Dr Rachel Pinney, founder of the Creative Listening Technique[2] maintains that: 'a person cannot give full attention to what is being said to them at the same time as assessing it and framing a reply. . . Therefore true listening rarely occurs.' Rachel Pinney goes on to say that despite this obvious fact, we go on trying to communicate as though such 'double attention' were possible, which of course it is not. 'The result is failed communication,' says Dr Pinney, 'or at best, part communication in which the two speakers may hear some of what is said'.

Take a few minutes to think about this statement from Dr Pinney:

'When two people meet to discuss **one** subject, what usually happens is that they really discuss **two** subjects, the two viewpoints that each one is putting forward. If full understanding is to take place only **one** subject should be considered at any one time.'

We might **think** we are discussing one subject, but because we do not **listen** to each other, being too busy formulating our own reply in our thoughts, even if we are too polite to actually verbally interrupt the other person, we do not **hear** what the other person says and go shooting off on our own tack – possibly a totally different one from the person with whom we are supposed to be communicating. Back come the basic theories of Six Steps to Dialogue and the cyclical flow of Dialogue discussed earlier in the chapter.

Let's look at just a few words which might aid the listening process for us at work:

MAKE ROOM	DON'T INTERRUPT
STOP TALKING	ASK QUESTIONS
LOOK AND ACT INTERESTED	TEST UNDERSTANDING
REMOVE DISTRACTIONS	SUMMARIZE
PUT THE TALKER AT EASE	CONTROL YOUR TEMPER
EMPATHIZE	DON'T ARGUE OR CRITICIZE
BE PATIENT	DON'T BE SIDE-TRACKED
	OBSERVE NON-VERBAL CUES

ACTIVE LISTENING

You will see from this list that listening and hearing do not mean that you need to keep completely silent. **Active** listening means that you play a part in the listening process. If the 'listening' signals fail to appear, or, having appeared then disappear, the effect on the person doing the talking can be disconcerting to say the least. Sometimes on television, we see exaggerated listening skills from interviewers – all smiles and nods. They remind me of those nodding dogs people used to have in the back of their cars. Whilst these people do not necessarily provide good models to follow, they do illustrate the importance of active listening skills.

Some rules for active listening:

- **Look:** at the person to whom you are talking. Do not glare at them with a dominating stare, and do not look away too much (or look over their shoulder which is an infuriating habit that some people have) because the person will think you are not interested. One needs to be fairly sensitive about how much eye contact to make depending on the type of conversation. For example, if someone is revealing something to you which they are finding difficult, it is sometimes easier for them if you look away. If it is just straightforward conversation, you should aim to make eye contact somewhere around 60 per cent of the time.

- **A tip** If you find it difficult to look at someone's eyes, try looking at the bridge of the nose – it will appear to the other person that you are looking them in the eye.

- **Smile:** naturally and sincerely. Do not grin like a Cheshire cat, but smile enough to show that you are interested in the person and encouraging them to talk to you.
- **Nod:** encouragingly, showing that you are following the speaker's communication and understanding it. (But don't overdo it!)
- **Make affirmative noises:** by saying 'Uh, huh' or 'Mmmm', or making other general 'listening noises' such as little grunts to show you are listening.
- **Use verbal prompts:** to encourage further speech and empathize with the speaker. For example, 'That must have been very difficult for you': 'How did you feel about that?'
- **Ask questions:** to motivate the speaker to give information, test understanding, clarify any ambiguity and so on (more about questioning techniques in chapter three).
- **Recap and summarize:** to show that you are listening and help the speaker to 'hear' themselves. This is not a mere repetition of the speaker's word: it is the listener's own words, making it clear to the speaker that the message has not only been heard, but also

understood. An example might be: **Speaker:** 'The meeting yesterday was a total disaster!' **Listener:** 'I am so sorry nothing good came out of the meeting'. More about this in chapter three, because it is a particularly useful counselling technique.

The point about active listening is that you concentrate on the speaker and what is being said, seeking to make their communication as effective as possible. You do not, however, immediately override their message with one of your own!

LISTENING LEVELS

There are basically three 'levels' of listening. Even if we do try to listen effectively, we may listen on one level only, misunderstanding the hidden feelings or real intentions of the speaker. To listen properly, we need to be paying attention on all three levels:

> * the head level:
>   listening to the thoughts and words;
> * the heart level:
>   listening to the emotion and feeling behind the words;
> * the will level:
>   listening to the intention and meaning of the message.

Head level

This means listening to the 'thinking' part of the message. What are the thoughts behind the person's words? What does the pitch of the voice or the pace of the speech tell you? For example, is the person speaking quickly or slowly; in a calm, logical manner or in a rambling 'beating about the bush' fashion? Does the way they are speaking mean they are feeling nervous, aggressive, confident or what does it mean? Is the language used factual and clear or full of adjectives and description – perhaps to the point of exaggeration? What does this tell you about the person, or about the message they are conveying? (Remember what we said earlier in this chapter about unspoken communication through the way people say things and the body language they use.)

Heart level

Sometimes, we find ourselves listening at heart level – that is, we hear and empathize with the feelings of the other person and it is possible to let the emotion of the situation cloud our rational judgement. This may possibly be a good thing on occasion, especially for managers who tend to be the 'hard bitten' type, tending to neglect people's feelings altogether. It can be less successful if we allow people to manipulate the situation and appeal to our 'softer' nature. Some employees can be very good at using emotion to their advantage. We do, however, need to listen to the feeling behind what people say because it does give us a much clearer understanding of their intention. We 'hear' a great deal about what they are not saying by listening to the emotional content of the message.

Will level

This is perhaps the most obvious level of listening because it is where the intention and meaning of the message is conveyed. However, if we consider the number of times the communication process breaks down, we can probably see that we do not always listen carefully enough to the willing intention to receive the meaning of the message.

Activity

Try the following exercise:

> Listen to the radio (or television with your eyes closed!) and try listening on one level at a time. Listen, for example, to the emotion and feelings behind the words being said, ignoring totally any meaning, syntax and so on. Listen like this for about five minutes and then try writing down what you have heard. There may be 'feeling' words actually used in the speech, but try to find words to describe the emotion lying behind what is actually being said, including the feelings of the speaker at the time. For example, the speaker may be nervous or anxious – did you 'hear' that in the way they were speaking? Just give totally concentrated time to this one level of listening.
>
> When you have tried this, listen for another five minutes, this time on the head level. Then listen a third time on the will level. You will be surprised how difficult it is to restrict your listening to just one level at a time, cutting out the other two levels completely.

Barriers to effective communication taking place

There are so many barriers. Barriers to sending and receiving messages. Barriers to accepting and understanding messages.

There are all kinds of reasons why communicators cannot get their message across. They may have inadequate communication skills or they may find it difficult to relate to people. They may not have sufficient knowledge about the subject they are trying to communicate, or they may provide incomplete information. The list of reasons for failure or breakdown of the message getting across is probably endless.

Similarly people receiving the message may have inadequate listening skills, they may have difficulty in relating to the person sending the message, or they may just be feeling tired or 'out of sorts'. They may know little or nothing about the subject being communicated and feel threatened and fearful, or even angry.

Then there are specific problems such as:

- **Language:** Language can be a barrier where the message cannot be understood; this may be caused by:

    foreign speech or foreign accent;
    regional dialect;
    the use of jargon or technical language (for people who do not understand it);
    the use of words with unspecific meanings or with ambiguous meanings;
    waffle;
    giving insufficient information;
    giving too much information (unnecessary detail).

- **psychological aspects:** There may be personality or emotional problems which prevent the communicator giving a clear message and the listener hearing it. There may be a 'personality clash' between the two parties. Just a few of the many factors under the heading of psychological barriers might be:

    shyness;
    aggressiveness;
    the use of emotive words and words which exaggerate and provoke both the communicator's and the listener's own attitudes, opinions, bias and prejudices;
    the prejudging of a situation;
    feelings of threat, fear and inadequacy.

- **physical situations:** again, there are all kinds of problems which hinder effective communication taking place. Some of these might be:

    physical disability or illness
    practical issues such as poor timing,
    interruptions, distance from the person receiving the communication, a noisy environment, inadequate space, too hot or too cold. . .

Even if they have heard the communication, receivers may put up barriers to action, either consciously or unconsciously. These might include poor memory/retention skills or the inability to accept what has been said – perhaps through attitude or opinion, or simply because of the lack of knowledge.

As well as interpersonal difficulties, there are organizational barriers too. These include siting of offices, factories or departments across a wide geographical area, large buildings with offices on different floors, the sheer size of the organization making lines of communication long and complicated, cultural barriers, technological problems, bureaucratic nonsenses. . . Sometimes I think the larger the organization the more difficult it is to make effective communication and I once left the employ of a public sector organization because I just could not stand the bureaucracy any longer. Any decision or response took at least three weeks and often a lot longer, and seemed to include endless memos, letters and meetings.

Personnel within different departments who do not talk to each other are a common source of problems in an organization. It seems to me from the experiences I have had, for example, that sales departments and manufacturing departments notoriously fail to liaise. How often was I involved in sales promotions for a specific product, only to find that when the customer demand rose as a result, no-one had thought to tell the production department and there was an insufficient supply of stocks available. It never fails to amaze me how the seemingly simple lines of communication do not seem to be in place.

In the consultancy work which I do, I am often asked to do a 'health check' on an ailing business and recommend solutions for their problems. I nearly always find that communication, or the lack of it, is somewhere at the root of the problem. I recently worked in a company where a very senior head of department was, frankly, in the wrong job. The professional skills were certainly there, but management skills were not and the person hated the management part of their role. (How often people with sound vocational skills are promoted into positions of management with little or no supervisory or management training or even aptitude for management. Yet they are expected to manage people!) The manager in question was under great stress because he was not coping with his job and knew it. His subordinates were in a state of conflict because they liked the manager as a person, but were totally frustrated by his inability to manage. Because of the manager's lack of confidence in the role, he felt powerless and, unconsciously or consciously, was attempting to obtain power by withholding information from subordinates, keeping it all to himself. The consequence of this was that communication from top management was not being disseminated to the workforce but was 'sticking' at departmental manager level. Virtually the whole of the organization's problems stemmed from this one person and the total breakdown in communication because of him.

Activity

Try making a list of barriers to effective communication you have faced at work:

- Who has been involved and what caused the barrier?
- How did you overcome it?

It will be interesting for you to see if there is any pattern in the communication difficulties you have experienced. Maybe it will be between the types of people involved, either by personal issues such as gender, age or personality type, or by role or status. This may say something about you as much about the other person or organizational problem.

The difficulty may be an interpersonal one. For example, if you have been conditioned from childhood to fear authority, it may be that you feel unconsciously intimidated by people 'above' you in status, or people who hold a role which you see as 'authority' such as a lawyer, a bank manager, a hospital consultant and so on. You may feel confident with certain types of people but not so with others.

Or it may be that your problems lie in specific task areas. You may have had difficulties with arithmetic when you were young which could mean that anything to do with finance or numbers scares you. I was very poorly taught the subject of mathematics at school and was absolutely terrified of my teacher. For years, I thought I was hopeless in the whole area of finance, but when accountancy was included in a degree course I did in my late thirties, the teaching was good and I soon realized I was perfectly capable. I have had trainees on computer courses with me who have been literally shaking with fear as they have sat down at the machine for the first time, terrified by technology and quite convinced that they would be failures (which of course they were not).

When you have made your list, try sorting the problems into sections of difficulty. For example:

- barriers put up by yourself through lack of confidence etc;
- barriers with other people;
- barriers with technological areas;
- barriers through lack of knowledge or skill;
- barriers with written communication (see part two);
- barriers with certain subjects (finance, language . . .);
- practical barriers within the organization;
- any other barriers you can think of.

Then try making an action plan to deal with your barriers. An action plan is not a 'statement of intent' (for example, 'I will try to be more confident'), it is what it says it is – a plan for **action**: 'Booked on an assertiveness course on (date) to improve my confidence' . . .

Where there are barriers beyond your control, or those you do not know what to do about, try talking to your line manager or someone who can help and advise you about self-development or supervisory management training programmes.

It seems to me that there are far more barriers to effective communication than smooth paths. As I have said before, the important thing is to remember that your communication is likely to fall at the first hurdle and check, check, check again that it has been received and understood in the way that you meant it.

The behavioural psychology of communication

You will have realized from all you have read so far that a great deal of communication – good or otherwise – results from our behaviour. I touched on this aspect in the Introduction, but I do feel it is worth looking at in a little more depth.

The behaviour we choose to use gives us great power. Every aspect of our behaviour is perceived by other people in some way – in other words, we communicate something by everything we say or do. Do not underestimate the power of your behaviour. You can make or break someone by what you say or do. The power you wield as a manager in the way you behave (that is, communicate), can be thrilling or it can be devastating. We will be looking at the ways in which supervisors choose to motivate their subordinates in chapter three, but here I want to think about the reasons **why** we choose the behaviour we do.

I wonder if you have ever thought about the fact that you choose your behaviour? We probably do not consciously think 'I am going to behave in a certain way because I want to have a certain effect on that person' but that is in fact what we do. So why do we behave in the way we do?

Behavioural psychologists tell us that our actions, characteristics, attitudes, prejudices and so on result from the input we receive from the environment around us, our experiences, learning, situations, influences and so on. If this is so, then the way in which we perceive ourselves in our surroundings must have an effect on our behaviour. If you like, the 'input' we receive affects our 'output'.

Let us return briefly to the story about the departmental manager who hated managing people. This person, you will remember, felt powerless and therefore withheld information from his subordinates in order to see himself as more powerful. The point about this story is that the man was not powerless, but **perceived** himself to be powerless. In reality he wielded a great deal of power in the organization (to the detriment of the firm's communication effectiveness).

Our behaviour towards other people (be it action, words or whatever) results from the way in which we see ourselves. Therefore, before we can think about managing others, we first need to be aware of who we are – we need to look at our own self-concept.

OUR SELF-CONCEPT

The concept we have of ourselves underlies the way in which we communicate, through behaviour, with other people. If, for example, we feel shy, lack confidence and see ourselves as fragile and powerless, we are likely to communicate this to others in the way we behave. Or, conversely, we will try to cover up our feelings about ourselves and 'put on a front' of being macho and aggressive. If we are, by nature, a highly introverted person, we learn to compensate for this in order to cope with our shyness and one often finds people whose behaviour seems 'over the top' who are actually very shy people, whereas they appear to be very gregarious and extrovert.

I like to think of these two people within us as **Real me** and **Role me**. That is, we all have a 'real' self somewhere inside. With some people it is locked away and only their nearest and dearest know that self – sometimes not even then. Other people reveal their real self more readily to others. The 'role me' self is the person we communicate to the world through our behaviour – our 'front' if you like. We all have one, but with some people it is a thicker crust than others. At work, it is likely that people present their **role me** rather than their **real me**, and as managers it is important to remember that. Sometimes we receive communication through behaviour from the people with whom we work which we find difficult to cope with, but we need to think **why** the people are behaving in such a way – what is the **real** meaning behind their behaviour?

The behaviour we display to others – our overt behaviour, be it verbal or non-verbal, conscious or unconscious, is like the tip of an iceberg. It communicates what they cannot see of us – our covert self; that which is below the tip of the iceberg. Remember that the largest part of the iceberg is below the

Role Me

Real Me

surface and cannot be seen – our thoughts, feelings, attitudes, beliefs, values and so on. Sometimes, our communication is presented as a 'mixed message' because our different behaviour components do not say the same thing. For example, our verbal language may indicate that we are cross, but the words we use are diffused by a smile to 'soften the blow' of the chastisement.

It is so important to remember that our communication includes more than just the words we speak or the letters we write. **All** our actions which people receive communicate something about what we are thinking or feeling. Peter Honey[3] points out that 'Behaviour breeds Behaviour'. In other words, the behaviour we use in communicating with others is likely to produce similar behaviour in return. (A smile to another is quite likely to produce a smile in return.)

The way in which we see ourselves has important implications on the way we see others, and the way in which we perceive that others see us.

Activity

- Choose one word to describe yourself, for example: shy, confident, exciting, professional . . .
- It is very difficult to choose just one word, but the one you choose tells you something about the view you have of yourself.

A successful career may depend more on how you feel about yourself than your talents. I always tell my management trainees that if they really believe they can achieve something, they will. We have all heard much about the Power of Positive Thinking in the last few years, but it really does work.

The concept you have of yourself will also affect your relationship with others. For example, you might see yourself as a warm, friendly person, yet your staff might see you as a loud offensive bore!

To be effective in your communication with other people, you need first to have a realistic (note that word) perception of yourself.

So, if the behaviour we use in communicating with others is based on the concept we have of ourselves, how do we form this self-concept?

There are four steps to building our self-concept:

- self-awareness;
- self-acceptance;
- self-actualization;
- self-disclosure.

SELF-AWARENESS

We already have some understanding of who we are which is derived from previous experience and interaction with other people. For example, we may see ourselves as intelligent, warm, generous and so on.

Not all beliefs about ourselves are realistic. Sometimes we see ourselves as that which we would like to be. The American psychologist Carl Rogers talked about this as our 'ideal self' – that which ideally we would wish to be. A woman may choose to see herself as fragile, elegant, sophisticated and incapable of physical effort. This may be true, but it may not. It is, however, the woman's chosen self-image, so whether it is her actual self or her ideal self is irrelevant. She will then accept experiences which reinforce this image she has of herself but reject those which do not.

If people respond to the woman's behaviour in like manner, this will be a self-fulfiling prophecy. If, however, they refuse to accept her communicated behaviour and respond to her in a different way (for example, as if she is silly and vulgar), she will either:

- reject the people providing the negative feedback; and
- seek out people who provide her with a positive reinforcement (her 'friends'); or
- change her self-image.

Negative self-concept

If people see themselves as failures and have a negative, pessimistic image of themselves, they will begin to act the part. Negative feelings feed on themselves and become a downward spiral, gradually encompassing all the person's thoughts, actions and relationships. People with negative self-concepts tend to complain constantly and find it difficult to accept criticism.

Positive self-concept

People who believe in themselves and are confident about their ability to deal with problems, make decisions and feel equal to others have respect for themselves and expect it from others. These are people who are realistic in their assessment of themselves and can admit to a wide range of feelings, behaviours and needs.

Of course, few people have entirely negative or positive self-concepts, but how we see ourselves does have a bearing on our role as a supervisor.

Activity

Try thinking about the following questions:

- How do you view life?

   Is the world friendly, unfriendly, threatening, exciting or what is it? The way you answer this question will depend on whether you have a positive or negative concept of yourself.

- How do you want to be viewed?

   Do you see yourself as a 'born manager' and wish to see that image confirmed by others? You will try to live up to that 'label'.

- How do you view others?

   We tend to view others in comparison with our own values and 'labels'. For example, if we set store by good time keeping ourselves, we will probably also expect it from others.

- How do you interpret messages?

   Do you accept messages which confirm your self-image but reject those that don't by misinterpreting, distorting or ignoring them? Remember that we are likely to see people around us in terms of how they respond to our image of ourselves.

The key to effective communication is
getting to grips with a more realistic view of ourselves.

To become more aware of who we really are is sometimes a painful process. There are various activities available to help you to do this which are outside the scope of this book, ranging from travelling down the Nile to 'find' yourself (which seemed to be all the rage some years ago) to exercises such as describing yourself as a musical instrument, a food and an animal (which sounds ridiculous but is actually quite revealing, especially when you get other people to describe you in the same way and compare notes).

SELF-ACCEPTANCE

Having become aware of who you really are, rather than the person you would wish to be, the next step on the self-concept journey is to accept yourself. This does not mean being smug, complacent, and uncritical. But it does mean building on the qualities you are satisfied with and working to change or improve the ones you are not happy with. It is not easy, particularly when you are constantly being evaluated by others – parents, children, partners, colleagues at work and so on.

Activity

Try carrying out a SWOT analysis on yourself. Divide a piece of paper into four and list as many things as you can think of about yourself under the following headings:

STRENGTHS	WEAKNESSES
OPPORTUNITIES	THREATS

Under Strengths: list the things about yourself which you feel really positive about and know you can rely on. These might be personality characteristics such as 'confident' and 'kind'; they might be skills that you possess such as 'good listener', 'good planner' and 'fork lift truck driver', or they might be practical things like 'childminder available' or 'I have my own car with a clean driving licence'

Under Weaknesses: admit the problems you have which you need to work on. Areas of doubt leading to lack of confidence: 'I do not communicate well', 'I have no word processing skills'. . .

Under opportunities: list the things which you could make use of, perhaps openings for promotion or development. For example, 'supervisory training programme available next month', 'management post coming up in new branch' . . .

Under threats: write the things which you see as a threat to you as a person, your relationships, your career and so on which need to be overcome. For example, 'new line manager from next month – difficult to work with', 'inability to speak out in meetings means my ideas don't get heard'. Usually threats include fear; fear of being passed over, fear of job loss . . .

Now look at the list of Weaknesses to see if you can write some kind of action plan to turn them into Strengths. For example, 'lack confidence' might mean that you book onto an assertiveness training programme; 'lack of word processing skills' could mean that you get some training to learn how to use a word processor.

Then see if you can look at your list of Threats with a positive attitude to try to convert them into opportunities. A new line manager could provide an opportunity for you to pursue new ideas and do things differently, especially if you can speak with confidence in meetings because you have been on an assertiveness programme! If he seems difficult to work with, remember that the behaviour he uses to communicate to you is his 'role me'. Ask yourself *why* he is difficult – it is probably some deep insecurity within himself that makes him present that outward front. Sometimes it is easier to cope if you know what makes the person tick.

Accepting yourself as you are does not mean that you do not aspire to achieve greater things. To have an 'ideal self' means that we are constantly striving to develop and reach goals, which is great. We would be very boring if we had no ambition or aspiration. We shall talk more about motivation in chapter three. However, if your 'self' as you see it at the present time is too far away from your 'ideal self' you will become dissatisfied, discontent and perhaps even irrational. Think of people who suffer from anorexia, for example. They cannot perceive themselves as anything other than overweight, even though the scales tell them intellectually that they are not. Their 'ideal self' continually nags at them, telling them that they must not eat because they must lose weight. This is an irrational state of mind and is all bound up with (amongst many other factors involved) the person not being able to perceive themselves as they really are, let alone accept what they are.

So, it is fine to aim high and aspire to greater things, whether it be personal issues, career issues, hobbies or relationships. If we set ourselves too high goals or standards which we cannot achieve, however, we may enforce a negative self concept. Likewise, we sometimes try to live up to an image, always trying to be perfect, or always attempting to meet standards and expectations set for us by others (often our parents, however long ago) – trying to gain their approval.

Self-acceptance is really all about **self-esteem**. Do we really esteem the person whose name we bear? Do we feel good about ourselves? Do we like ourselves? It is all very difficult for most people, because most of us have been conditioned to put ourselves last and taught that it is wrong to think highly of ourselves.

Note for encouragement:

- **You have permission to think highly of yourself, to accept yourself as you are (warts and all) and to esteem yourself as a good, acceptable and worthy individual. Because you are! If anyone else thinks differently, that is their problem, not yours!**

SELF-ACTUALIZATION

This is a term used by Maslow in his motivation theory (see chapter three). I prefer to use the term 'Self-realization' because I think it is easier to understand. This step on the self-concept route involves growth and development motivated from within you. It is a willingness to pursue your 'ideal self' on your own, for yourself, to grow and to change because you think it is important.

This is where you take steps to make things happen for you. You know your potential and you actively pursue it. You know what you want to do, what is right for you and consequently you set and maintain personal standards and are open to new experiences.

I think it is very sad when I meet people who have closed minds to new experiences in life; people who are firmly stuck in their rut and are not prepared to tread outside it, often through fear.

Whatever age and whatever circumstance, life is a challenge and it can be very exciting. Change is hard for most people, but the one thing in life that you can be sure of is that there will be change. You can opt out if you choose and do a 'Miss Haversham' (do you remember the old lady for whom time had stood still since her fiancé abandoned her on their wedding day – Charles Dickens' Great Expectations?). Or you can push open the doors and see where they lead you.

Three things are necessary:

- you are willing to stand on your own feet and take responsibility for yourself, capitalizing on your strengths and opportunities;
- you trust yourself, believing you can make decisions for yourself;
- you are flexible, willing to broaden your interests by experiencing as much as possible; you are not afraid to change when you see certain decisions or alternatives are wrong for you.

SELF-DISCLOSURE

Having become aware of who you really are (as you are now, and as you see your 'ideal self'), having accepted that person as a perfectly good and capable human being, and having decided on how you are going to work towards 'actualizing' or developing towards your 'ideal self', you are now a pretty confident individual. The final stage towards a mature self-concept is how you are going to **reveal** yourself – and this is where communication through behaviour comes in again. You need to 'know yourself' well before you can disclose or reveal anything to others about your 'real' self. Usually we talk about ourselves to a friend or near relative. Revealing ourselves involves risk – difficult with people at work or with new acquaintances. There has to be trust before we can reveal our innermost thoughts and some people have had such trust betrayed in past experiences and their ability to disclose their true self has been damaged.

Yet, it is only by revealing our 'real self' to others that we begin to build trust. I am not suggesting that we should share intimate personal matters with colleagues at work, far from it. But the nearer we can get to communicating from our 'real self' rather than our 'role self', the more the rapport between us and our colleagues will be a trusting and worthwhile relationship.

The more we reveal about ourselves to others, the more we learn about ourselves. The more truth we are able to accept from others, the more accurate our self-concept will be. Many people spend a lot of time and energy trying to avoid becoming known by others. One might ask what they are afraid of:

- rejection?
- failure to gain reinforcement of their (faulty) self-concept?
- hurting someone else, or being hurt themselves?
- no-one being interested in them?
- or?

Are **you** afraid?

THE JOHARI WINDOW

Two psychologists, Joseph Luft and Harringon Ingham (hence the name of the concept), developed an interesting diagram to identify four kinds of information about ourselves that affect the way in which we communicate. Think of the whole diagram as representing your total-self as you relate to others.

	Information known to self	Information not known to self
Information known to others	OPEN AREA	BLIND AREA
Information not known to others	HIDDEN	UNKNOWN

This diagram shows four 'window panes', but you can change the size of the 'panes' according to your awareness and the awareness of others of your behaviour, feelings and motivations. Whilst the size of the panes can change according to different levels of awareness, the size will also be different for different people you interact with because your behaviour, feelings and motivations are different. Every relationship you have can be described by a Johari window and no two would be alike. Compare, for example, the types of window you would have with a work colleague and a member of your close family.

The open pane

The size of the open pane reveals the amount of risk you take in relationships. As relationships become deeper the open pane gets bigger, reflecting your willingness to let yourself be known (that is, to disclose about yourself). It includes things you know and are ready to admit about yourself.

The blind pane

This pane consists of all the things about you that other people perceive but that are not known to you! Others may see you as aggressive and unpleasant, while you see yourself as charming and affable. You may think your behaviour communicates confidence and self-assurance, but unconscious nervous mannerisms may convey to others your insecurities. The more you learn about what is in your blind pane, the more you will be able to control the impressions you make on others, understand others reactions to you and learn to mature and grow beyond them.

The hidden pane

This is where you exercise control. It comprises all your behaviours, feelings and motivations that you prefer **not** to disclose about yourself to others. It could include experiences that have happened to you that you do not want known, or particular aspects of your lifestyle that you prefer to keep to yourself.

The unknown pane

This is the area of your life where everything about you is unknown to you or to others. We all learn more about ourselves all the time (if we are prepared to), but this pane will always be there no matter how small it gets – it will never completely disappear. It includes all your future potential, as yet untapped resources, all that currently lies dormant. The more you interact and communicate with others, the smaller this pane becomes because without others, much of your potential may remain unrealized (or 'unactualized', to use the jargon).

The important thing about the Johari window is that the interdependence of the panes means that a change in the size of one will affect all the others. For example, if, while talking with a colleague, you discover something about yourself you never knew before (that therefore existed in the blind pane), this would enlarge the open pane and reduce the size of the blind one.

It can be rewarding and satisfying to add to your open pane, but it can be very painful too. It also involves some risk. Discretion is sometimes called for, because an inappropriate disclosure can be damaging whether you are giving or receiving it. You need to be sure about the 'safety' of your environment and the possible consequences before you try to empty hidden and blind panes into your open pane.

OUR EGO STATES

At this point, I think it is worth a look at the way in which we inter-relate with each other by using behaviour patterns. By this I mean the patterns which were recorded by our brains during infancy and childhood through all the feelings and experiences we were exposed to. These patterns are observable as three distinct modes of behaviour – ego states – which considerably affect our communication style and its effectiveness.

We all have three ego states:

- Parent;
- Adult; and
- Child.

It is interesting to observe the way in which each mode of behaviour causes us to change our communication style.

Parent

Whether or not we are physical parents, we all have a part of us which is a 'parent'. To complicate the issue, the school of Transactional Psychology says we are two kinds of parent:

- the nurturing parent;
- the controlling parent.

- **The nurturing parent** – the part of us that:

   encourages, praises, motivates, protects, loves, smiles, is concerned for others;

   uses words like 'good', 'nice', 'well done'

- **The controlling parent** – the part of us that:

   criticizes, disciplines, moralizes, judges, makes rules and regulations, is disapproving and finger wagging;

   uses words like 'bad', 'should', 'ought', 'don't', 'must'

This is not to say, of course, that the controlling parent is all bad, because we would probably all agree that rules and discipline are necessary. If you think about management styles, however, you will be aware of the kind of manager who motivates by kindness and caring, and the manager who drives by fear.

Child

Again the child in us divides into two:

- the natural child;
- the adapted child.

- **The natural child** – the part of us that is spontaneous, has fun, is creative and imaginative, loves and trusts, is curious and enquiring, is selfishly hedonistic, is free and easy and joyful; uses words like 'fun', 'want', 'mine'. In other words, the natural child in us is the person we were born with before the influence of experience caught up with us and we became
- **The adapted child** – a little child learns that certain behaviour is acceptable and other behaviour is unacceptable; he or she learns to behave in a certain way in order to gain a certain response from others. Thus we 'adapt' our natural child to respond to people and situations around us. We sometimes see this child in adults through fear, anger, rebelliousness, manipulation and 'game playing', trying to get one's own way, pouting, whining, aggressive or submissive behaviour, with the use of words such as 'can't', 'won't', 'please', 'thank you'.

From the last three words above you can see that some of our learned experiences make for living in society a little easier!

Adult

- **The adult** – Sigmund Freud maintained that the adult ego state was a state of maturity which held in balance the child-like instinctive impulse state (which he called the ID) and the controlling parent-like punitive conscience (which he called the Super-ego). This state of maturity is nothing to do with age, but rather maturity of personality. The adult ego state is one of rationality and assertive behaviour, which can plan, make decisions, give and receive information, evaluate, make sound judgements, set goals and targets, reasons. The adult is confident and remains calm, is straightforward in communication, does not manipulate or play 'games'

The ego states play an important part in communication because they have a considerable effect upon the way in which we relate to others:

- whether we are concerned with our own goals at their expense and always have to 'win';
- whether we are frightened of upsetting or hurting others, or need to gain their approval;
- whether we are concerned with getting a job well done, but at the same time encouraging others and helping them to achieve their own goals.

We need to examine our **motives** in behaving towards others in the way we do. **Why** do we need to beat others? **Why** do we need to always succeed? **Why** do we need the approval of others? And so on.

I remember when I was first at college, I was not satisfied with anything less than an 'A' for an essay. I thought that I was setting myself high standards and surely there is nothing wrong in that. One day, I was feeling particularly despondent because I had worked really hard on a particular piece of work and the tutor had given me a 'C'. OK it was a pass, but 'C' smacks of 'satisfactory' as opposed to 'excellent'. A wise old friend said to me 'I think you need to examine your motives as to why you always need to get an 'A' for your work.' I remember being most offended at the time, but when I thought about it afterwards, my motives were quite revealing (if uncomfortable).

Of course, there is nothing wrong with high standards, but if we always need to be top because we cannot bear our status to be threatened, perhaps we need to examine our motives for our behaviour. As managers, you are communicating daily with subordinates in all kind of ways. Are you the kind of manager who gets to the top and pulls the ladder up behind him? Or are you a manager who is delighted when subordinate staff you have nurtured and encouraged go on beyond you?

Think about this for a moment:

What motivates you to behave in the way that you do when communicating with:

- your subordinates?
- your superiors?
- your peer group ?

Bearing in mind all that we have said in this chapter about communication and the important part our behaviour plays, behaviour that is based on our underlying attitudes, prejudices, values, beliefs and feelings, before we move on to the next subject, try the following activity as a summary to the chapter.

Activity

Interpersonal Communication Inventory

I do not know who devised the following questionnaire, but it is a useful exercise, providing you with an opportunity to make an objective study of patterns of communication in your interpersonal relationships. It will enable you to better understand how you present and use yourself in communicating with people in your daily contacts and activities. You will find it both interesting and helpful to make this study.

COMMUNICATIONS INVENTORY

DIRECTIONS

- The questions refer to persons other than your family members or relatives.
- Please answer each question as quickly as you can according to the way you feel at the moment (not the way you usually feel or felt last week).
- Please do not consult anyone while completing this inventory. You may discuss it with someone after you have completed it. Remember that the value of this form will be lost if you change any answers during or after this discussion.
- Honest answers are very necessary. Please be as frank as possible, since your answers are confidential.
- Use the following examples for practice. Put a tick (✔) in one of the three boxes on the right to show how the question applies to your situation.

EXAMPLE

	Yes (usually)	No (seldom)	Sometimes
Is it easy for you to express your views to others?	✔	☐	☐
Do others listen to your point of view?	☐	☐	✔

- **The Yes Column:** is to be used when the question can be answered as happening most of the time or usually.
- **The No Column:** is to be used when the question can be answered as seldom or never.
- **The Sometimes Column:** should be marked when you definitely cannot answer 'yes' or 'no'. Use this column as little as possible.

- Read each question carefully. If you cannot give the exact answer to a question, answer the best you can but be sure to answer each one. There are no right or wrong answers. Answer according to the way you feel at the present time. Remember, do not refer to family members in answering the questions.

COMMUNICATION – INVENTORY

	Yes (usually)	No (seldom)	Sometimes
1 Do your words come out the way you would like them to in conversation?	☐	☐	☐
2 When you are asked a question that is not clear, do you ask the person to explain what they mean?	☐	☐	☐
3 When you are trying to explain something, do other persons have the tendency to put words in your mouth?	☐	☐	☐
4 Do you merely assume the other person knows what you are trying to say without explaining what you really mean?	☐	☐	☐
5 Do you ever ask the other person to tell you how s/he feels about the point you may be trying to make?	☐	☐	☐
6 Is it difficult for you to talk with other people?	☐	☐	☐
7 In conversation, do you talk about things which are of interest to both you and the other people?	☐	☐	☐

	Yes (usually)	No (seldom)	Sometimes
8 Do you find it difficult to express your ideas when they differ from those around you?	☐	☐	☐
9 In conversation, do you try to put yourself in the other person's shoes?	☐	☐	☐
10 In conversation, do you have a tendency to do more talking than the other person?	☐	☐	☐
11 Are you aware of how your tone of voice may affect others?	☐	☐	☐
12 Do you refrain from saying something that you know will only hurt others or make matters worse?	☐	☐	☐
13 Is it difficult to accept constructive criticism from others?	☐	☐	☐
14 When someone has hurt your feelings do you discuss this with them?	☐	☐	☐
15 Do you later apologize to someone whose feelings you may have hurt?	☐	☐	☐
16 Does it upset you a great deal when someone disagrees with you?	☐	☐	☐
17 Do you find it difficult to think clearly when you are angry with someone?	☐	☐	☐
18 Do, you fail to disagree with others because you are afraid they will get angry?	☐	☐	☐
19 When a problem arises between you and another person, can you discuss it without getting angry?	☐	☐	☐

	Yes (usually)	No (seldom)	Sometimes
20 Are you satisfied with the way you settle your differences with others?	☐	☐	☐
21 Do you pout and sulk for a long time when someone upsets you?	☐	☐	☐
22 Do you become very uneasy when someone pays you a compliment?	☐	☐	☐
23 Generally, are you able to trust other individuals?	☐	☐	☐
24 Do you find it difficult to compliment and praise others?	☐	☐	☐
25 Do you deliberately try to conceal your faults from others?	☐	☐	☐
26 Do you help others to understand you by saying how you think, feel and believe?	☐	☐	☐
27 Is it difficult for you to confide in people?	☐	☐	☐
28 Do you have a tendency to change the subject when your feelings enter into the discussion?	☐	☐	☐
29 In conversation, do you let the other person finish talking before reacting to what she says?	☐	☐	☐
30 Do you find yourself not paying attention while in conversation with others?	☐	☐	☐
31 Do you ever try to listen for meaning when someone is talking?	☐	☐	☐
32 Do others seem to be listening when you are talking?	☐	☐	☐

	Yes (usually)	No (seldom)	Sometimes
33 In a discussion, is it difficult for you to see things from the other person's point of view?	☐	☐	☐
34 Do you pretend you are listening to others when you are not?	☐	☐	☐
35 In conversation, can you tell the difference between what a person is saying and what he may be feeling?	☐	☐	☐
36 While speaking, are you aware of how others are reacting to what you are saying?	☐	☐	☐
37 Do you feel that other people wish you were a different kind of person?	☐	☐	☐
38 Do other people understand your feelings?	☐	☐	☐
39 Do others remark that you always seem to think you are right	☐	☐	☐
40 Do you admit that you are wrong when you know you are wrong about something?	☐	☐	☐

INTERPERSONAL COMMUNICATION INVENTORY – SCORING KEY

INSTRUCTIONS

Look at how you responded to each item in the inventory. In front of the item write the appropriate score from the table below.

e.g. if you answered 'Yes' to No 1 you would score 3 points.

When you have scored each item, total the scores at the end of your questionnaire.

SCORE TABLE

	Yes	No	Sometimes		Yes	No	Sometimes
1	3	0	2	21	0	3	1
2	3	0	2	22	0	3	1
3	0	3	1	23	3	0	2
4	0	3	1	24	0	3	1
5	3	0	2	25	0	3	1
6	0	3	1	26	3	0	2
7	3	0	2	27	0	3	1
8	0	3	1	28	0	3	1
9	3	0	2	29	3	0	2
10	0	3	1	30	0	3	1
11	3	0	2	31	3	0	2
12	3	0	2	32	3	0	2
13	0	3	1	33	0	3	1
14	3	0	2	34	0	3	1
15	3	0	2	35	3	0	2
16	0	3	1	36	3	0	2
17	0	3	1	37	0	3	1
18	0	3	1	38	3	0	2
19	3	0	2	39	0	3	1
20	3	0	2	40	3	0	2

How did you score ?

- 0 to 40 You have a low sense of self-awareness; your interpersonal skills need quite a bit of development;

- 41 to 59 Your sense of self-awareness is fairly low. You may find difficulty in some areas of interpersonal relationships; you need to identify areas where you find communication difficult and do some work on them;

- 60 to 79 You have a fair self-concept of your interpersonal skills. There may be a few areas of communication where you need to do some work;

- 80 plus You have a good understanding of how you interact with others and are an effective communicator. Build on your strong areas of communication skills.

The researched answers to the Proportion of Communication pie chart exercise on page 9 are:

- the words used – approximately 7 per cent
- the way the words are spoken (tone) – approximately 38 per cent
- the body language – approximately 55 per cent

This means that your pie chart should look something like this:

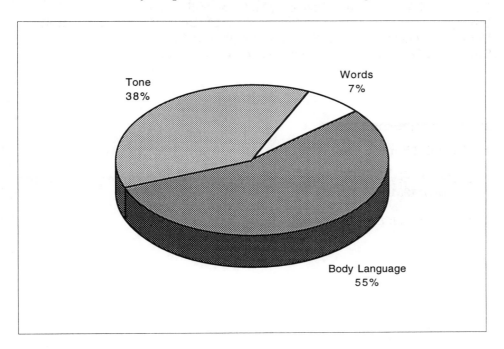

The suggested answers to the moods and feelings expressed by the facial drawings on page 13 are:

1	indifferent	7	tired, lethargic
2	hostile, sarcastic	8	a little cross
3	happy	9	pretending happiness
4	very angry	10	very sad, distressed
5	sad, sullen, surly	11	doubting, sceptical
6	naively happy, childish	12	deep sorrow

BIBLIOGRAPHY

For further reading:

Berne, E., *Games People Play*, Penguin, 1964
Berne, E., *I'm OK, You're OK,*
Burniston, C. & Parry, J., *Direct Speech*, Hodder & Stoughton, 1987
Honey, P., *If Looks Could Kill*, Video Arts, 1986
Honey, P., *Solving People Problems*, McGraw Hill, 1980
Pinney, R., *Creative Listening*, 3rd ed. A to Z Printers & Publishers, 1981
Rogers, C., *On Becoming a Person*, Constable, 1961
Storr, A., *The Integrity of the Personality*, Pelican, 1960

1   Christabel Burniston and John Parry, *Direct Speech,* Hodder and Stoughton, 1987

2   Rachel Pinney, *Creative Listening*, A to Z Printers and Publishers Ltd, 3rd Edn (revised), 1981

3   Peter Honey, *If Looks Could Kill*, Video Arts, 1986

CHAPTER TWO

Effective Presentation

IN THIS CHAPTER WE WILL LOOK AT THE FOLLOWING AREAS:

- Preparing your presentation:

    the objective;
    know your audience;
    collect and arrange your material;
    the structure of your presentation;
    your notes;
    visual aids.

- Making your presentation:

    style;
    voice;
    breathing;
    body language in presentation;
    use of language;
    managing your presentation.

- A postscript for the big day itself.

Having considered behaviour and how it affects our attitude towards communication with others, together with some of the techniques for communicating verbally and non-verbally, we now turn to more formal communication – that of speaking in front of a group of people or presenting a topic in public.

Most people are quite terrified when they tackle this subject, but as with all good communication, it comes down to a few basic techniques backed up by a lot of confidence coming from positive thinking and belief in oneself. We talk about some of the techniques in this chapter, but good presentation comes from experience and practice (like any skill) –the more you do it, the easier (and hopefully better) it gets.

A few basics to start with:

- don't expect to get it right the first time you do it;
- don't worry if you get 'butterflies'; a few nerves are not necessarily a bad thing – they keep you on your toes;
- do prepare thoroughly;
- do rehearse your speech or presentation beforehand, preferably looking in a mirror;
- don't write your material in full prose, you will read it out if you do and there is nothing more boring.

Perhaps the most important point above is to prepare thoroughly. I cannot stress enough the importance of preparation. To really know what you are doing and what you are going to say is a great comfort and confidence booster. It stands you in good stead when you rise to speak and suddenly feel the spotlight upon you. Your throat goes dry, you cannot remember a word, your breath seems to stop altogether and the panic hits you! You have, however, thoroughly prepared your opening lines and you hear yourself saying them. The sound of your voice in the 'air' will give you confidence and away you go, just using your notes as trigger points because you have already planned what you are going to say. Let us then look at preparation.

Preparing your presentation

Whether you are giving a formal presentation in public, leading a team meeting, briefing staff or talking to clients, the key to success is in your **preparation**. Let us consider what is involved:

OBJECTIVE

First you need to be very clear about what you want to achieve. Are you informing, persuading, instructing, explaining, selling – or any combination of these? It is essential that you know what you want to have achieved by the end of your presentation and it is a good idea to commit your objectives to paper. (If you are not clear, your audience won't be either.)

Sometimes it seems easy to set down a subject which you wish to talk about, but one of the main faults of presenters is to have too broad a subject title which means they waffle and are vague. You need to home in on the precise part of your topic which you intend to cover, and you need to bear in mind the time you have in which to speak – we will cover the ratio of how much you need to fill the time later on.

I was once asked to speak at a conference about the success (or otherwise) of the Equal Opportunities Act. I asked how long the organizers wished me to speak for and was told 40 minutes. Now, I could have spoken about the pros and cons of the Equal Opportunities Act for three days, so I asked for a more concise brief – what part of the Act did they wish me to cover?

You get the idea. You know a great deal about your subject, otherwise you would not be speaking about it, but the old saying 'You cannot tell anyone everything about anything' comes into play here. You must be ruthless in defining as concisely as you can the objective/s you wish to cover in the particular talk for which you are preparing and you must be clear whether you are seeking to provide your audience with information, training or whatever.

Supposing your subject is the painter Monet, you can quite simply write down something like:

The objective I intend to achieve is:

To entertain the audience with information about:

a)   Monet's early life;
b)   His time at Giverny;
c)   The water lily paintings.

All your preparation thereafter will be confined to these specific objectives and you will not be tempted to try to cover all aspects of Monet's life and work which would come across as waffly and ill-defined and would take you at least a week to do any justice to at all.

**You must be absolutely clear on your objective/s for
your talk and so must your audience**
(see Introduction on page 76).

KNOW YOUR AUDIENCE

It is a good idea to know as much as possible about the audience you are going to address because you can prepare accordingly. For example:

- How many are there likely to be?
- Who are they?
- Why are they there?
- What do they want from the presentation?
- Will they be enthusiastic, interested, hostile, neutral?
- How much do they know about the subject already?

It is certainly helpful to know why the audience is there; for example, have these people been 'sent' or are they there of their own accord? This often has a bearing on their attitude towards you before you even start. It is lovely to have a warm, receptive audience, but there will probably be times when you face a defensive and possibly even hostile one and it is as well to be prepared. Do you know the people who are likely to be there or will they be strangers? This may have a bearing on the tone you take and how formal or informal your talk will be.

> **The more you know about your audience,
> the better the rapport you will be able to build with them.**

COLLECT AND ARRANGE YOUR MATERIAL

There are two steps to this one:

a) Assemble your material

Bearing in mind your objective/s, assemble all the material you can find. Brainstorm all the possible things you might talk about and get them down on paper. Some people like to make a 'list' at this stage, others find that this prioritizes things at the top of the page, so they prefer to make a spidergram:

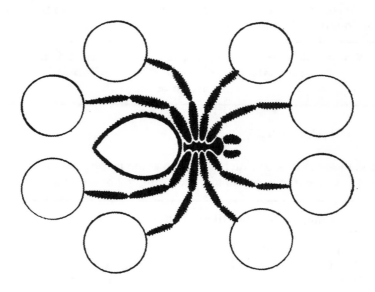

This is the stage where you research, check your facts, gather together all your material, using only very rough notes.

When you've done this, go through your notes and decide what the KEY points are in the light of your OBJECTIVE/S. These will be the points which you will work on in the next stage. Remember that most people can only take in perhaps three key points from a presentation. What three points would you like your audience to remember?

b) Sift and sort

The second stage of arranging your material is to review your rough notes and ruthlessly discard anything which is not strictly relevant (always bearing in mind your objective/s).

One of the most useful tips I know at this stage is to sort your material into two categories:

- need to know;
- nice to know.

'Need to know' are key points which you cannot afford to miss out. 'Nice to know' are anecdotes, stories – interesting tit-bits you can use if time is dragging, but can happily leave out if you are short of time. The secret is to write your notes in two colours – one for the 'needs' and one for the 'nices'. If, for example, your time is passing too quickly and you have to cut something out, you can glance at your notes, skip the next lines written in black (assuming your 'nices' are in black) and go straight to the next red point (the 'need to know' points). This saves you having to spend time with your head down in your notes trying to decide what you can leave out. It also gives you the peace of mind that you will not be missing out anything vital.

Conversely, if you find time is dragging, glance at your notes to pick up a 'black' point and launch into an entertaining anecdote, or give a role play exercise if you are training, or whatever is relevant to the situation.

**Sift and sort your mass of rough notes into logical,
workable material, with separated
'Need to know', and
'Nice to know' points.**

THE STRUCTURE OF YOUR PRESENTATION

Now consider your reviewed notes to make sure they directly support your key points. Have you included practical examples that relate to your audience? Above all, are you still sticking to your objectives?

Before you can write your final notes, you need to consider timing. The structure of any presentation will have similar shape and include an Introduction, a Main Content section and a Conclusion.

The opening and closing sections are very important and will probably be remembered by your audience more than the middle.

It is useful to remember the old maxim:

- **Tell them what you're going to tell them** (in the introduction to your presentation);
- **Tell them** (in the main content section);
- **Tell them what you've told them** (in the concluding summary).

Introduction

This should state the purpose of your presentation and relate to your audience's needs and interests. You need to think of a good opening line. If you are the kind of person who has a ready wit (you are indeed fortunate), then you might try a joke, but can I make a plea that if you are not (and most of us are not), then don't try!

I knew one lady who stood up to speak and fell over the flip chart stand. She certainly had everyone's attention! Now she does it 'accidentally on purpose' at the beginning of all her talks. I am not advocating that, but you need to find an 'attention getter' which works for you and suits your personality.

Introduce yourself, if the audience does not already know you. There may be 'housekeeping' things to talk about such as fire regulations, location of lavatories, arrangements for food and so on; if so, these come into the introduction. State the objectives for your talk and what you hope will have been achieved by the end of it. You may choose to take questions as you go along, or you may wish your audience to keep any questions until the end of your talk. You can indicate this in the introduction.

When preparing your Introduction, ask yourself questions such as:

- What sort of opening will I have (factual, a quotation, a question, a story, something practical. . .)?
- Can I cope with a joke that misfires? (If in doubt, don't!)
- Can I build any benefits to my audience into the opening?
- When do I want to take questions?

Main content

This section is where you give your audience the main information and this should be ordered logically and clearly into your key points. Make sure that you explain anything which might be misunderstood, including 'jargon' and abbreviations. (It is very easy to go wrong here because you are talking about something which you know very well and tend to slip into language which you use every day, often including words and phrases which at the best could be ambiguous and at worst could have no meaning at all for your audience.)

Throughout the main content section, remember your 'Need to know' and 'Nice to know' information.

Sometimes, you will have a part of your presentation which is almost separate from the main content and that is a **Consolidation** section.

This is used to reinforce the main content by re-stating it in a different way. It is important to remember that **no new information** is given in the consolidation.

For example, when I am training in counselling skills, I give a theoretical input first (main content) and I then consolidate by showing a video which reinforces all that I have said (with visual impact as well as oral), and I further consolidate by asking the participants to take part in role play exercises. The video and the role play do not provide any new information, but they reinforce that which has already been given to them.

The consolidation may be literally separate as I have outlined, or it may be interwoven with the main content, perhaps by a discussion or question and answer session at the end of each key point.

> **A Consolidation section is useful to reinforce what you have said in your Main Content because it is unlikely that your audience will remember anything they hear just once.**

One last point in the 'main content' section. People often ask where to pitch the level of knowledge in an audience of mixed experience. If you can avoid this happening, do so, because it is always difficult, but if you cannot, then my advice is to pitch slightly lower than middle. If you pitch at the people who have little or no knowledge about the subject, you will bore the 'experts' in the audience. If you pitch at the latter group, the former will not understand anything.

You can help the situation a little by explaining the problem in your introduction, stating that you will try to keep the people with little or no knowledge in the picture as much as possible, but suggesting they come to you afterwards if they would like clarification. You can, if you wish, suggest they ask a question if they don't understand, but I doubt that they will, because people are always afraid of looking silly and always think they are the only one who doesn't understand (mistakenly, actually). You should be 'reading' people's understanding of your communication by watching eyes, body language and so on. When people don't understand, they tend to look down, afraid to meet your eyes.

Another way of handling the situation is to suggest that the 'experts' take the question: 'Mary, this is your field – would you like to take Peter's question?' This not only makes Mary feel good, but also gives you breathing space.

Speakers often assume a basic level of knowledge in their audience which just is not there. They think they will patronize their audience if they give them the basics. If you do not know the level of your audience's knowledge, it is probably better to give them information which to you may seem obvious, but which to them may be quite new and unless they have it, the rest of your presentation will be lost. I always remember being present at a word processing lesson where the lecturer assumed her class had a basic knowledge and tried to teach how to move a paragraph from one place to another. In fact, the students did not even know how to switch the machine on and get into a typing area.

It is true that there is a danger of patronizing your audience. Just because they don't know much about the topic you are presenting (otherwise they wouldn't be there), do not assume that they are less intelligent than you. I hate presenters who 'talk down' to their audience, don't you? There is a lovely quote which puts this into perspective:

'Never overestimate your audience's knowledge, but never underestimate their intelligence.'

C.P. Snow

Your Conclusion

The aim here is to summarize by reiterating the objectives you gave in your introduction. You need to do this in such a way that you leave a long-lasting impression with your audience. Take care not to keep giving signals of your close:

People often ask me if 'Questions' should come before or after the close. I suppose there is no hard and fast rule about this, but my own feeling is that it is a pity to make a superb close with a real punch-line ending and then rather feebly say 'Any questions?' If there are not, it is an anti-climax and even if there are, what do you say at the end of the questions? Do you give another close? No, I think it best to put questions before the close, then you can end with some kind of climatic end that they will remember, thank them for listening and sit down (to deafening applause perhaps).

Timing

As I said earlier, people tend to have too much material for the time they have. When people are asked to speak, say for half-an-hour, they think it is an eternity and they will never have enough to fill it. Therefore, they tend to prepare too much material. We need to consider the amount you need for a given presentation time:

The following is an example of content amount for an half hour presentation:

Introduction	–	5	minutes
Main content	–	12	minutes **
Consolidation	–	10	minutes
Conclusion	–	3	minutes
		30	minutes

** The main thing to note here is that the Main Content (that is, the only time you introduce new information) is never more than half the total time you have to speak.

Consolidation may be interwoven with the main content or a totally separate section. Depending on the situation, it may be a similar length to the main content or it may be a little shorter.

The order in which you prepare the various items within the presentation is a matter of personal choice, but I would recommend:

Order of preparation   Item:

1	Set objectives
2	Decide on evaluation process *
3	Prepare introduction
4	Prepare conclusion
5	Decide on consolidation process
6	Write main content

* You should always think of a method to evaluate that your objectives have been achieved.

People are often uneasy about this order of preparation; they feel that the main content should be written first. But, I don't think you can do that until last. If, for example, you know what form of consolidation you are going to use (for example, a video), you write your main content accordingly. It is only when you are fully aware of the methods you are going to use that you can logically decide what you are going to say!

Your notes

This is a very personal thing and everyone does it differently, but there are a few basic points which might help. You can either have your notes written out in full, or you can work from shortened notes. We have all listened to people 'reading' to us from a complete script and we would probably all agree it is not the most successful method. The most interesting speaker to listen to is some-one who (seemingly at any rate) is speaking 'off-the-cuff' and spontaneously responds to audience participation. This can only be done with the confidence of thorough preparation, a thorough knowledge of the subject and of well-written notes.

Most people do need to use notes, but ideally they should be merely trig-ger points – headings to remind you of topics about which you want to speak. Shortened notes may result from fully written scripts which are gradually whittled down by reading and revising notes, each time more going into the memory and less going down on paper – a bit like the revision notes we pre-pared for college exams!

If you have well written notes, you do not need to hide them. The audience will expect you to use notes and – if you use them well – will hardly notice them at all. A confident, natural flow of speech comes from a thorough knowl-edge of your material which then allows you to concentrate on your presen-tation skills: your body language, your rapport with your audience and so on.

To prepare your shortened notes:

Divide up what you want to say into sections:

- Choose or prepare a sentence which summarizes each section; pol-ish it up and you'll have the key sentence for your notes which will unlock the whole section for you;
- Consider what are the supporting points on which you'll need to enlarge from the key sentence;
- Take a card (ruled index cards are ideal) or paper (not as big as A4 – it flaps about when you're nervous!) and write out your key sen-tence in block capitals at the top (in your 'Need to know' colour);
- List your supporting points below. These are prompts and need to be only one or two words for each point.;
- Prepare a personal shorthand system so that you can give yourself cues – any visual aids you want to use; if you propose to ask the audience a question at a certain point. . . (I use abbreviations in a circle in the left hand margin – anything I see there I know is a note to me and not to be spoken.) You can also give yourself graphic or text messages. A little 'smiley' face at the top of each card reminds you to smile, for example – the best form of relaxation I know (and lovely for your audience!). I was once taking a piano examination and playing a particularly rhythmic piece of music; I wrote 'Sit still'

across the top of each page (for obvious reasons). Until you become experienced, it is a good idea to put timings into your notes, say every five minutes, to remind you approximately where you are within your total presentation time.

- Always write on one side of the card only and put only one theme or idea on each card. Finally, number each card (saves disaster if they **should** fall on the floor) and ideally punch a hole in the top left hand corner (right side if you are left handed) and string together with a 'treasury tag'. This allows you to turn over the card without getting snagged up with paper clips or staples.

Always put your notes where you can easily see them. Ideally, you should be able to glance down and scan the next point without losing your flow of speech or losing communication with your audience. You cannot do this if you cannot see the notes! Write large enough to be able to see the words without bending down (otherwise the audience will have a great deal of communication with the top of your head, which doesn't do a lot for the rapport). It is a good idea to use a table lectern for your notes (or perhaps even a standing one if it is a formal presentation), particularly if you are tall or short-sighted! Some people prefer to hold their notes, but if you do this make sure they don't create a barrier between you and your audience.

A very important point here is that when we are nervous we tend to regress to needing our childhood 'security blanket'. We find speakers clutching their notes, burying their noses into them and not making eye contact with their audience, becoming totally engrossed in their visual aids (how many times have you seen a presenter gazing fondly or even indicating a blank white screen where once an overhead slide projected!) – anything but full interaction with their audience! As you make a rapport with members of your audience by eye contact, smiling, nodding and so on, you will probably find that they interact with you by smiling back when you meet someone's eye; certainly they should be looking interested if you are presenting well. Therefore, your concentration should be on them, what they are receiving from you, what they are feeling and interpreting about what you are saying. Most of the time, you will find that your audience is supportive and sympathetic and your audience alone should be the focus of your attention.

Question:	Who should be our 'security blanket'?
Answer:	The people in our audience!

VISUAL AIDS

Sight is the most powerful of our learning senses and it is often an advantage for your presentation to be as visual as possible, especially if you have a complicated concept to project, or a fairly heavy subject which can be lightened with graphics or diagrams. Providing the visual aids are well made, they add a professional and businesslike touch to any presentation. However, visual aids can be a pitfall of disasters to any presenter who is not comfortable with or efficient in their use. Visual aids should **enhance**, not **dominate** the presentation and a lot of speakers hide behind their visuals, allowing them to 'take the heat off' them by directing the audience's attention elsewhere. (This links in with the 'security blanket' syndrome already discussed.)

Some time ago, I went to hear a very well known management guru speak about his theories. He is a very well known man in management development circles and has written some excellent books. I was really looking forward to hearing him, but seeing him go onto the platform with a great pile of overhead slides under his arm, my heart sank. True enough, his whole presentation consisted of slide-after-slide-after-slide and we heard very little of the man himself. (It is an easy way of doing things, of course, because your 'notes' are there on the overhead slides and you can reproduce the same talk time after time.) I felt cheated and disappointed – and, significantly, it is that message that stayed with me, not anything he said!

Visual aids should be minimal and should only be used when they will truly help to clarify, interest or enlighten the audience, not because the speaker takes the easy way out or feels the presentation will be thought of less because they have not used visual aids. As Anthony Jay says,[1] 'visual aids are a means, not an end'. There is, for example, no point in using overhead slides bearing a list of words. In fact it can be insulting to an audience to read out text which they can easily read for themselves. Graphic or diagrammatic visuals are the best because they give a visual image of what is being said (you need only to think of the power of television advertising to realize the advantages of this).

Visual aids are what they say – an

A I D

to understanding;

to effective communication taking place.

They should *not* be a substitute for the presenter's input.

Golden rules for visual aids:

- Do not feel you have to use visual aids, only use them when they truly enhance your presentation;
- If you do use them, they must look professional and be absolutely clear;
- Use them sparingly and keep them simple;
- Everyone in the audience must be able to see them;
- You must be totally comfortable with their use and know what to do if equipment goes wrong;
- Graphics are better than text.

The most commonly used forms of visual aid include:

- Overhead projector;
- Flip chart;
- White or black board;
- Photographic slides;
- Physical Objects;
- Working models;
- Video.

Of these, the overhead projector and flip chart are the most often used, so let us look at some advantages, disadvantages and pitfalls that you are likely to encounter:

Advantages	**Disadvantages**
Overhead projector	
Looks professional	Can break down
Can have professionally made slides	Professional slides cost money
	Needs practice to use well
Saves time – no writing	Needs setting up in advance
Presenter controls the pace	Equipment not easily portable
Slides are portable	Can take presenter's mind
Framed slides are durable	off audience
Flip chart	
Easy to prepare and portable	Takes time to write up during
Can be done in advance	presentations
No special equipment	Sheets are easily damaged
Inexpensive	Writing needs to be good
Nothing to break down	May be difficult to see in a large
Saves time if prepared in advance	or odd shaped room

Tips for use

The following guidelines apply to overhead projector slides, but some of them relate to flip chart work too, together with white and black boards:

- **Not too much** – Keep each visual simple. No more than eight lines of text, using key words only.
- **Not too little** – single word, phrase or symbol can be condescending to the audience.
- **Not too many** – Limit the number of overhead slides for real impact.
- **Write big** – Remember that every member of the audience must be able to see the visual from wherever they are sitting. Typed copy is unlikely to be big enough for overhead slides. As a guide, use 1 inch lettering for every 30 foot depth of audience.

- **Colour adds interest** – Don't go overboard, but sometimes try an additional colour or two, reserving red for the main points you wish to emphasize. Experiment with colours – some show up better than others.
- **Words are not visual** – Use your imagination to create visual images that will register in the minds of your audience. Line drawings, cartoons or diagrams are good attention holders.
- **Always, always check it out** – As with all visual aids, check and double check beforehand: are there any spelling mistakes on your slides? (Even one little spelling mistake looks huge when it is magnified onto a big screen!) Is the grammar correct? Have you checked to make sure the projector is focused and the image square? Do you know how to change the bulb if it blows – and do you have one to hand? Can the visual be seen by everyone? Is any part of the overhead projector blocking someone's view? Are YOU blocking anyone's view by standing in their line of vision? (Can the person at the back see the brochure you are holding up? If not, don't use it!)

The amazing thing about using visuals such as an overhead slide is the ease with which you can control the direction of your audience's attention. Switch on the light and every eye will transfer to the screen – but remember that while the light is on, that is where the audience's attention will be, so remember to turn it off as soon as you have finished speaking to that particular slide. When you turn off the light, every eye will revert back to you.

Another golden rule for all visual aids:

As soon as you have finished with the visual, get rid of it!

- Switch off the light (overhead projector);
- turn over the page (flip chart);
- wipe off the lettering (white or blackboard).

Always be sure of the techniques of using whatever visual aids you choose. They will only enhance your presentation if you are totally comfortable with their use (and therefore the audience will feel comfortable with them too).

With overhead projector work, for example, you should always place the slide onto the projector (having rehearsed beforehand which way up it goes!) **before** you turn on the light. When you change the slides, the sequence should be:

1 turn off the light;
2 remove the slide;
3 put the next slide in place;
4 turn on the light.

There should at no time be a blank white light showing on the screen.

People sometimes take me to task over this. They say that the continual switching on and off of the light is a distraction to the audience. My answer to this is in that case the presenter is using far too many slides! Some modern projectors have a dimmer slide which avoids the click of the switch.

Rehearsing with the overhead projector before the presentation is essential (even for seasoned presenters) because you need to be confident that your slide is in place and in focus. This allows you to keep your eyes on the slide itself as it lies on the projector, rather than looking behind you at the screen.

One of the classic mistakes when using overheads is to look at the screen, thus turning your back on the audience, and even to speak to the screen rather than your audience (there is the 'security blanket' again). There is something to be said for directing your audience's attention to a particular point on the screen by looking at it yourself, but otherwise you should avoid it.

It is sometimes helpful to 'point' your audience to a particular item on the overhead. There are three ways of doing this:

---

1 use a reveal;
2 use a pointer on the glass of the projector itself;
3 use a pointer at the screen.

---

1 **A reveal** is a method of covering the wording on the slide so that only your chosen item is visible on the screen. If you have a list of topics, for example, and wish to talk about one of them, it is unhelpful to have the full list on the screen because the audience's attention may well be focused on items other than that which you are addressing. A reveal is usually a piece of paper or card which is drawn down the slide to 'reveal' another item as you wish. (Too flimsy a piece of paper will often fall onto the floor, or be blown there by the projector fan.) The reveal should be placed in position on the slide **before** the light is switched on.

2 **Never use your finger** to point out something on a slide. Nervous, trembling hands are magnified on the screen and may block the projected image. Use an object such as a pen, laying it flat on the slide and leaving it alone. (This also avoids you bending down over the projector and losing eye contact with your audience.)

3 **A long wand or pointer pen** can be used by the presenter, who stands back against the screen to 'point' out the relevant item. The disadvantage of such wands is that one has to be very careful not to 'conduct the audience'! It is also important to specifically point to the item concerned, rather than vaguely wave the wand up and down, refraining from tapping the pointer on the plastic screen.

Make sure that any notes are at the side on which you are standing. Once the light is on, you should not walk across in front of it. It may be most comfortable to stand on the side of the projector switch or slide, rather than having to lean across to switch on the light, when your shadow will be projected onto the screen.

You can build up a diagram or picture of a complex subject by laying one slide on top of another. It is useful to secure the slides so that you do not have to take time getting them in the right place.

All these tips about using an overhead projector may put you off for life if you haven't tried using one, but it's like anything else, 'practice makes perfect' and overhead projectors are really extremely useful visual aids providing you are in charge of them and they are not in charge of you!

Two final points on visual aids:

• **Always have Plan B ready in case the equipment breaks down!**

• **You must control them, they must not control you!**

Making your presentation

If you have done all your preparation as well as you can, have a thorough knowledge of what you want to say and what methods you are going to use, you are well on the way to a first class presentation.

There are a few other things you need to think about, though, so let's now look at some guidelines for ensuring that all goes well on the day.

STYLE

You have spent a long time preparing what is about to happen. All could be in vain if your message is not delivered well.

People often say to me that they are far too shy to speak in public. Sometimes I think that shy people make the best presenters. The secret is to know your material well and then act the role. For a long time, I was terrified of speaking in public, but because my work demanded it, I had to do it. In chapter one we talked about the 'Role me' – the 'front' that we show to other people, and the 'Real me' – that real self that we hide away inside and which some people reveal only to their nearest and dearest. I recently worked with a young woman who was an expert in computer aided design, but who felt her career was being threatened because she had to present her findings to senior management and was so terrified that she continually dried up with panic. She came to me for help and asked if I thought she should go for elocution classes. I told her that in my opinion that was the last thing she should do. If she wanted to do something to help her nerves, she could best join an amateur dramatic society and learn to act – to 'play the role'.

When you first start presenting and feel you are going to dry up, fear you will not be able to breathe, dread that you will forget what you are going to say and so on (and we have all been there, believe me), it is helpful to learn by heart the first part of your speech, and 'do your King Lear bit', as I tell my trainees. You need to forget yourself (which is why I do not think that elocution helps) and concentrate on conveying your message to your audience. Commit yourself to them, believe in them and spread the gospel of your subject. Eventually, the techniques you are practising will take over and you will be able to relax and enjoy your presenting (you may not believe this at the beginning, but I assure you it is true!).

The need for rehearsal prior to the presentation is very important. If you can find another person (or even the dog) to listen to your presentation beforehand, it will improve your confidence on the day. As I said at the beginning of this chapter, it is a good idea if you rehearse looking at yourself in a mirror, because if you think about it, you are the only person who never sees your face and other body language when you are presenting. It is quite useful to know what your face is conveying and what mannerisms you have!

Let's consider some general points about your presentation style:

- If you are an inexperienced presenter, don't apologize about it.
- When you begin, smile at your audience and look directly at them as individuals – look at **all** of them, not just the friendly faces.
- Maintain eye contact throughout, making sure you encompass the whole audience by moving your eyes naturally around them (do not concentrate on one section of the audience alone, even if they are the ones who are giving you visual feedback or asking the most questions).
- Be enthusiastic about your subject – it's catching.
- Treat your audience with courtesy and respect (never use bad language or language which could offend).
- Don't be too theatrical, but use gestures naturally.
- Move about with purpose, but don't prowl around like a caged lion.

One secret of relaxed, fluent presentation style is to speak to your audience – whether six or six hundred – as though you are chatting to a friend, sitting at the kitchen table over a cup of coffee.

We have probably all sat and listened to speakers who bored the pants off us. We need to consider things which make the presentation enjoyable for us, or, conversely, what inhibits presentations for us. Then we can put ourselves in the shoes of our audience and make sure we don't make similar mistakes, but build on the things we know make for good listening.

Some of the points which inhibit or facilitate good presentations are listed below, but you can probably think of a lot more yourself.

INHIBITORS	FACILITATORS
Common usage (we are used to communicating and therefore take it for granted we will be understood)	Awareness of inhibitors Knowledge of subject Knowledge of audience (attitudes, expectations and so on)
Misunderstanding	Honesty of presenter
Ambiguity	Sincerity of presenter
Misinterpretation	Commitment to audience
Suspicion (on the audience's part)	Clarity of **WHAT** (the objective) " of **WHY** (the required outcome)
Amount (too much or too little can have an adverse effect)	" of **HOW** (the best way to obtain the required outcome)
Timing	
Speaker – boring voice mannerisms (verbal and non-verbal) lack of skills lack of knowledge poor appearance	" of **WHEN** (timing and frequency)

The last item on the 'Inhibitors' list above is something I feel should be mentioned under the heading of 'style'. Although I know there is a lot of controversy over what people should wear on certain occasions, I do think one needs to give some attention to this. All I will say here is that in my opinion a presenter should bear in mind two things when deciding what to wear:

1   what is appropriate for the occasion;
2   what is comfortable.

Whether this means suits and ties or casual dress for men, or suits and heeled shoes or trousers for women, I leave to you. The other thing about appearance which I think is important is the personal hygiene issues such as:

- clean hair (no dandruff on collar)
- clean finger nails
- clean shoes
- BO (or lack of it!)

AND NEVER, NEVER, NEVER EAT GARLIC BEFORE YOUR PRESENTATION!

Lots more could be said about style, but I guess we have covered the main points - the rest I leave to your good sense and your own personality, because that is what is most important. To be the natural 'you' is essential. If you try to learn style from a book you will come across as stiff and unnatural.

A THOUGHT:

Communication is not difficult – we just do it badly!

VOICE

The sound of the presenter's voice is extremely important. If we are aiming for a pleasant, positive voice, we need to think pleasantly and positively, because our voice reflects our psychological thought. As we all know, one of the problems of being nervous is that our voice sometimes shakes (because we are **thinking** shakily). If you feel nervous before you speak, sit down comfortably, take some good deep breaths and look around you at your audience, becoming interested in **them** and forgetting yourself. Most people enjoy 'people watching' – now is your chance. You can get to know a lot about your audience by observing them before you stand up to speak.

The easiest voice to listen to is one of fairly low, full tone, with plenty of variety in pitch, inflection and rhythm. It will flow naturally, without jerkiness and without the common fault of anticipating the ends of sentences. By this I mean that many people (possibly because they psychologically wish the talk would soon come to an end) begin a sentence at a certain register of their voice and soon drop to a lower pitch as if ending a sentence, but continuing to speak at that same point. Using the musical stave this could be graphically represented:

We are all aware of the difficulty of listening to people who speak on a monotone, or at a certain pitch of their voice for a long time, thus:

You should try to use the full range of the register of your voice, not in a false unnatural way, but in an interesting, dynamic sense:

We all use a much greater range of our vocal register when we sing than when we speak. Research the full range of your speech by reading aloud and taping your voice (Charles Dickens provides excellent material for this, with narration followed by a variety of character voices). Lock yourself in the bathroom and experiment!

If you listen to different people talking, you will hear the 'music' in their voice. Some nationalities have more musicality in their voices than others. Welsh people, for example, speak with a beautifully lyrical tone, with a lift at the end of sentences. French people, too, are dramatic in their speech, with a variety of dynamics of pitch.

Another problem that we often encounter is speakers who start each sentence on the 'same note' and drop the ends of their sentences to exactly the 'same note':

Listen to yourself reading aloud on tape and see if this is happening to your voice. Try experimenting with more variety of pitch, especially at the ends of sentences. A full stop, for example, may take you to a slightly lower pitch than, say, a colon or a semi-colon.

As well as the beginning and end of sentences, think about the interest of your voice in the middle. The value of inflection can help here, to stress certain syllables or give added meaning to important words. Inflection can also change meanings and has an effect upon the rhythm of the sentence.

You will remember the following example from chapter one:

'Will you come down **Here** and have your breakfast?'

has a different meaning from

'**Will** you come down here and have your breakfast!'

Another reason for a voice being boring to listen to is where there is no variation in pace of speech. Sometimes a person uses a varying range of pitch but their voice still seems monotonous because. . . they. . . always. . . speak. . . at. . .exactly. . . the. . . same. . . pace. When you are describing something or chattering away generally you can speed up a little, then. . . **Pause**. . . (slower) you. . . can. . . make. . . your. . . point. You can have people on the edge of their chairs with the use of the pause – it can be very dramatic and a great 'attention getter'. Speakers are sometimes frightened of leaving silence, but they need not be because although it sounds like an eternity to them, it actually gives the audience time to think about what the presenter has just said (or is going to say).

Another perennial worry for presenters is volume. Some tend to think you need to shout to reach the back of the room or hall in which they are speaking. Actually, shouting tends to distort sound, as those of you who have had any dealings with deaf people will know. What is much more important is clarity, particularly of consonants. If you breathe properly (see below), the sound of your voice will be supported by a reservoir of air. Your lips shape the sound the air makes as it is catapulted out of your mouth and it is your lips that send the sound to the back of the hall. It is called **Projecting** the voice.

The importance of sounding consonants cannot be stressed enough. Not only do they shape the sound and determine its clarity, but they ensure that the sound is made at the **front** of the mouth.

Activity

> Experiment with making the following sound at the back of your mouth as though you were 'swallowing' the sound:
>
> 'AH' (as required by the doctor!)
>
> Now put an M in front and try to get the sound just behind the front teeth (try smiling – it is difficult to get it wrong then because the muscle structure of the face pushes the sound forward):
>
> 'MAH'
>
> Now try this exercise, saying it several times aloud:
>
> 'The tip of the tongue and the lips and the teeth'
>
> really making the lips work hard (particularly the top lip muscle) and projecting the sound from just behind the front teeth.

I often encounter difficulties with men with moustaches when I am training presenters. They seem to be conscious of this great weight of hair on their top lip which prevents them moving it adequately and the clarity of their speech is greatly affected. I was working with a fellow recently who seemed to contradict this theory. He had a moustache, but his top lip worked well. I commented on this (to the amusement of all present) and he told me that he sang in a professional choir and had learned to loosen his top lip so that it was very flexible – hair and all!

If consonants work for clarity, vowels work for tone. We are after that sonorous resonant tone we remember from great actors such as the late Sir Laurence Olivier and Dame Peggy Ashcroft. Good tone is produced by the combination of vowels, breath and resonance found within the sinal cavities (did you know that most of your head is space – it's wonderful for filling with breath to create beautiful sound).

We must mention dialects and accents at this point. Some presenters feel that it is important to speak the 'Queen's English' or, if you like, standard English. What does that mean? Different regions have acquired so-called 'accents' over the years, which usually relate to vowel sounds rather than consonants. Should public speakers try to rid themselves of regional accents or dialects, or should we preserve them as assets of heritage? This is a very personal thing and my own view is that, provided the audience can understand what the speaker is saying (which is fundamental to effective communication taking place) and the accent is not in itself a distraction, then regional dialect is not important. However, you must make up your own mind about this and if you choose to change your vowel pronunciation, then you can do so with patience and practise. Language is learned, not innate; we learn to speak by imitating others and therefore we can equally learn new vowel construction.

It is not easy, however, because as Christabel Burniston says in her excellent book *Sounding out Your Voice and Speech*:[2] 'Fine shades of differences of vowel sounds are not discernible by the speaker himself. Any correction needs a good teacher who is both patient and exacting and a speaker with infinite self-criticism and will-power.'

Verbal mannerisms are always cropping up in presentations. Habit words and phrases such as 'Right?', 'OK?', 'The thing is. . .', 'Basically. . .', 'You know?', together with, of course, the 'Ahs, 'Ers', 'Ums' and the regular clearing of the throat.

When these become a distraction to the audience because of their regularity, something must be done to eradicate them from the speech pattern. It seems to me there are three main reasons for such verbals.

First, there are what I call 'punctuation habits'; every time the speaker comes to a full stop, they automatically say 'Er' or 'Um'. If that is the motive, the speaker can make a deliberate effort to do something else every time there is a full stop – such as compress their lips, or squeeze their thumb and finger together.

Secondly, the hesitation 'words' may come about because the speaker does not know what they are going to say next. This may become a habit pattern, or it may genuinely reflect a 'blank' memory gap. With the confidence of knowing the subject and having prepared thoroughly, and with the commitment to and rapport with their audience, these verbal mannerisms will disappear with experience. It is my opinion that the more you dwell on trying to get rid of 'Ers' and 'Ums' when this is the motive for them, the more conscious you will become of them and the more you will hear yourself saying them! Don't worry about them (unless they really are a very bad distraction), they will go away as you become more confident.

Thirdly, the reason for verbal mannerisms such as 'OK?' and 'Right?' is because the speaker is trying to check the audience's understanding of the communication. There are better ways to do this and it is a matter of consciously thinking through how you can monitor that your audience is receiving your communication effectively. You could ask them questions, for example, or encourage them to participate in discussion. If the presentation is a formal one, or the audience numbers too big for individual participation, you should be 'reading' the audience's understanding by their body language, their facial expression and by direct eye contact with as many of them as possible.

Six words to remember:

PITCH   ENERGY
PACE   ENTHUSIASM
PAUSE   CONVICTION

BREATHING

Breathing is all-important, not least because it calms your nerves. As we have already said, the sound that comes out of your mouth is dependent upon your breathing. Most people breathe shallowly when they are nervous and the voice comes out of their mouth as a thin, timorous, reed-like wobble! Have you ever had that experience of hearing this horrible sound and realizing it was coming out of your own mouth? I have! Even worse, I have been in situations where no sound has come out at all! All this is down to breath control.

When we breathe shallowly at the very top of our chest (where there is very little space for our lungs to expand anyway as it's mostly full of bone and muscle), our shoulders get higher and higher until they reach our ears, tensing all the time as they go, until eventually there is nowhere else to go so we cannot breathe at all, we are as tense as a board and we may start to hyperventilate. What breath we do have cannot be controlled and so it emerges through the sound we make like a cracked organ pipe.

If you think about your anatomy for a moment, you will be aware that the place where you should be breathing is in your diaphragm. This is a great balloon-like reservoir which, when full of air, can strengthen the most nervous person with the confidence of hearing steady, supported sound coming out of their mouths in spite of the nerves they may be encountering. Make no mistake about it, beautiful and dependable sound comes from correct breathing. If you are not used to breathing correctly, it will take some practice. Be aware of your diaphragm expanding, lifting your rib cage and making you feel secure and strong within yourself. Stand with both feet on the ground, put your hands either side of your abdomen and think yourself into your diaphragm as you breathe. Breathe in with your mouth open a little, opening the back of the throat as you do so. The uvula (the dangly bit at the back of your throat) should lift if you are doing this correctly. Practise in front of a mirror.

As you now speak, the breath is forced up the trachea, vibrating across the vocal chords as it does so, producing the sound. However, even now we are not finished, because a sound made 'on the throat' is a harsh, strident sound. Teachers often lose their voice a week into a new term because they shout 'on the throat' at their pupils.

Activity

Try saying the following nursery rhyme wrongly, using the very hard, strident sound of the throat:

> Mary had a little lamb
> Whose fleece was white as snow
> And everywhere that Mary went
> The lamb was sure to go.

Does your throat feel sore? Yes, because you were using your voice wrongly. To understand the correct use of the voice, try humming with your fingers either side the bridge of your nose and see if you can feel the 'buzz'. . . . These are the spaces we want to use to improve the resonance of tone and to use the voice correctly. This is a difficult concept to get across in a book. It is a psychological rather than a physical one. The most descriptive I can be is to ask you to imagine that you are a unicorn and where your single horn sprouts from the top of your head is the place where you are going to 'think' the emergence of sound. If you can do this, with a supportive reservoir of breath in the diaphragm, your voice will sound wonderful and you will never get a sore throat. This, together with your lip work we have already discussed, will make for excellent speech production. It takes a lot of practice, but then everything worth doing. . .

BODY LANGUAGE IN PRESENTATION

Whatever you say and no matter how heart-stopping your voice, if your body is giving the wrong signals, your communication will not be effective. We discussed the importance of body language in communication in chapter one and all the things said there hold good in presentation skills. There are one or two points that should be made here, however, which apply particularly to presenting.

You should be 'saying' with your body what you are saying with your verbal language. It is no good verbalizing the most profound concepts which can change the world if your body is giving every indication that you wished you were somewhere else and the last thing on earth you want to be doing is talking to these people in this place at this time.

Good posture and stance is essential, not only to convey the right message to your audience, but also to support your voice and breathing mechanics. If you stand on one foot, slewed to one side, your whole breathing capacity is affected adversely. You should stand on two feet, possibly with one foot slightly in front of the other, with feet slightly apart.

Unless you are giving a formal presentation from a lectern or particular place behind a table (do avoid that if you can – it really does act as a barrier between you and your audience), try walking around a little, but do not pace up and down at regular intervals. It makes it interesting for your audience if you move about, especially if you feel confident enough to leave your notes behind you and walk towards your audience, perhaps as they participate or ask questions.

Make sure you make eye contact with everyone in the room if numbers permit, moving your eyes around the audience (but not with the regularity of watching a tennis match). If you have a large audience, by ranging your eyes around the room and making direct eye contact with different people from time to time, it will appear to members of your audience that you are making personal contact with them. You must do this. The old method of looking at the wall at the back of the room just above the heads of your audience will really not do. You have to establish personal rapport with every member of your audience from the word go and eye contact is the most vital part of this communication process. It is also essential for 'reading' your audience's understanding and reception of your pearls of wisdom.

When it comes to mannerisms, people get very worried about distracting their audience – and rightly so. It is a good idea to watch yourself on video because it is only then that you really become aware of all the funny things you do, especially when you are nervous. Trainee presenters are often appaled by seeing themselves tapping feet, clicking fingers, stepping from side to side as though they are on guard duty, pushing spectacles up their noses, women flicking back their hair at regular intervals, men playing with their tie or jingling the loose change in their pocket (or worse!), clicking tops of pens on and off monotonously and so on. I know there are so many things to think about. It's a bit like learning to drive a car. Will you ever be able to do everything at once – the gear, the steering, the clutch, the indicators, the mirror, the brake. . .? Will you ever be able to think of what you have to say, when to switch on and off on the overhead projector, when to turn over the flip chart, what you are doing with your hands, where your feet are taking you. . .? But, just as we eventually **do** learn to drive the car and all the things we worried about individually become second nature to us, so – with practice – will all the skills involved in presentation fall into place.

Many teachers of presentation skills encourage their trainees not to use their hands. Some even make their students stand with their hands behind their back. I think, personally, this makes for a very rigid presenter. I would far rather see people using their hands naturally. An important point here is to use your hands within the bounds of your own natural personality. If you are a person who would find it over the top to wave your arms about, then don't. If, however, you find it excruciating to keep your hands still, then by all means use them **unless** they become a distraction to your audience. Then you must curtail the movement. My own opinion is that the distraction comes, not so much from natural movement of the hands, but of using them in a very symmetrical way. If the presenter does exactly the same thing with both hands all the time, it becomes difficult. If you watch an amateur musical conductor and then a professional one, the difference you will see is that very often the amateur carries out exactly the same movement with both hands at once. If the right hand goes out to 'three o'clock', the left hand goes to 'nine o'clock'; if the right hand points to 'two o'clock', the left hand points to 'ten o'clock'. The professional conductor, however, has learned hand independence. The right hand may use the baton to beat time while the left hand brings in the violins at a certain point, followed by the trombones at another point.

Therefore, if you are going to use your hands – and I hope you are, because it is far more natural than standing with them stiffly at your side or behind your back (let us not even consider the thought that you might put them in your pocket), try to work on hand independence so that they do not emulate each other every time to move into a symmetrical position.

There are lots of tips as to ways you can help nerves by relaxing various muscles. The best way I know is to **smile**. Smiling not only helps audience rapport (watch them smile back at you), but it completely relaxes your face muscles, thus easing out all the tension and stress of nerves. Christabel Burniston talks about 'thumb clutchers' – people who grip one thumb with their other hand which tenses the whole upper body. She says (op cit p7):

'Avoid clenching your teeth; relax your mouth by releasing the jaw bone 'hinge' as much as possible. Lips should touch lightly in moments of repose but behind the lips the teeth should be apart – only then is the jaw relaxed.'

Remember the tip about chatting to people as if you are speaking with friends over a cup of coffee – the same movements of head, face, body, gestures, pitch and pace of voice – and above all, think of **them**, not of yourself. Only then will you forget your nerves and become the natural, fluent, entertaining presenter that you wish to be.

USE OF LANGUAGE

Over and above that which I have already said about language in presentation, there are one or two points which you might find helpful.

There is a term used in professional presentation circles known as **signposting**. When you write, you begin a new paragraph to indicate to the reader that you are about to begin a new theme or idea. When you speak, however, you cannot do this, so you need to find a way of signposting your audience, advising them that you are about to begin a new 'paragraph'. One way of doing this is to summarize the idea about which you have just been speaking: 'So what we have seen so far is.. ' Then indicate to your audience that you are about to start a new subject by a verbal 'sub heading'. Rhetorical questions are good for this: 'So what do we know about . . .?'

There is also the 'three point sermon' idea. In the introduction you may choose to indicate to your audience that you will be presenting three points during your talk. Then, at the respective points during your content, say 'firstly', or 'my second point. . .' In this way, your audience knows where they are in your talk and it will be structured rather than a woolly mass.

A further thought at this point is about the use of complex, wordy sentences in spoken English. Although one may choose to use long words and a superior vocabulary in written English (where at least the reader has the opportunity to use a dictionary if necessary), when you are speaking it is much more natural to use simple language with short sentences.

The obvious example of this is Sir Humphrey in the television programme 'Yes Minister'. He may say something like 'I will give my attention to ensure that you have adequate sound reception facilities'. What is he really saying? Probably something like 'I will make sure you can hear properly'! Why not just say what you mean? (Remember my advice about your presentation style resembling a chat over a cup of coffee with a friend?)

MANAGING YOUR PRESENTATION

The responsibility for managing your presentation and its timing is yours and yours alone. This means that you have to ensure that your talk, together with any questions and responses from your audience during the presentation itself, finishes on time. There is nothing worse than a presenter who runs over time, often affecting following speakers or the organiser's arrangements for refreshments.

People often say to me 'How do you know how much time to leave for audience participation and/or questions?' The answer is, of course, that you don't, so you have to plan accordingly. I have already written about 'need to know' and 'nice to know' indicators so that you can fill in or leave out material as you go along without losing the structure of your presentation or the logical flow of your topic content. You can choose to take questions during your talk, or you can leave them until the end. Either is quite acceptable, but if you are going to leave time at the end, you need to tell your audience in the introduction. You might say something like 'Please feel free to ask questions as I go along', or you might prefer to say 'I will leave time at the end for questions, so perhaps you could keep anything you would like to ask me until then'.

Some presenters are frightened of questions, but I always welcome them. If you know your subject well, there is nothing to fear. This doesn't mean to say you will always know the answer. We cannot possibly know everything. You will not lose credibility if you say 'I don't know the answer to that, but it is a very interesting point and I will find out for you and let you know'. (And you must let them know, otherwise you are being 'dishonest' to your audience.)

If a person in the audience asks a question, there is a tendency to direct your answer to that one person and a dialogue ensues. There is then a danger that you will 'lose' the rest of your audience. They will either switch off altogether or, worse, they will start talking among themselves. The way to get round this is to address your initial response to the person who asked the question (perhaps walking towards the person if it is a small group and it is convenient). After a few seconds, glance around the rest of your audience, nodding and making eye contact with them to include them in your answer. It is your responsibility to keep your audience with you at all times.

There is a pneumonic for handling questions which I find very useful:

TRACT

T-hank the person for asking the question;

> 'Thank you for asking that question, it is a good point. . .'

R-epeat the question;

> for three reasons:

> 1   to make sure everyone has heard the question (what is worse than hearing an answer from the speaker, but you didn't hear the question in the first place);
> 2   to make sure that you have understood what the questioner means;
> 3   to give yourself time to think of the answer!

A-nswer the question;

> (if you can – don't bluff; if you lie and someone asks you another question leading from your answer you will get deeper and deeper in the soup. If you don't know the answer, say so);

C-heck that you have provided a satisfactory answer for the questioner;

T-hank them for the question

> 'Thank you for raising that point, it was most helpful. . .'

If you get someone in your audience who dominates the whole presentation with interjections and questions, perhaps to the point where he or she is threatening to take over from you, you may need to 'take back the reins'. You can do this by an assertive comment such as 'Thank you, John, for your points. I am sure they have been most helpful. Jane, could you give us your views?' As you say the name 'Jane' (someone you have picked from the other side of the room from where John is sitting), you turn away from John to face

Jane. This body language confirms your verbal message to John to 'shut up'! Never, however, put down or humiliate a person by being aggressive by actually saying 'Shut up' or something which means that!

A postscript for the big day itself

Always make sure you allow plenty of time to get there. Allow for punctures, traffic hold ups, train delays and so on. It is just awful to arrive in a great state of hassle because you are late. You need time to have a little space to prepare yourself and you do need time to set up shop. Check out the room you will be using. You will probably have been asked previously how you want the seating, whether you want an overhead projector, flip chart and so on, so now make sure everything is there as you requested it. It is your responsibility to ensure that the environment is as good as it can be (including seating, heating, equipment and so on). Make sure that everyone in the room will have a clear line of sight to you and any visual aids you use. Check that the overhead projector bulb is working (and you know where there is a spare and how to put it in), that the flip chart pens are in good condition, that you have waterproof/non-waterproof pens as appropriate for the white board. (How many of us have found that we have written on the whiteboard indelibly and our words of wisdom are there for everyone to see for a very long time!) Ask for water to be made available for you if it is not already there (nerves often dry the throat and a tickly cough is often a hazard for presenters).

Make a final check that your notes and visual aids are in the correct order and that you know where you are going to put your notes and where you are going to stand.

If it is a fairly informal presentation, welcome individuals as they arrive. If you wait passively for people to gather, it makes for a cold, formal atmosphere and it becomes even harder to win them over!

BIBLIOGRAPHY

For further reading see:

Burniston, C, *Sounding Out Your Voice And Speech,* The English Speaking Board, 1989

Jay, A, *Effective Presentation*, British Institute of Management, 1971

Jay, J, *Making Your Case*, Video Arts, 1982

Leigh, A & Maynard, M, *The Perfect Presentation*, Century, 1993

Marks, W, *How To Give A Speech*, Institute of Personnel Management, 1980

1   Jay, A., *Effective Presentation*, British Institute of Management, 1971

2   Burniston, C., *Sounding Out Your Voice and Speech*, The English Speaking Board, 1989

CHAPTER THREE

More About Verbal Communication

IN THIS CHAPTER WE WILL LOOK AT THE FOLLOWING AREAS:

- communicating on the telephone;
- communicating effectively in meetings;
- interviewing and questioning techniques.

Communicating on the telephone

FIRST IMPRESSIONS

Did you know that you can hear a smile? If you smile when you answer the telephone your voice changes in tone – it sounds warm, relaxed, friendly and helpful. Everyone should smile when they answer the telephone. This is just one technique that can make a radical difference to the way callers assess you and your organization when they ring up. The other day I rang up a company because from what I had read in the trade press I thought they might be able to help me with a particular project – I was a potential customer. For a start, neither of them smiled when they greeted me. Then, from the way they questioned who I was and what I required, they sounded suspicious of me rather than interested and helpful. Early on in the call I wondered if they actually wanted customers – and by the time I put the receiver down I had decided that if they did, I would not be one of them.

This story illustrates three important points:

- Quite often the first point of contact with a company is over the telephone.
- If a caller does not receive a clear, friendly greeting, they form a poor opinion of the organization
- The first impression of an organization is a lasting one.

You might say – so, what's the loss of one customer? Does it really matter? I saw Tom Peters, the management guru, give one of his lectures on television. He pointed out that if you get one satisfied customer through the door, many more customers follow, and they bring with them more customers, and these customers bring more customers and as a result your business flourishes. If you lose one customer, you potentially lose hundreds of others. These days, when customer care is at the top of every company's list of priorities, good telephone techniques are essential. This doesn't just apply to the telephone sales team or receptionists, it applies to everyone.

It is surprising how, by following a few simple telephone guidelines, the impression you and your organization gives to other people can be improved dramatically.

- The telephone should be answered within six rings, three is better.
- Avoid picking up the receiver while you are involved in another conversation. It sounds inefficient and rude to the caller to hear the tail end of another conversation before you can find the time to talk to them.
- As you pick up the receiver get into the mind set for a telephone call. The tone of the initial greetings you are about to give is important, so a smile is essential. For those of you reading this who have to say the same greeting over the telephone hundreds of times a day, I know it is difficult – but for the caller this may be the first time they have been in touch – so your greeting needs to sound fresh, precise, clear and courteous – not garbled or bored.
- Many business books on telephone techniques tell you that a greeting is a waste of time – get down to business. However, in my experience a caller needs some 'tuning in time' – so a quick response, or instant factual information such as the company name, is inappropriate. Start with a greeting such as 'Good morning', 'Good afternoon' or 'Hello'.
- Now that the caller is 'tuned in', no need to wait for a response, speak slowly and clearly, giving information about the company or person they are speaking to: 'This is the Palmer Group, can I help you?' or 'This is Valerie Butterfield speaking.

TRANSFERRING CALLS

This sort of incident should not happen:

- Passing a caller from one person to another in an attempt to answer a query;
- Leaving the caller on a ringing line where no-one answers, often with the result that they have to call again to talk to someone else;

- Transferring the caller while they are still explaining what they want.

These experiences are infuriating for the caller, and let's face it, the only conclusion they can draw from them is that your organization is inefficient. As a result they could take their custom elsewhere. Staff need to be trained so that they know what buttons to press in order to carry out the transfer effectively.

- When a person transfers a call, they should give the caller's name and request to the new extension, so that the caller does not have to repeat their business again.

- If there has to be a delay before a transfer can take place the customer should be informed every few seconds of the progress the operator is making with the transfer.

- If the caller wishes to speak to someone who is absent they should be asked whether they would like to speak to someone else, ring again later, leave a message, or be rung back by the person they wished to speak to.

The important point here is that the call is the responsibility of whoever has answered the call, until a satisfactory conclusion is reached. So, for example, if a receptionist takes the message that the caller wishes to be called back by the person who is currently unavailable, then it is the receptionist's responsibility to not only make sure the message is conveyed but that it is also followed up. Only then, as the receiver of the call, has their part of the transaction been completed.

TAKING MESSAGES OVER THE 'PHONE

Never trust your memory when it comes to taking a telephone message. Always write down the following points:

- the date and time of the call;

- the name of the person the caller wanted to speak to;

- the caller's name, company or address and telephone number;

- details of the caller's message.

An example TELEPHONE MESSAGE SHEET:

Incoming call:

From: (Name, company and phone number);
Telephoned/left message on answerphone:
Message:

Please ring (note any specific day or time)/caller will ring back (note any specific day or time)
Any further action required/Additional notes:

Day of call   Date of call   Time of call

Message noted by (name):

LEAVING MESSAGES ON THE ANSWERPHONE

A lot of us hate answerphones. I know it makes me feel self-conscious and I hate the thought of what my voice sounds like on a recording. Lots of people I have spoken to have the same problem. Also, because in most cases, you expect to speak to the person at the other end, suddenly you have to take a different tack because they are obviously not there, or too busy to answer your call. Answerphones may be horrid, but they can be very handy for ensuring your message gets through to the person you want to talk to. It's useful if you use the above checklist for the message you leave.

Do listen to the recorded answerphone message to make sure you have got the right number. I have received some very interesting messages, one in particular stands out in my mind. The caller had a lovely rich, rural voice, with a lurking chuckle behind it. The sort of voice I imagine a retired sheep trial commentator might have. I could imagine he was quite a character, with red rosy cheeks. In his telephone message he commented on my 'jazzy answerphone message' which he obviously had not really listened to because he went on to leave a message that was not meant for me at all. 'Well, there's a group of about 20 of us and looking forward to seeing the sheep on Saturday. So I hope that's all-right then. Get the hay bales out and we'll see you then.' As he did not leave his full name and address or telephone number, I could not set him right. I hope that when the fateful Saturday arrived the poor person he thought he had forewarned was prepared to receive 20 unexpected guests!

There are two morals to this story:

- Always listen carefully to the recorded answerphone message to check that you have called the right person;
- Always leave your name and number, and enunciate them very clearly as messages always sound a bit muffled on answerphones.

This message would have been more useful:

'Hello, this is Bernard Chapman from the Western Amateur Sheep Trials Club. I was hoping to speak to Sarah Adams to tell her to get the hay bales out – 20 of us are coming along!. I'm leaving this message on Monday the 24 August at 9 am. I wanted to confirm our visit to Ballards Farm, for Saturday 30th. Please could you ring me at home this afternoon, or any time on Wednesday just to confirm that this is still all-right. This is Bernard Chapman, Chairman of the Western Amateur Sheep Trials Club. My telephone number is 0181–3456 7891. I'll say the number again: 0181–3456 7891. Thank you. Goodbye.'

CHATTING ON THE 'PHONE

When the caller is a person you know, it is natural and considered polite in our Western culture, to start the conversation with some general sociable chat, perhaps about the weather, how their weekend was, or if you know them well, the family. This is part of encouraging the business relationship between yourself and caller — it is not a waste of time. However, it should not go on for too long, because as they say 'time is money'.

MAKING THE 'PHONE CALL

If you are making a call remember that a business call should be planned in the same way that you plan a business letter. If there are any papers you may want to refer to during the call, get them out so that they are easily accessible. It is a good idea to have a call sheet and note down the topics you want to cover before you make the call. During the call you can also note down any conclusions that were reached. Afterwards file the sheet as a record of the call.

Whether you are making or receiving the call, give it your undivided attention – it is always obvious to the person at the other end if you are trying to do two things at once. Also listen carefully to what they have to say – sound interested even if you feel the call has been transferred to the wrong section or you are recovering from a bad hangover.

Remember that time seems to get exaggerated on the telephone. The person at the other end may only have to wait 10 seconds for you to find some information – but to them it probably feels more like 10 minutes. This means that if you have to leave your desk or if you are interrupted you must explain to the caller that they will have to wait. For example, 'Excuse me, I just have to deal with a quick query, I won't be long.' Make sure you only take a few seconds, and when you get back to the caller apologize for the interruption before continuing the conversation. If your interruption means that you are going to be longer than a few seconds, say you will ring back, and make sure you do.

Also remember that on a normal telephone a caller cannot see what you are doing. You might be doing something relevant to the call such as finding a letter you have filed – but as far as the caller is concerned there is nothing happening and you have left the line dead. Therefore, if they must wait while you find some information, give them a running commentary of what you are doing to assure them that you are still on the end of the line: 'Right, I have the file in my hand. . . I've just got to find the right section now. . . here we are, I can see the copy of the letter now. . . and if I just refer to the second page. . .' and so on.

WHAT TO SAY AND WHAT NOT TO SAY

Even the most confident and articulate speaker can make the most appaling mistakes simply by careless choice of words. Samuel Goldwyn, the Hollywood producer, became well known for his 'Goldwynisms' such as: 'A verbal contract isn't worth the paper it's written on'. It is very easy to fall into such traps and, especially because we have no 'body language' to speak with on the telephone, we need to be especially careful in choosing our words in order to reduce the risk of misunderstanding or ambiguity. A common communication failure on the 'phone is talking in jargon. The following example is paraphrased from British Telecom's guidance booklet on telephone techniques: *The Language of Success*:

Talking in jargon

Most people use jargon these days. Usually, it is a form of shorthand between people sharing common experiences. Sometimes, it is used to deliberately convey the impression of privileged knowledge or even to hide a lack of knowledge. Whatever the case, it hinders communications, so avoid it.

Always Keep It Simple and Straightforward

'The agreement states that Alice, the party of the first part, agrees to sell her business as hereinafter defined to John, the party of the second part.'

By deleting the 'legalspeak' this confusing statement becomes much clearer:

'The agreement states that Alice agrees to sell her business to John.'

ENDING THE CALL

At the end of the call, always check back facts to ensure your understanding and the accuracy of your notes. This goes for any details you take down whether it be telephone numbers, items ordered, or actions you have agreed to take. Take particular care with words with the same vowel sounds such as 'five' and 'nine'. If someone is spelling out something, take care to check in particular 'S' and 'F' which sound the same over the 'phone, and also letters like 'P', 'B', 'V', 'D' and 'T' or 'M' and 'N' which can be confused with each other: 'So, the recipient's name is Mr Node – so that's spelt "N"for Nellie, "O"for Oliver, "D"for David, "E"for Edward?'

The official Telecom alphabetical code is as follows:

A for Alfred	J for Jack	S for Samuel
B for Bejamin	K for King	T for Tommy
C for Charlie	L for Lucy	U for Uncle
D for David	M for Mary	V for Victor
E for Edward	N for Nellie	W for William
F for Frederick	O for Oliver	X for X-ray
G for George	P for Peter	Y for Yellow
H for Harry	Q for Queen	Z for Zebra
I for Isaac	R for Robert	

An aggravating ending is when people say 'goodbye' and then suddenly think of another topic they wanted to cover. For the person at the other end this is confusing and sounds inefficient. If you jot down the headings of topics you want to cover before you make the call this won't happen.

Some people seem to be afraid of putting the receiver down at the end of the call. They prolong the agony by repeating 'goodbye' or variations of it so that you get a string of meaningless endings: 'See you then. . . thank you again. . . bye then. . . nice to talk to you. . . bye. . .' and then the receiver reluctantly put down. This is not very business-like.

Once the subjects of the call have been covered, say 'thank you' and 'good-bye', hear their 'goodbye' and put the receiver down gently, not too fast. You should only need to say 'goodbye' once.

HANDLING DIFFICULT CALLS

British Telecom's booklet 'The Language of Success' mentioned above gives five types of difficult people you might find at the other end of the telephone line:

The Bulldozers

They will try to crush anyone who stands in their way and will never admit they are wrong. You have to be quick to get a word in, but they rarely listen anyway.

How to handle them

- Avoid challenging their imagined expertize (which may be seen as a personal attack;
- Assemble all your facts and figures before phoning them;
- Don't interrupt but make your point when you get the opportunity: 'May I suggest. . .?' (By asking permission, the caller will feel important and you will be able to have your say.)

avoid challenges and don't interrupt

The Passives

Talking to passive people is like talking to a sponge. Your conversation flows down the line and the only (occasional) response you get is 'Mmmm' or 'I see'. You have no idea how your communication is being received.

How to handle them

- Don't be thrown by their silence;
- Press on with what you want to say even in the face of seeming indifference;
- Ask direct questions and wait in silence for the answer; this compels a response;

press on and ask direct questions

The Yes'ers

These people always agree with what you are saying, but you get the feeling when you have finished that they have no intention of acting on your calls.

How to handle them

- Ask questions which challenge their understanding of the conversation;
- Try to commit them to times and dates, if relevant;
- Confirm the conversation in writing after the call, possibly by fax (always a good idea anyway).

ask challenging questions and confirm conversations

The No'ers

These people say 'No' to anything suggested, almost as a matter of principle. It can be a depressing experience. . .

How to handle them

- Be positive and use encouraging and enthusiastic language;
- Do not get into an argument with them as it will cement their determination to say 'No';
- When they respond positively or even uncertainly, react warmly and tell them how valuable their co-operation is.

be positive and don't resort to a slanging match.

The Snipers

Instead of being openly angry or aggressive they use innuendoes and sarcasm.

How to handle them

- Do not react with sarcasm and don't acknowledge innuendo (that is what they want you to do);
- Break down their hostility with words like 'I'm sorry if you feel that way';
- Do not accept their version of events use.

subtlety not sarcasm.

THE MANY DIFFERENT USES FOR THE TELEPHONE

People in your workplace probably use the telephone for a number of different things. The techniques for good general communication apply to telephones, although it is difficult to gauge the effect of your communication on a standard telephone because you cannot see the other person's body language.

Staff should not waste time on unnecessary conversations and should not use business lines for private calls except in special or urgent cases. There should be a policy on this in your company which should be known to all the staff and enforced by all of them.

There are more telephone techniques for special types of communication over the 'phone, such as telephone sales and marketing, negotiating over the 'phone, handling telephone queries, specific telephone etiquette for calls abroad – and there are courses available to help staff do these activities effectively.

Activity

---

1   Find out and list the different uses your telephones are put to on a daily basis. List them below.

Sales, customer queries, anything else?

2   Ring up your organization with a query and appraise it against the telephone techniques listed above.

Communicating effectively in meetings

Most managers spend a great deal of time in meetings and if this time is to be spent effectively and the objectives of the meeting are to be met, it is essential that the members of the meeting communicate well. Rachel Pinney (op cit) points out that in discussion groups and meetings, interruptions often occur and repartee take place, causing disruption and irritation. The over-talker over-talks, the under-talker under-talks; both are frustrated and neither is fully heard.

The success of a meeting (and the criteria by which I define the word 'meeting' in this case is when three or more people come together for at least 30 minutes to achieve a result) is dependent on two major factors:

1   The mechanics

such as:

- the presence of clear objective/s;
- the quality of the agenda;
- whether the 'right' people are present;
- whether members have received adequate notice of the meeting, the correct paperwork and so on;
- suitable accommodation.

2   Behaviour of the members

- what the chairperson and members say and do before, during and after the meeting

In discussing communication techniques, we need to look at the second of these.

People often find it difficult to behave assertively and contribute effectively in meetings, even though they may be perfectly confident on a one-to-one basis. Perhaps they feel their performance will be 'judged' in some way? Many people see meetings as challenging, uncomfortable and stressful and this often leads to a change in normal behaviour. Those who are usually confident, assertive people may become aggressive or submissive in a meeting, which may say something about how they feel about themselves, or perhaps they are unclear about their rights as members of the meeting.

There are three stages when this uncomfortable feeling may occur – before, during and after the meeting. Before the meeting, a person may have thoughts along the lines 'I'm obviously going to be in a minority in the meeting, so there is no point in my saying anything'. Conversely, a person may feel quite aggressive towards another who will be present at the meeting and may plan to 'put him on the spot'. A more effective way of approaching these thoughts would be (respectively) 'I may well be in a minority at the meeting, but I will put my point across as well as I can. I may not succeed in influencing the others but I will have done as much as I can.'; 'I feel really angry with John about the way he has introduced a new procedure without consulting me, but I will see him on a one-to-one basis about it rather than putting him on the spot at the meeting.'

During the meeting, a person feeling inadequate and submissive may wish to put forward an opinion or idea, but may think 'It's only my point of view and the others will not want to hear that', rather than taking an assertive approach such as 'I have the right to put my point of view and be listened to. The others may not agree with me, but they will respect what I have to say.' Or, 'I don't understand what has just been said, but if I ask a question they will think I am stupid' rather than 'I cannot contribute effectively if I don't understand and I have the right to ask for clarification. It doesn't mean that I am stupid.' You get the idea?

After the meeting, some people who have been brave enough to speak assertively, put forward their ideas and views, challenge others' opinions and so on, often chastise themselves: 'I wish I hadn't said that'; 'that must have sounded really silly'. . . nine times out of ten what the person contributed was justifiable, respected and worthwhile, but such people have to carry out the self-flagellation and postmortem. If you are such a person, perhaps you need to examine the reasons why you punish yourself in this way.

You may find the following helpful:

A BILL OF RIGHTS FOR MEMBERS OF A MEETING

I have a right to:

- give my opinions and ideas;
- be listened to and reacted to;
- understand what is being said;
- spend my time in meetings productively;
- disagree with others' views and opinions;
- make my contribution without being interrupted;
- know in advance the objective/s of the meeting;
- know in advance the approximate length of the meeting.

As with all rights, of course, it depends whether you feel able to accept them, because whether you do accept your rights as a member of the meeting, or whether you fail to accept them will have a direct bearing on how you behave at the meeting.

TIPS FOR COMMUNICATING EFFECTIVELY IN MEETINGS

You have an important responsibility in meetings – that of *controlling your behaviour*. Your choice of behaviour is entirely yours. If you choose to lose your temper, become aggressive, thump the table, dominate everyone else and deny anyone else the right to speak, you are not behaving as a responsible and effective member of the meeting, whose responsibility it is to move the meeting forward to a satisfactory conclusion in achieving its objectives. Nor are you doing so if you choose to sit in a silent, submissive heap, contributing nothing and whining afterwards that you did not agree with the outcomes. Make sure that your behaviour helps rather than hinders the effectiveness of the meeting.

NINE AIDS TO EFFECTIVE MEETING CONTRIBUTIONS

1   *Be prepared*

Prepare beforehand so that you are well briefed and well informed about the various items on the agenda to be discussed. Arrive punctually for the meeting with the relevant agenda and papers.

2   *Keep your contributions short*

If you ramble on with a long, complex speech your message will be diluted. Make one or two succinct, relevant and constructive points and shut up!

3   *Avoid interrupting others and do not let others interrupt you*

The only excuse for interrupting others is when the meeting has a poor Chair and it becomes necessary for someone to stop a long, rambling monologue.

Otherwise don't. Providing you are not guilty of providing such a monologue, you have the right to prevent interruption – 'I would like to finish the point I'm making. . .'

4   *Keep non-verbal behaviour assertive*

It is pointless getting the words right if your tone of voice, body language, eye contact and so on do not complement them. Too quiet and you will be interrupted and not taken seriously (especially if you fiddle with your papers, put your hand over your mouth while speaking and avoid eye contact with anyone). Too loud, with staring eye contact and aggressive gestures means you will not be 'heard' and will not be respected.

Eye contact is very important. Use it wisely: to catch the Chair's eye to let him/her know you want to speak; distribute it between Chair and members while speaking, especially to those for whom the contribution has most relevance. It signals you want a response and it also enables you to see their reaction to your contribution.

Keep your voice calm and medium paced, with an even pitch and volume. Maintain an approaching, but not dominating body position, leaning forward slightly (not dominatingly) and be aware of what your facial expression is 'saying'.

5   *Timing your contributions*

It is not just what you say that counts, but when you say it. The impact may be lost if you do not make your point at the relevant time on the agenda, or if you wait until the very last moment before putting an opposing point of view. If the members are on the verge of a decision, they will be irritated and may become aggressive towards you.

6   *Changing your mind*

People tend to believe that it is weak to change one's mind. On the contrary, it can be an extremely strong thing to do if, for example, having held a particular view, you hear facts put forward which make you realize that you were wrong. You do not need to apologize for it. Just be honest and open: 'In the light of what you have said, Tom, I realize that I was wrong. I will change my view and would like to vote in favour of . . .'

(If you stick defiantly to your original view because you think by changing your mind you will come across as weak or indecisive, you are actually behaving aggressively.)

7   *Falling in with the majority*

Even though you may not fully agree with a decision, it is sometimes necessary to go along with the majority in order to enable the meeting to reach an effective conclusion.

If you stick to your guns come what may, you may be labelled as 'awkward' and people may fail to listen to you or take you seriously on other occasions. If you feel really strongly about something, then obviously you should make your view known, but if you feel able to go along with the majority on a particular issue you could say something like 'I do not see a way around this. I would really prefer. . . but in view of time, I am happy to go along with the idea'.

8   *Not falling in with an apparent majority*

Have you ever been in a meeting when one or two dominant members have spoken in such a way that it would seem everyone agrees on a certain point. You may not agree, but as everyone else seems to, you keep quiet.

After the meeting, you hear other members saying 'I didn't agree with John or Joy, but I didn't like to say so because everyone else seemed to.' Whereupon others say 'I felt the same' and it becomes apparent that the majority did not agree with John or Joy, but they were so influential in their contribution that no-one challenged them. Therefore, a decision was made with only a minimum of support.

9   *Helping the meeting to improve its effectiveness*

If you accept the right to spend your time productively, you will take on a degree of responsibility for the way the meeting is organized. This is not just the prerogative of the Chairperson (who may be a poor one!).

For example, if no-one has allocated a finish time for the meeting, you could suggest that this be done; you could suggest that a flip chart be used to write up ideas; you might suggest that items on the agenda be tackled in a different order for some pertinent reason.

You will not embarrass the Chairperson if you use:

'I' statements –

'I would find it really helpful if we could have five minutes to read this information.'

Responsive assertions –

'How about spending no more than half-an-hour on this item?'

You can also help by influencing others' behaviour. For example, you could ask a quiet member to contribute when you see he or she is unsuccessfully trying to catch the Chairperson's eye – 'Kay may have a view on this?'. But do not try to take over the Chair – that is not responsible member behaviour!

BEHAVIOUR WHICH MAKES A COMMITTEE MEMBER INEFFECTUAL IN MEETINGS

1 Irregular attendance, frequently late in arriving and early in leaving;
2 Not being prepared, forgetting agenda and papers; ill-informed on issues to be discussed;
3 Uninterested, apathetic approach; not being prepared to take part in the discussion;
4 Aggressive, dogmatic behaviour; wanting to dominate the discussion and get their own way; putting other people down; being disruptive and trying to take over the role of the Chair;
5 Failure to listen to others or discussion about items in which they are not interested; only attentive during the parts of the Agenda in which they are personally involved;
6 Having their own 'hidden agenda' or their own goals for the meeting.

Activity

Step one –

Sit quietly with your eyes shut and visualize yourself at an imagined business meeting. You are communicating in a way which makes you feel really good.

- What are you saying?
- How do you sound?
- How do you look?
- How do you feel?

Step two –

Now think about a meeting which you have been at recently where you did not behave in this way and ask yourself why you didn't. Think about the topic of the meeting, the people there, how you felt about things and so on.

Step three –

Finally, ask yourself what you need to do to overcome the fences you identified in step two so that you can behave in the way you imagined and felt good about in step one. What rights do you need to give yourself? What responsibilities should you be taking as a member of the meeting? What are your thoughts before, during and after the meeting?

Remember – meetings are there for you to communicate your views, ideas, opinions and feelings. But you have to make them work for you.

CHAIRING A MEETING

It is quite possible that as a manager you will be involved in chairing meetings. The role of Chair is not an easy one. Let us look at some of the responsibilities of this position.

Responsibilities of the person chairing the meeting

1 Before the meeting, the Chair should liaise with the secretary about arrangements for the meeting, including the date, time and place, the contents of the agenda, any papers which need to be circulated prior to the meeting and ensure that the correct information is circulated to the members of the meeting at the correct time.

2 The Chair should open the meeting (on time) and make sure everyone has their relevant papers and a copy of the agenda, and that people know how long the meeting is likely to last. It is the Chairperson's responsibility to keep the meeting to time, while allowing sufficient time for each item on the agenda.

3 At a formal meeting the Chair will ask the secretary to give any apologies from absent members which have been received. The secretary will then be asked to read the Minutes of the last meeting, or these may be 'taken as read' (that is, when they have been circulated previously), at the conclusion of which the Chair will ask the members if they agree the Minutes as being a true record of the previous meeting, make any necessary amendments and sign them as approved. The Chair will then ask if there are any 'matters arising' – that is, any matters to be reported on arising from the previous meeting's Minutes which do not appear on the agenda for the current meeting.

4 It is unlikely that the Chairperson will give a personal view on the matters under discussion (unless it is a formal meeting and the membership is equally divided when voting on a decision, when the Chair will give a 'casting vote'), although in an informal meeting the Chair may possibly enter the debate. The Chair must remain objective at all times.

5 It is the Chair's responsibility to allow and encourage members to speak and he/she should constantly watch for those wishing to speak, especially those who are rather reticent to speak. The Chair should also restrict the contributions of those who tend to ramble so that all who wish to speak may do so. Members should be encouraged to speak to others through 'the Chair'.

   This helps to avoid 'free-for-all' discussion and prevents mini-meetings taking place between a few people.

6 Having allowed sufficient discussion on an Agenda item, the Chair should bring the subject to a conclusion by summarizing what has been said. If a decision has to be made, the Chair will usually take a vote. In a formal meeting this may take the form of someone to propose the motion, someone to second it and a vote to find the number of members in favour of the motion and those against it.

7 The Chair will introduce each item on the Agenda in turn and may decide to alter the sequence of items or postpone others to the next meeting if time is running short.

8 At the end of the meeting, the Chairperson is responsible for fixing the date, time and place of the next meeting and for liaising with the secretary on any action necessary. After the meeting, the secretary usually gives draft minutes of the meeting to the Chair for approval before he/she circulates them to the members.

It is important that a Chairperson is well prepared before the meeting. The objectives of the meeting should be clearly understood and the more sensitive or controversial items on the Agenda prepared for. The Chair should ideally know the members who will be present and be able to recognize the 'stronger' and 'weaker' members. They should be insightfully aware when discussion on a particular item is no longer fruitful and bring such discussion to a meaningful conclusion.

The role of Chairperson is so important in meetings that it is true to say that the effectiveness of the meeting, whether it meets its objectives, and whether the members feel that it has been worthwhile, is largely the Chair's responsibility. We have all been in meetings which we have considered a total waste of time, with very little having been achieved except a great deal of frustration on the part of everyone present. If you think about such meetings which you have attended, think about the performance of the Chairperson and how effective it was. (Perhaps you were the Chair yourself!)

TYPES OF BUSINESS MEETINGS

1   Annual General Meeting

If the organization is a limited company, the law requires it to hold an Annual General Meeting for all interested parties (such as the directors and the shareholders). This constitutes an annual appraisal of the company's performance and affairs.

2   Extraordinary General Meeting

An Extraordinary General Meeting is called when it is demanded by a certain percentage of the voting shares and its purpose is to consider any abnormal matter which appears to those shareholders to give cause for concern.

3   Board Meetings

The Directors of an organization will meet at regular intervals to discuss the policy affairs of the company.

4   Management Meetings

Management meetings of various kinds take place to discuss the implementation of the Board's policies. (Note, the Managing Director is the link between the Board of Directors and the Management of the company as he/she is a member of both bodies.) Senior, middle and junior managers may all be involved in management meetings of various kinds.

5   Departmental/Team Meetings

The manager of a department or team, having attended the Management meeting, will probably hold a departmental meeting to brief his team as to their involvement in implementing the company policies and strategies. These are operational meetings, literally concerned with the hands-on day-to-day operation of the business.

6   Meetings held for specific reasons

Most of meetings held within an organization revolve around particular topics. There are numerous reasons why people call meetings. They may be working parties, specific committees (such as the sports and social club), or ad hoc meetings – those arranged for a special purpose.

Written meeting procedures (notice of meeting, agendas, minutes and so on) will be found on page 167 in chapter six.

Interviewing and questioning techniques

As first line managers, at some point you will undoubtedly become involved in interviewing. I am defining 'interview' here as a face-to-face meeting and discussion between two or more people for a specific purpose. We can take the communication which takes place in the interview to mean that which we have talked about previously: the transference of ideas, facts and feelings between the people involved in order to achieve an understanding between them. In an interview, however, the conversation is directed towards its objective or purpose by the interviewer.

Each interview will, of course, be different depending on its purpose and on the individuals concerned, but there are a few common general points which apply to all of them:

The three P's:

Purpose of the interview

- establish the objectives to be achieved.

Preparation
- gather the facts;
- ensure privacy and no interruptions;
- allow adequate time;
- plan your approach.

Procedure

- put interviewee at ease and establish rapport;
- explain the purpose of the interview;
- encourage the interviewee to express his or her views;
- use open questions;
- listen and watch;
- investigate and clarify areas which are not clear;
- take notes but do not be 'glued' to your notepad;
- check information before taking a decision;
- judge as impartially as possible – avoid personal bias;
- summarize at regular intervals;
- conclude on a positive note by stating what action will be taken and by what date.

The skills of interviewing

A good interviewer will control an interview without doing all the talking. The object of the exercise is to get the interviewee to talk in order to provide you with the information you need to make decisions

---

An effective interviewer needs to be able to:

- build rapport;
- show empathy;
- get the interviewee to open up;
- listen actively;
- use appropriate questioning techniques;
- retain control of the interview;
- be non-judgmental;
- be perceptive;
- take minimal but accurate notes;
- follow a structure.

QUESTIONING TECHNIQUES

'I keep six honest serving men
(They taught me all I knew);
Their names were What, and Why, and When
And How and Where and Who.'

So wrote Rudyard Kipling in the Just-so Stories and this verse gives us all we need to know about the use of so-called 'open' questions.

Open questions are those which elicit more than a 'Yes' or 'No' answer from the person giving the response (which are known as 'closed' questions and have their purpose as we shall see).

Activity

Can you form a question beginning with the words What, Why, When, How, Where or Who to which you can give the response 'Yes' or 'No'? (Answer at the end of the chapter.)

The purpose of questioning an interviewee, in whatever kind of interview you are conducting, is to get the person talking in order that you may gain certain information. You may want facts, opinions, details of their skills, knowledge or experience, feelings. . . information which will help you to make some kind of decision. Without the correct information, you cannot make that decision. It is obviously important, therefore, that you phrase your question clearly and unambiguously in order to provide a framework for the intervie-wee to respond with the information you require. Questions can often be thought through before the interview begins.

I said earlier that closed questions also serve a purpose. Once having gained a full verbal response from the interviewee, the interviewer can clar-ify understanding or gain confirmation by paraphrasing back to the intervie-wee what they have said in a way which enables the person to say 'Yes' or 'No'. If it is 'No', the interviewer can use further open questions to gain fur-ther understanding or whatever.

For example, supposing you asked a candidate at a selection interview 'Why did you decide to apply for this post?' (open) to which your interviewee responds with information about the job they currently hold, but which does-n't stretch them, you can then confirm and clarify his or her response by ask-ing 'So you feel that this job would give you the opportunity to use the skills and experience you have gained in your present post and at the same time give you more responsibility?' (closed) to which the person has to answer 'Yes' (that is, you've got it right) or 'No' (you've got it wrong, in which case you would proceed with more open questions to gain further information).

Open questions, therefore, are used to get the interviewee talking about ideas and feelings as well as facts. They are good questions to use in a non-directive situation.

Closed questions are used to summarize or to bring back the conversation to the subject if the discussion has wandered. They are also used to clarify understanding. In addition to open and closed questions, there are a number of other types of questions which can be used in interviewing.

For example:

Specific questions – 'On what date did you join your present firm?' These are used to find out facts and take a directive approach. (They are useful to curb an over-talkative interviewee!)

Reverse questions – 'You are not too happy with your present post then?' Questions which reverse a statement by rephrasing it and sending it back to the interviewee, keeping him talking. They avoid personal involvement or subjective bias.

Leading questions – 'I suppose you would not have approached the situa-tion in that way?' What other answer can the interviewee give but 'No' – the answer is given in the question. (A question can become a leading question not just by the use of words, but also by the inflection or tone of voice, or even by a hesitation.) Leading questions can be useful for relaxing a nervous per-son at the beginning of an interview: 'I expect you are feeling a little nervous?'

Hypothetical questions – 'If I were to offer you a job with this company, would you be interested?' 'Supposing you were the marketing manager now, what would you be doing?' These are good for testing possible reactions and examine the thinking power of the interviewee. They ask for reasoned answers based upon theoretical facts.

Reflective questions — the interviewee asks 'What should I do?' to which the interviewer responds 'Well, what do you think you should do?' This response turns the question back to the asker. This technique is particularly useful in the counselling interview.

PREPARATION FOR AN INTERVIEW

Some of all of the following may apply, depending on the type of interview you are conducting:

- consider timing and length of time needed;
- consider a suitable location;
- ensure privacy;
- ensure no interruptions (people or phone);
- arrange tea/coffee, tissues available etc;
- collate all facts and information required;
- plan your approach and meeting structure;
- plan possible questions to ask;
- consider possible responses and outcomes;
- anticipate likely questions and your responses;
- check company procedures;
- check any legal requirements;
- notify others concerned.

CONDUCTING AN INTERVIEW

Throughout the interview, ensure that you adopt the right style. Your style is likely to be different in a variety of interview situations, such as disciplinary, selection, appraisal, counselling and so on.

Display positive body language during the interview and make sure that the tone of your voice matches the words you are saying. For example, if you are disciplining an employee, your words will not carry meaning if you adopt a 'there, there' attitude and carry out a friendly chat perched on the edge of your desk or over a cup of coffee in the canteen. (Many managers take this approach in disciplinary interviews because they find this part of their role hard – possibly because they wish to remain popular with their staff, or are afraid of being seen as 'ruthless'.) Conversely, to listen to someone in a counselling interview who is pouring their heart out while you sit behind your desk displaying defensive body language is hardly encouraging (although perhaps understandable for some managers who feel threatened by hearing about feelings and cannot face emotion).

The Introduction

- Put the interviewee at ease and establish rapport;
- Explain you are going to take notes and the reasons for them (this may not be necessary or acceptable in a counselling interview);
- Clarify the purpose of the interview;
- Set the scene and establish the ground rules.

The main part of the Interview

- Ask open questions (see above);
- Make statements to clarify and give information;
- Listen actively;
- Observe the interviewee;
- Maintain eye contact with the interviewee, but not constantly so that the person feels threatened or uncomfortable (around 30–60 per cent is about right);
- Allow 'pause' time for the interviewee to reflect and consider before they speak;
- Check understanding of both parties as you go along.

The conclusion

- Summarize and ask if the interviewee has any further questions;
- Discuss any follow-up action and confirm dates and times if relevant;
- Conclude the meeting.

After the interview, run through your notes to make sure that you have all the information you need in writing. You may think you will remember things about an interview, but it is probable that you won't. If you are seeing more than one person in a session, check that your notes are complete before the next interview.

A few interview don'ts

- get personal;
- be aggressive;
- get involved in arguments;
- rush the interviewee;
- interrupt/finish sentences for them;
- be flippant;
- laugh at the interviewee;
- be sarcastic;
- raise your voice/display anger;
- prejudge/assume;

- display boredom/lack of interest;
- display your own prejudices/bias;
- digress/lose purpose of the meeting.

TYPES OF INTERVIEW

Interviewing is not just about job selection. You will probably also be involved in some or all of the following:

- disciplinary interviews;
- grievance interviews;
- appraisal/development interviews;
- counselling/coaching interviews;
- feedback interviews;
- fact finding interviews;
- redundancy and other termination interviews.

Some of these which are more commonly undertaken by line managers are discussed in more detail below.

Selection interviews

The purpose of a selection interview is to establish if a person is suitable for a position and meets the requirements of a predetermined job description and employee specification.

It is also to provide information to the interviewee so that he or she can decide whether the job is for them, should it be offered to them.

Let us assume that the job description is already written, the post advertised and a short list of suitable candidates drawn up for interview. It is possible that a member of the personnel department will have carried out initial interviews, tests and so on and that you, as the line manager involved, may then meet the candidates to make a final choice.

You must make a decision about the essential criteria within the job description which you consider most important and the type of personality you are looking for. Sometimes, a person may have all the right qualifications, skills and experience for a job, but may not 'fit' into an existing team. On the other hand, a person could perhaps have fewer skills or experience, but be the type of personality who would immediately enhance the team. It may be a more satisfactory appointment and the skills developed with training.

Selection interviewing techniques can be drawn from those given above, but care must be taken to avoid personal bias and it is important that you do not ask 'sensitive' questions which may cause offence or may contravene the Equal Opportunities Act.

Try to concentrate on the interviewee and listen to what they say. It is all too easy to fall into the trap of thinking what you want to ask next and therefore you fail to listen properly to what the candidate is saying. Respond to their questions clearly and unambiguously, but avoid losing control of the interview. Some candidates ramble on at great length – possibly through nerves – and it is the responsibility of the interviewer to 'hold the reins' and manage the structure of the interview.

Another trap which interviewers tend to fall into is failing to stick to their selection criteria and making sometimes instant subjective judgements about a person following 'intuition' or 'feelings'. The latter are not necessarily wrong in selection interviewing, but snap decisions are not always the best ones.

Try to keep an open mind until the interview comes to an end. If you are interviewing a number of candidates, consistency in questioning is important. Try to ask the same kind of questions of each candidate so that the results are comparable.

The Seven-Point plan

Devised by Professor Alec Rodger of the National Institute of Industrial Psychology, this plan can be regarded as a check-list of the main factors to be considered in preparing a 'person specification' before the interview and a reminder during the interview.

- **Physical make-up**: appearance, build, speech, eyesight;
- **Attainments**: educational qualifications, experience relevant to the post;
- **General intelligence**: ability to understand and deal with complex problems: is the person required to be 'quick on the uptake' or is the thinking process slow?
- **Specialized aptitudes**: manual dexterity, musical ear, languages, mechanical aptitude, numeracy etc;
- **Interests**: social/leisure, solitary or social, active or passive in leisure organizations?
- **Disposition**: very important if the job requires dealing with others inside and/or outside the organization. Does the job require a leader or a follower? Patience, concentration, suitability for confidentiality.
- **Circumstances**: stability, domestic situation, mobility, readiness to work irregular hours, are own tools or finance or car required?

Not all jobs will require consideration of all parts of these factors.

Selection interviewing is a topic which deserves a book of its own and, of course, many books have been written on the subject. If your job is going to involve you in selection interviewing, it is recommended that you undertake specialist training in the skill and practise your techniques on a willing 'guinea pig' before trying it 'for real'.

Disciplinary interviews

The purpose of a disciplinary interview is to examine the situation concerned, with a view to establishing the facts prior to deciding if disciplinary action is required. It is also to inform and correct unacceptable behaviour or performance to prevent recurrence, helping the person to improve and giving guidance. It may be necessary to provide official warnings to the employee concerned. A model for giving constructive critical feedback is given in the next section. It may also be helpful in carrying out disciplinary interviews.

The subject is not developed further because it is unlikely that first line managers will be involved in carrying out disciplinary interviews to any degree. If you are required to do this, it is recommended that you read specific books on the subject.

Appraisal interviews

Appraisal, or review interviews are usually carried out by an employee's line manager. They provide an opportunity to discuss the employee's work performance over a period of time, often the past twelve months, evaluating it against previously agreed objectives, targets and performance indicators. Opportunities for improvement, training and development can be identified, and targets and goals can be set Appraisal interviews should be two-way sessions which give both parties an opportunity to put their point of view and discuss any issues which arise.

There is no one way of carrying out appraisal interviews, but they should be a fairly formal process with recorded notes of the meeting signed by both line manager and employee as a true record. Some organizations have a points system whereby the line manager assesses the employee and marks are given to grade the employee's performance. Occasionally, organizations do this without the employee being given the opportunity to know their grade, but usually it is an agreed grading between the two people concerned. The grades are sometimes used in future salary reviews, or when the employee may be considered for promotion.

Most companies use a printed appraisal or review form, but this is not strictly necessary. Usually, the employee receives part of the appraisal questionnaire to complete prior to the interview and the manager likewise. They then compare their thinking and discuss the outcomes. Both sign the final document to agree their acceptance of its content.

Line managers are often asked to appraise their staff with little or no training in how to do it. The usual techniques apply of open questions to encourage the employee to give their own views, identify any problems they may have, any training and development issues and so on. The manager may need to give constructive feedback on something he or she wishes the employee to improve. Here, the 'praise sandwich' is useful – praise the person for something which they have done well, suggest areas where they might improve and finish with further positive comments so that the person leaves the meeting feeling it was worthwhile.

Such feedback on the part of the manager should always be given constructively, rather than negatively. There is a good model for this, although I have to confess it is not mine and I do not know its source.

Giving constructive feedback:

Constructive criticism or feedback is particularly useful in situations where you would like someone to modify or change their behaviour. A structured format is suggested as a way of practising the skill, but as you become more experienced, you will be able to develop a more natural style that includes the necessary components, which are:

1 **When you. . .** Describe the behaviour – behaviour is a person's actions – what they say or do. Be specific about what you saw or heard the person do (the objective facts), but leave out your judgements and interpretations (these are open to being questioned and make the person defensive). Give a recent example of what you are referring to. Avoid using generalizations (always, never) and references to the number of times the problem has occurred (frequently, repeatedly, often).

2 **I feel. . .** Share your feelings – this part of the message conveys the importance of what you are saying. You need to find a feeling word which captures the type and level of the emotion you feel in connection with the person's behaviour. Don't go over the top – 'I feel outraged' when you really mean 'I am irritated' will not be taken seriously. **Own your feelings**. Don't say 'You make me feel. . .' – others are not responsible for creating your feelings. Do not use this part of the statement to convey judgements – 'I feel that you are thoughtless' is a judgement.

3 **Because. . .** Describe the effect of the behaviour on you – you need to ensure that the person understands the purpose of your raising the issue. That is, their behaviour is affecting you in a negative way. Specify the effect as concretely as possible. Do not exaggerate – the person is likely to accept that their behaviour causes you certain problems but is unlikely to believe that your job is impossible because of it.

4 **I would prefer. . .** Say what you want to be different – this part of the message may seem obvious, but people are more likely to agree to modify their behaviour if you make it very clear exactly how you would like them to behave differently. Say what you want rather than what you don't want.

Let us take an example of the above model. Supposing you were carrying out an appraisal interview with a member of your staff who continually gossiped about others in your team and thereby caused a lot of ill feeling in the department (and wasted a lot of everyone's time). You might try the following:

'**When I heard you telling Peter and Parvin about Jo's marital problems when you were standing by the photocopier yesterday** (*specific incident, without 'always' 'frequently' etc even though you might feel like saying that!*), **I was disappointed** (*try to find a word to describe your feelings which is not over the top but pertinent to the situation*) **because** (*describe the effect of the behaviour on you, not on Jo – you do not know how she felt, after all*) **you were gossiping about your colleague's private life which is nothing to do with people here unless she chooses to discuss it herself. I would prefer you to keep any knowledge you have on the subject to yourself and, in any case, to concentrate on your work in working time.**' (*You could have said 'Do not. . .' but remember that this part of the model suggests that you say what you want rather than what you don't want.*)

Now, admittedly, you would be unlikely to discuss such an incident as this at an appraisal interview, but it is an example of how to use the model to give constructive feedback.

Activity[1]

Choose a member of your staff whose performance is not as good as it should be and write down what you would say if you were to speak to the person, working through the following points. Be as precise as you can and always constructive, avoiding prejudice, bias and subjectivity.

1   What targets were set and what performance indicators used?
2   Which targets were met and which missed? What have been the implications of these successes and failures?
    (From this you can arrive at an overall evaluation of the year's performance.)
3   How could you sincerely offer praise for the successes?
4   Summarizing the reasons for the failures which have become apparent in the appraisal, how could you put these across to your employee without appearing threatening? (Make it clear, where relevant, that you are aware that they may have occurred because the person is dependent upon others doing their job properly (including, perhaps, yourself).
5   Summarize the changes needed (personal and organizational). If there are a number of changes to be made, how would you prioritize them?
6   Specify the rewards and punishments contingent upon subsequent performance. Clarify what organizational resources are available to support the changes.

Coaching interviews

The purpose of a coaching interview is to discuss with and advise on problems an employee has, probably work-based, but not necessarily, with a view to solving or alleviating the problem or to help the person come to terms with it.

Counselling interviews

The purpose of a counselling interview is to provide a safe environment for the employee to talk about their problem(s), without fear of judgement or recrimination, in order to find their own way through to a solution or alleviation of the problem. The interviewer is not there to advise or provide solutions, but merely to listen, paraphrase back to the interviewee what they have said in order to clarify and confirm understanding, and – by the use of open questions – encourage the interviewee to fully explore their feelings.

One of the basic differences between coaching and counselling interviews is that whereas the interviewer would advise and suggest solutions to problems in a coaching situation, **at no time** would this ever happen in a counselling interview, where the interviewee is totally responsible for working through their problem and coming to a solution for themselves. (This is very difficult for managers who are used to making decisions and providing solutions to problems!)

Another difference is that coaching interviews involve 'head thinking'. That is, the discussion which takes place intellectualizes the situation by thought processes. Counselling, on the other hand, involves 'heart searching'. The interviewee is encouraged to explore **feelings** rather than thoughts.

FINALLY ON THE TOPIC OF INTERVIEWING. . .

Some barriers to the communication process in interviews:

- **The Environment:**

  The room – its size, warmth, comfort, tidiness;
  The layout of the furniture – large desk, small chair. . .;
  Bad positioning of the interviewee such as sun in their eyes;
  Interruptions by people or the 'phone ringing;
  Distractions – visual or aural, or from the interviewer themselves (mannerisms such as pencil chewing, hand/foot tapping. . .).

- **The Psychology between interviewer and interviewee:**

  Lack of understanding;
  Misunderstandings;
  Prejudice and bias;
  Status;
  Lack of confidence;
  Displayed boredom, impatience or irritation;
  Losing control of the interview.

- **Language**

> *Use of jargon;*
> *Too much talking by the interviewer;*
> *Speaking down to the interviewee;*
> *Failing to pitch conversation at the right level and failing*
> *to establish rapport;*
> *Interrupting interviewee;*
> *Poor questioning techniques;*
> *Failing to answer interviewee's questions adequately.*

First impressions may be misleading – avoid snap decisions

Answer to the Activity on page 98

There are only two questions beginning with the words What, Why, When, How, Where or Who to which a 'Yes' or 'No' answer applies:

What is the opposite of the word 'Yes'? Answer = 'No'
What is the opposite of the word 'No'? Answer = 'Yes'
(Sorry, trick question!)

BIBLIOGRAPHY

For further reading on the subjects in this chapter see:

Blanchard, K. & Lorber, R., *The One Minute Manager*, Fontana, 1982

Blanchard, K. & Lorber, R., *Putting The One Minute Manager To Work*, Fontana, 1984

Breakwell, G.M., *Interviewing*, British Psychological Society & Routledge, 1990

Chisholm, P., *Count on Confidence*, Macmillan, 1990

Lewis, D. & Fielding, G., *The Language of Success*, British Telecom

Lockett, J., *Be The Most Effective Manager In Your Business*, Thorsons Publishing Group, 1987

Stubbs, D.R., *Assertiveness At Work*, Pan, p 207, 1985

---

1 With acknowledgement to Breakwell, G.M., *Interviewing*,The British Psychological Society and Routledge Ltd, p 67, 1990

PART TWO

HOW WE COMMUNICATE THE MESSAGE THROUGH THE WRITTEN WORD

CHAPTER FOUR

Sorting Out the Grammar

*If language is not correct, then what is said is not what is meant;
if what is said is not what is meant, then what ought to be done
remains undone.*

Confucius

IN THIS CHAPTER WE WILL LOOK AT THE FOLLOWING AREAS:

- recent changes in acceptable 'rules' of grammar;
- sentences and paragraphs;
- some potential grammar 'trips' to watch out for;
- punctuation;
- spelling;
- titles and forms of address.

When considering what to put in this part of the book, I came to the conclusion that we really need to look at some basic grammar before we come on to written communication such as letter writing. In my experience, many managers find written communication difficult because they do not have the fundamentals of English grammar and therefore find syntax, punctuation and spelling eludes them. This is not a criticism as many will have not had the opportunity to acquire this knowledge. One of the constructive aspects of management is that one can become a manager by the skill of managing people, without necessarily having had a particularly academic education. This, however, becomes a great handicap when it is necessary to communicate through the written word.

It you think that you have a thorough grasp of the English language, feel free to skip this chapter and go on to the next one which looks at writing business letters and reports.

Most of us remember English lessons at school, struggling with obscure concepts such as finite verbs, the use of the semicolon, and 'i before e except after c'. Some of us grew to love the use of the English language and the way it is expressed. Others, probably because they were badly taught in the first place, grew to fear grammar, got into bad habits and the effectiveness of their communication suffered as a result. More recently, parts of the educational system went through a 'grammar rules are not important' phase. At the time, I was teaching secretarial and business studies in further education and it was extremely difficult trying to train people who would be required in the future to correct **their** boss's spelling and punctuation when they had no idea themselves. It was not their fault, of course, the educational system had failed them, but it was hard work for them to get to grips with rules and principles which they could have acquired much more easily when they were younger.

Whatever your situation, use this chapter as a reference guide. It is unlikely that you will want to read it word for word straight through. Rather, use it to dip into when you wish to check something or there is a particular grammar point that you are not sure of.

Recent changes in acceptable 'rules' of grammar

We used to have a lot of rules about words which could not be used at the beginning of paragraphs. It is still considered rather *infra dig* to use the word 'I' as the very first word of a letter, but it is now considered suitable as a word to begin the second and following paragraphs.

In the autumn of 1995, Oxford University Press published 'The Plain English Guide' which attempts to lay down the current rules of good English. It dismisses many of the old English usage rules as mere 'schoolroom mythology'.

Conjunctions such as 'but', 'and' and 'so' were once frowned upon as words with which to open a sentence, but we are now told that this is acceptable.

'There are many examples of fine writers breaking the rules,' says the guide's author, Martin Cuts, research director of the Plain Language Commission. 'Many good authors over the last few hundred years have ignored the [conjunction] myth. Jane Austen begins sentences with 'but' on almost every page and occasionally uses 'and' in the same position'.

Another major grammatical evolvement is the acceptance of the split infinitive. Most of us were taught at school that it was heresy to split our infinitives! This usually involves the use of an adverb between the word 'to' and the verb. Perhaps the most famous example of this is at the beginning of the television series 'Star Trek' – 'To boldly go . . .' The new Guide intimates that the rule against splitting infinitives is a favourite target for linguistic inverted snobs and egalitarians. They maintain that such 'non-rules' (as the OUP calls them) merely serve to distinguish the educated from the ignorant, so that we may condescend to the latter. Language belongs to everyone, they argue, and the only authority is general usage.

I am not completely convinced by this argument, being of the school which finds the English language extremely elegant as it is. I can see, however, that slavish adherence to the rules of grammar for no other reason than 'it has always been so' is plainly ludicrous.

Whatever your view on this, it is true to say that linguistic styles and principles are constantly evolving and it is difficult to keep up to date with what is acceptable and what is not. However, modern usage of written English is definitely moving toward the simpler, oral style and many of the old rules are – for better or worse – on the decline.

Sentences and Paragraphs

Keep sentences fairly short. They should not take the place of a paragraph; rather a paragraph should consist of several sentences. The average sentence should be about 20 words, but the length should be varied to keep the document interesting. Sentences should not contain more than one topic, otherwise they become confusing.

When several sentences have been written on the same theme and you begin one on a totally different subject, start a new paragraph. Paragraphs usually contain three or four sentences, although there is no hard and fast rule. The main thing is to contain a paragraph to one idea or subject. As soon as the subject moves to a different idea, start a new paragraph. One sentence paragraphs should be avoided, although they are becoming more common than they were.

Sentences must have a subject and a verb. A subject of a sentence is the person or thing that is doing what the sentence is talking about:

- **John** went to work.
- **I** am a good cook.

The subject need not necessarily come at the beginning of the sentence:

- When the meeting had finished, **the manager** made two 'phone calls.
- Having typed the letter, **she** took it to her manager for signature.

The trick to finding the subject of a sentence is to ask yourself who or what is doing or being something.

A sentence must have a finite verb. That means, it must have a verb that is doing or being something:

- John **went** to work.
- I **am** a good cook.
- When the meeting had finished, the manager **made** two 'phone calls.
- Having typed the letter, she **took** it to her manager for signature.

Many people become confused about present participles: 'ing' words. In the last example above, the word 'Having' is a present participle – it is not sufficient in itself to act as a verb necessary to make a complete sentence. (It is not a doing or being word.) One often finds business letters which contain phrases such as 'Having read your letter of 1 January.' This is not a sentence because 'having' is not a finite verb. Try saying the phrase aloud and you will find that the sentence seems unfinished. You would need to write 'Having read your letter of 1 January, I find that I cannot attend the meeting after all.' Therefore, after a present participle (an 'ing' word), it is necessary to use a comma followed by a subject and finite verb.

Activity

Find the subjects and verbs in the following sentences:

1 The grass outside my window is beautifully green.
2 The boy hopped from one cracked paving stone to the next.
3 Thinking you were not coming, I went ahead to the bus stop.
4 Having looked at my diary, I realize I cannot make the next meeting.

(Answers at the end of this chapter)

SYNTAX

Syntax is the way in which words are ordered within a sentence. Very often the meaning of the sentence is made clear by the order in which the words are arranged. The rule is easy enough to state, but not so easy to carry out.

It is not always easy to identify which words are 'most nearly related' and we are writing them. How much less clear to our readers! For example:

The order of words within a sentence:

The words most nearly related should be placed in the sentence as near to each other as possible, so as to make their mutual relation clearly appear.

- We held a meeting last night to discuss the worrying of hens by foxes in the farm kitchen.

might be better written:

- We held a meeting in the farm kitchen last night to discuss the worrying of hens by foxes.

Sometimes the object is a long way from the verb and this makes the meaning very difficult. For example:

- Be careful that you change when you come home your shoes.

rather than

- Be careful that you change your shoes when you come home.

where 'change' is the verb and 'shoes' is the object.

People often run into trouble with **pronouns** when it comes to word order and it is true that written communication can be ambiguous in meaning because of them. Although hopefully obvious in meaning, the following sentence from Otto Jespersen[1] is an example:

- If the baby does not thrive on raw milk, boil it.

The general rule for pronouns is that the pronoun applies to the immediate preceding noun. In other words, the 'it' in the example above applies to the 'milk'.

In theory, it is possible to put the pronoun **before** the noun to which it relates, but it is difficult for the reader to catch the meaning – he cannot understand until he comes to the noun itself. For example:

- As he cut it, he realized his hair was going grey.

Until you come to the word 'hair' you do not know what is meant by the word 'it'. It is therefore best to use the pronoun after the noun has been stated.

Some potential grammar 'trips' to watch out for

'Only'

Where to place the word 'only' causes great problems to many people. Consider the following five statements, in each of which the word 'only' changes the meaning:

- Only I went to see him.
- I only went to see him.
- I went only to see him.
- I went to see only him.
- I went to see him only.

The final two statements are similar in meaning, the final one intensifying the meaning of the fourth.

The word 'only' can, of course, equally mean 'as recently as' (only last night I discussed it with him).

Lie or lay?

What problems these two words cause some of us – in verbal as well as written communication. It seems to me that people from certain parts of the country tend to use the word 'lay' instead of 'lie' almost as a kind of dialect. For example, the expression 'lay-in' instead of 'lie-in' (to have an extra stay in bed in the morning!) is in common use in certain areas, which does not, however, make it correct.

- **Lie:**

     Apart from the meaning of the word 'lie' as something which is untrue, the word also means 'to lie down'. The confusion that arises between the two verbs 'to lie down' and 'to lay down' stems from the fact that the past participle of the verb 'to lie' is 'lay'. (The past participle of the verb 'to lay' is 'laid') 'I lay down' is the past tense of the verb 'to lie down'. Other than this use of the word 'lay' you should use the word 'lie' when referring to yourself. For example:

  - I am lying on the bed (present tense).
  - I was lying on the bed (imperfect tense – you go on doing it).
  - I shall be lying on the bed (future tense).
  - I lay on the bed (past tense – see note above).
  - I want to lie on the bed (the infinitive).
  - Lie down! (present imperative).

- **Lay**

     The verb 'to lay' means to put something or someone down (to lay turf, to lay an egg). You do not do it to yourself. For example:

  - The hen is laying an egg (present tense).
  - The hen was laying an egg (imperfect tense).
  - The hen will lay an egg (future tense).
  - The hen laid an egg (past tense).
  - It is necessary for the hen to lay an egg (infinitive).
  - Lay an egg! (present imperative).

Activity

Complete the following sentences:

1 The carpet is . . . on the floor.
2 The fitter is . . . the carpet on the floor.
3 The fox was exhausted, so he . . . on the ground.

4 The fox . . . the chicken on the ground.
5 I . . . on the grassy bank and looked at the blue sky above me.
6 I am . . . on the sofa.

(Answers at the end of this chapter)

I or me?

Use 'I' when there is an actual or an implied verb following (that is, where the word 'I' is the subject of the sentence). For example:

- Jane and I arrived at the house at the same time.
- No-one could be better than you and I [could].

Use 'me' when it is the object of the sentence. For example:

- It was given to Ruth and me.
- The dinner is being given for Jonathan and me.

Check this out by leaving out the other person's name. It would be incorrect to write 'It was given to I' or 'The dinner is being given for I'.

While on the subject of 'I' and 'me', there seems to have been an uncomfortable incorrect usage of the word 'myself' creeping into our language recently. I recently received a letter from my bank which said, 'I should be grateful if you would kindly sign and return the enclosed form to myself . . .' This use of the word 'myself' is incorrect and should have been 'me'. 'Myself' should be used only for emphasis ('I went there myself') or as the reflexive form of the personal pronoun ('I have cut myself').

She or her?

The rules are similar to 'I' and 'me' in that 'she' is used when there is an actual or an implied verb following (that is, where the word 'she' is the subject of the sentence). For example:

- It wasn't I (implied: 'who did that'), it was she (implied: 'who did that')

More often than not, you would hear 'It wasn't me, it was her' – both 'me' and 'her' are incorrect in this case.

The word 'her' is used as an object, as with the word 'me'. For example:

- It was given to her.

Fewer or less?

- 'Less' refers to degree, quantity or extent or the noun to which you are referring.
- 'Fewer' refers to number (has to be something you can count).

For example:

- I made a quantity of scrambled egg using a number of (3) eggs.
- If I had made less [scrambled egg] I would have used fewer eggs.

This can be further clarified in that 'less' takes a singular noun, 'fewer' a plural noun For example:

- I had less opportunity than did my brother.
- There are fewer opportunities open to me.

Shall or will?

The general rule is that to express the future tense, that is, what is actually going to happen, one uses 'shall' in the first person and 'will' in the second or third:

- I shall give.
- You will give.
- He will give.

If, however, motive is brought into the picture, and we are talking about obligation, expectation or wishing, it becomes the other way round:

- I will give (I am determined to, I want to).
- You shall give (you are allowed to, you must).
- He shall give (he is permitted to, he must).

Who or whom?

Use 'who' when you are referring to the subject and 'whom' to the object. The rule is quite straightforward, but for some reason it causes confusion. This is possibly because writers throughout ages have insisted on breaking the rule. Some people feel that 'whom' is archaic and should disappear from our language altogether. If you choose to use 'whom' correctly, as I hope you will, the following are some examples to help you on your way:

- To whom shall I go for a decision?
- Who will go to the exhibition?

- It depends on who is meeting him.
- May I ask to whom you are referring?
- Who is it that you are meeting today?

Either or neither?

Use 'either' when looking at positive alternatives, and remember that 'either' goes with 'or':

- It is either the red one or the green one.

Use 'neither' when looking at negative alternatives, and remember that 'neither' goes with 'nor':

- It is neither one thing nor the other.

DO NOT USE A PREPOSITION TO END A SENTENCE WITH!

I have put this slight 'red herring' in at this point because I want to tell you that you may use a preposition to end a sentence with! Old grammar rules taught us to turn the sentence around so that we read, for example, that we 'should not use a preposition with which to end a sentence'. How clumsy that sounds. Most people agree these days that it is best to follow your ear and write words which flow naturally and easily. Sir Winston Churchill apparently made a note in the margin against a sentence that was clumsy in trying to avoid ending with a preposition, 'This is the sort of English up with which I will not put!'.

There is a well-known story about a nurse who managed to get four prepositions at the end of a sentence when she asked her patient, 'What did you choose that book to be read to out of for?'

Still better, perhaps, is a verse by an American poet, Morris Bishop, who published in the *New Yorker*, 27 September 1947:

> I lately lost a preposition;
> It hid, I thought, beneath my chair
> And angrily I cried, 'Perdition!
> Up from out of in under there.'
>
> Correctness is my *vade mecum*
> And straggling phrases I abhor,
> And yet I wondered: 'What should he come
> Up from out of in under for?'

DOUBLE NEGATIVES

Although historically two negatives in a sentence do not cancel each other out (viz Shakespeare's Kind Claudius: *'Nor what he said, though it lacked form a little, Was not like madness'* it is accepted these days that they do. For example:

- I shouldn't be surprised if it didn't rain.

rather than:

- I shouldn't be surprised if it rained.

A speaker in the House of Lords was heard to say:

- 'There is no reason to doubt that what he said in his statement . . . is not true.'

What he actually meant, of course, was:

- 'There is no reason to doubt that what he said in his statement . . . **is** true.'

Punctuation

Full stop

Every sentence should begin with a capital letter and end with a full stop (unless it ends with a question mark or exclamation mark).

Question mark

Direct questions need question marks; indirect questions do not. For example:

- Have you read the minutes of the meeting?
- I am writing to ask you whether you have read the minutes of the meeting.

Exclamation mark

An exclamation mark is an alternative to a full stop. Use it when you wish to exclaim in an emphatic manner. It can also highlight something unusual or surprising. For example:

- Good gracious!
- No!
- Well I never!
- Poof!
- It was not like that at all!

Comma

Some people use more commas than others. There are two definite places where commas should be used:

- within a list:

  Commas are placed between each item in the list except the last two which are joined by 'and'. For example:

  The colours of the rainbow are red, orange, yellow, green, blue, indigo and violet.

  The same applies to a list of adjectives preceding a noun, such as:

  It was a lovely, dark green, fluffy jumper.

- round a sub-clause Where an extra phrase or clause is included in the sentence we use a comma at either end. For example:

  The rain prevented us from doing any gardening.
  The rain, which the weather men had forecast, prevented us from doing any gardening.

  The first sentence is a straightforward, simple one. The second includes an extra sub-clause: 'which the weather men had forecast' and this is placed between commas.

  An easy check on whether you have a sub-clause which should go between a pair of commas is to read the sentence aloud without the extra phrase and if it makes sense, the words you left out are the sub-clause.

  Words like 'however', 'perhaps', 'therefore' and 'of course' count as sub-clauses and are usually placed between two commas. For example:

  It would seem, however, that you have not yet typed the letter.

  Test the sub-clause by reading the sentence without the word 'however'. It still makes sense, so put 'however' between a pair of commas.

  It is not true, of course, to say that the moon is made of green cheese.

Commas are not always easy because, apart from the two rules above, there are no hard and fast rules. (Note the sub-clause between two commas in that last sentence.) Commas are there to help the reader make sense of the text.

They are usually used after an initial phrase of a sentence when the subject and verb is not immediately introduced. For example:

- Having read your letter of 2 March 1996, I feel that we need to meet.
- If the ground is too wet to dig, let us leave the planting of the tree until next week.
- In practice, it has been found advisable to do it this way.

Most of us were taught not to put a comma before the word 'and'. There are exceptions to this rule, however, where the comma helps to clarify the meaning, such as:

- The car was dirty, and muddy paw marks from our cat did not help. You can see how the comma after the word 'dirty' helps to make sense of the sentence. Without it the car could have been dirty and muddy.
- The meeting included the Bishops of Salisbury, Bristol, Winchester, and Bath and Wells. Without the commas before 'and' in this sentence, it would not be clear whether the Bishop of Bath and Wells was one or two people.

Another place where commas are usually placed is preceding a conjunction – words such as 'but', 'which', 'while'.

Semicolon

Some people never use a semicolon because they are not quite sure where to use it. I always think of a semicolon as something more definite than a comma, but not so final as a full stop. Where there is a clause followed by another clause which is closely related to it in meaning, it is best to use a semicolon rather than a full stop. For example:

- We shall be holding a salary review at the next meeting; the 1997 budget will be considered.
- The girl had a great mane of curly auburn hair; it reminded me of a flaming, red torch.

The semicolon is sometimes used instead of commas to differentiate between items in a list. With the example of 'The Bishop of Bath and Wells above, you can see that commas could lead to possible confusion with several 'ands'. To overcome this problem, use semicolons – but note that you do not need to use the word 'and' between the final two items in the list:

- The menu will consist of soup; melon cocktail; smoked trout; lemon sorbet; roast beef, Yorkshire pudding and vegetables; apple pie and cream; coffee with petite fours.

Colon

Like the semicolon, the colon is used less than it used to be, but it has two particular parts to play.

- colons can introduce a list. For example:

   The objectives of the programme are to:

- identify the skills delegates already have;
- identify new ones which they need;
- improve on existing skills;
- acquire new ones.

   Some people put a dash after the colon when it is used in this way (:–) but the dash is superfluous and adds unnecessary clutter.

- colons can be used in the middle of a sentence to divide it into two, where the second half develops the first. For example:

   The bread was not fit to eat: it was covered in a green mould.

Hyphen

Hyphens are used at the right hand edge of text when part of a word carries over to the next line. They should not be used in this way if the word has only one syllable ('edge') or if the word is a proper name ('Southend, Jonathan'). Where a word is already hyphenated ('first-class'), the break should come at the existing hyphen. Otherwise, the hyphen should split the word at a convenient place, possibly between syllables ('edu-cate', 'book-let') or between a double consonant ('daf-fodil', 'accom-modate').

Hyphens are also used in compound adjectives ('first-class', 'part-time') but only when they precede a noun, not when they follow it. For example:

- The balance-of-payments difficulties;

- BUT;

- The difficulties are over the balance of payments.

In addition, hyphens sometimes link words with their immediate neighbours to clarify meaning. For example, the omission of a hyphen between the words 'Council' and 'financed' in the following sentence confuses the reader:

- The Council financed projects in the last financial year . . .

Note, there are no spaces before and after a hyphen.

Dash

Dashes are used in **pairs** to indicate a kind of parenthesis (brackets, see below). They set apart a phrase in the middle of a sentence, either to emphasize it, or to explain what has just been said. For example:

- There were two dogs in the yard – both in superb condition – and we ran down the path to greet them.

As with phrases between commas (see above), the sentence will make sense if read without the phrase between the dashes.

A single dash is often used towards the end of a sentence if you need to add something which is almost an afterthought. For example:

- There are nine bananas in the fruit bowl – one is bad.

Note, the dash has a space before and after it.

Parenthesis (brackets)

A parenthesis is used to insert an additional piece of information of any sort into a sentence that is logically and grammatically complete without it. It can be marked by commas, dashes or brackets. Brackets are ideally used when the piece of information is a complete sentence within itself, but they tend to be used in the same way as a pair of dashes. For example:

- When you come to see me (I do hope it will not be too long) I will show you the photographs of my holiday in Turkey.

We usually use curved brackets to illustrate a parenthesis ( ), although sometimes square brackets are used [ ], especially when printing a verbatim quotation where something has been implied but not actually said. When put into print it may be ambiguous and the words in brackets aid clarification. For example:

- It was said at the Annual General Meeting: 'The shareholders' dividend for the year [1995/6] has been set at 5 per cent.

When two or more items or figures are bracketed together, { } brackets are usually used.

The Apostrophe

There are two kind of apostrophe:

1   those which indicate omitted letters;
2   those which show possession

1 Apostrophes as an indication of missing letter/s

When one or more letters are left out of a word, we put an apostrophe in place of the missing letters. For example:

- Let's go (Let us go);
- Don't you know? (Do not you know?);
- Can't you do it this way? (Cannot you do it this way?);
- Couldn't we go tomorrow? (Could not we go tomorrow?);
- I'm sure I did tell you (I am sure I did tell you);
- They're really nice sweets (They are really nice sweets);
- It's a nice day (It is a nice day).

Note, that the word Its does **not** carry an apostrophe before the 's' when it is possessive – Its coat was red.

There are one or two words which alter in construction when abbreviated such as 'won't' (will not) and 'shan't' (shall not). The word 'shan't' should, strictly speaking, have two apostrophes – 'sha'n't' because the apostrophe is in place of the letters 'll' and 'o'.

Most words which are shortened in this way, although used in speech, are not written – at least not in business correspondence. Sometimes we need to restructure a sentence because we cannot use the full form of words like 'can't' (cannot you . . .) and 'didn't' (did not you . . .) which sound rather quaint in business letters.

2 Apostrophes which show possession

If the owner of the item does not already end in 's', place the apostrophe **before** the final 's'. For example:

- Jenny's bag;
- The leader's suitcase;
- The children's books.

If the owner of the item already ends in 's', place the apostrophe **after** the final 's' which is already there. For example:

- The girl's bicycle (a single girl);
- The girls' bicycles (more than one girl);
- The boss' secretary;
- The dress' buttons are green.

Note, when the word already ends in 's', you do not need to add another 's' after the apostrophe, **except** when writing names. For example:

- St James's Church;
- Chris's shoes.

However, there is no hard and fast rule about adding a further 's' to ordinary nouns:

- The boss's secretary;
- The dress's buttons are green,

are both acceptable if you think it looks better.

Quotation Marks

These used to be called 'inverted commas' because that is what they looked like – commas upside down, but with the advent of modern typefaces this is no longer necessarily so. One can use either double or single quotation marks. Which you choose to use depends on style. Most publishers now call for manuscripts using single quotation marks, but your organization's house style may be to use double. Both are equally correct for marking direct speech or for quoting what someone has said.

When writing prose containing direct speech, the words spoken go within quotation marks, with any narrative between. For example:

- 'It is the middle of the night,' she said angrily.
  'How dare you knock at my door,' the stranger replied urgently,
  'An avalanche has started up in the mountain – you are in grave danger.'

Note, that a new line is started for each person who speaks and that each piece of speech starts with a capital letter, even if it follows a comma.

Use quotation marks also to mark a person's actual speech where you quote in the middle of a sentence. For example:

It was reported in the minutes of the last meeting that John said there were three clients to be seen 'before the end of June'. What he actually said was 'before the end of July'.

The words which have been quoted here are 'before the end of June' and 'before the end of July'. (It is not necessary to add additional punctuation as in direct speech.)

What about spelling?

It is not possible in a book like this to cover the subject of spelling, but we need to look at a few basics and commonly misspelled and confused words.

FIRSTLY, SOME OF THE BASIC GUIDES:

i before e except after c (but only when it rhymes with key)

Did you know the last bit of that ditty? I didn't for years and couldn't make out why it didn't always apply (eg 'height', 'weird', 'foreign').

- Words like 'grieve', 'friend', 'belief', 'relieve', 'wield'
- and after 'c' – 'deceive', 'receive', 'conceive', 'ceiling'

There always have to be exceptions, of course. Think about 'seize' (but note 'siege'), 'efficient' . . .!

Adding a suffix

1 Where you add a suffix beginning with a vowel (eg 'er', 'ing', 'y', 'es') to a word of one syllable ending with a single consonant, the consonant doubles. For example:

- sad = sadder; dig = digging; sun = sunny; pass = passes.

- Exceptions to this rule include 'focused'; 'buses'; 'gases'.

2 Where the suffix begins with a consonant (eg 'ly') the consonant does not double. For example:

- sad = sadly

3 Where a suffix is added to a word of more than one syllable ending in a single consonant, the consonant doubles only if the **last** syllable of the word is stressed. For example:

- begin = beginning; prefer = preferred; submit = submitted; occur = occurred; forget = forgetting.

Whereas words stressing **other** syllables do not double the final consonant when adding a suffix. For example:

- budget = budgeting; benefit = benefiting; gossip = gossiping.

But again there are exceptions (eg travel = traveller).

4   Where a suffix is added to a word ending in a silent 'e', if the suffix begins with a consonant (eg 'ty'; 'ly'; 'ness'; 'ment'; etc) the silent 'e' remains. For example:

- safe = safety; immediate = immediately; same = sameness; wide = wideness; judge = judgement; acknowledge = acknowledgement.

If the suffix begins with a vowel (eg 'ing'; 'ity';) the silent 'e' is dropped. For example:

- bake = baking; sane = sanity; decide = deciding.

These are guides only, and there are always exceptions: ('duly' rather than 'duely'; 'mileage' rather than 'milage'; 'likeable' rather than 'likable'; 'moveable' rather than 'movable').

5   The suffixes 'able' and 'ible' cause confusion. The general principle is that when a word ends in a silent 'e', the 'e' is dropped and the suffix is '–able'. For example:

- advise = advisable; move = movable.

- (exceptions – force = forcible; collapse = collapsible; reduce = reducible.)

Where the word ends in 's', the suffix '–ible' is used. For example:

- accessible; admissible; divisible.

- (exception – passable)

WORDS WHICH BECOME CONFUSED

Advice/advise

'Advice' is the noun; 'advise' the verb (I gave him advice; I advised him).

Affect/effect

'Affect' (always a verb, never a noun) is to influence or to produce a change in ('The leadership has an affect on their morale'); 'effect' is to bring about or to result in (verb), or a consequence (noun).

Ante–/Anti–

'Ante–' is a prefix meaning 'before' ('ante-natal'); 'anti–' is a prefix meaning 'against' ('anti-nuclear movement').

Biannual/biennial

'Biannual' means 'half-yearly' (that is, twice in the year); 'Biennial' means 'every two years'.

Compliment/complement

'Compliment' as in 'David paid Christine a compliment'; 'complement' literally means 'that which completes' as in 'The staff has its full complement'.

Councillor/counsellor

A 'councillor' is a member of a council; a 'counsellor' is someone who gives counselling or advice.

Dependent/dependant

'Dependent' is an adjective, ('dependent relative'; 'dependent on the weather'); 'dependant' is a noun meaning the person who is dependent on another ('she has several dependants').

Desert/dessert

'Desert' is a place ('we wandered in the desert'); 'dessert' is a course of a meal ('we had strawberries and cream for dessert').

Didn't ought to/Didn't used to

Although not two confusable words, I have put these in here because they are often used but are incorrect. The first should be 'I should not have' or 'I ought not to have'; the second should be 'I used not to'.

Disinterested/uninterested

'Disinterested' means the person has no self-interest in the subject; he derives no personal advantage from it. 'Uninterested' means he is 'not interested'.

Eatable/edible

If something can be eaten, it is 'edible'. However, if it may not be 'eatable' (for example, it may have been burned in the cooking) – it is 'uneatable' or 'inedible'.

Ensure/insure

To 'ensure' is to make certain or make safe; to 'insure' is to pay a sum of money for an insurance policy to cover loss or damage to your property.

Especially/specially

'Especially' is an exception or to an exceptional degree ('exceptionally loud'); 'specially' is for one special purpose (it was a 'special' day).

Lightening/lightning

'I lightened her load by carrying her bag'; 'I am afraid of thunder and lightning'.

Practical/practicable

Practical is to be useful – 'It was a really practical handbag because it had three different sections'; practicable means that which is feasible to be carried out – 'It was practicable to go by the lower road because although the ford was high, it was passable and it cut six miles off our journey'; or it's opposite: 'It was impracticable to use the bicycle on rough ground as its tyres were too thin'.

Practice/practise

'Practice' is the noun; 'practise' is the verb. Thus:

- Mary practises the practice of counselling.

Principal/principle

'Principal' (noun or verb) is the 'chief' ('the principal of a college', the 'principal event'); 'principle' (noun only) is a theory or an ideal ('he was a man of principles'; the 'principle behind it is this').

Stationery/stationary

'Stationary' means not moving; 'stationery' is the paper you write on. (A stationary piece of stationery.)

Suit/suite

A 'suit' of clothes, but a 'suite of furniture' or an hotel 'suite'.

Their/there

'Their' is a possessive pronoun ('their car'; 'their words'); 'there' is connected with place ('over there'; 'neither here nor there'); or is used as an adverb ('there are/is'; 'there stands').

Unsatisfied/dissatisfied

'Unsatisfied' means that a desire has not been fully gratified (eg hunger); 'dissatisfied' means to be discontented.

SOME TRICKY SPELLINGS:

absence	belief	consistency
access	believed	consistent
accommodate	benefited	contemporary
accommodation	biennial	correlate
achievement	budgeted	correspondence
acquaintance	budgeting	correspondent
acquiesce	bureaucracy	councillor
acquire	business	counsellor
address	calendar	courteous
agreeable	chaos	courtesy
amateur	co-operate	criticism
amiable	co-ordinate	cumulative
analyze	colleague	deceive
analyzes (pl)	colour	decision
analysis (sing)	commitment	definite
ancillary	committed	definitely
anonymous	committee	dependant
arrangement	comparative	dependent
ascertain	compatible	deterrent
assess	conscience	develop
awful	conscientious	development
bachelor	conscious	disappear
beginning	consistency	disappoint

disapproval
disapprove
discipline
discrepancy
dissatisfied
distributor
efficiency
efficient
eighth
embarrassment
eminent
equipment
equipped
erroneous
especially
exaggerate
excellent
exercise
existence
extremely
favourite
feasible
February
foreign
fulfil
fulfiled
fulfilment
gauge
government
grievance
guarantee
guard
harassment
honourary
honour
honourable
humourous
humour
hurriedly
immediately
immigrant
imminent
implement
incidentally
incipient
incompetent
independence

independent
indispensable
influential
inseparable
install
installment
intelligence
irrelevant
irreparable
itinerary
judgement
judicial
knowledge
liaison
loose
loosen
lose
losing
lying
maintenance
manoeuvre
marriage
minimum
miscellaneous
movable
necessary
necessitate
negligence
negligible
negotiable
negotiation
niece
noticeable
occasionally
occur
occurred
occurrence
offered
omission
omit
omitted
paid
parallel
parliament
patience
patient
permanent

permissible
persevere
personal
personnel
persuade
piece
possess
practical
practice (n)
practise (v)
precede
precedence
preceding
preference
preferred
prejudice
prejudice
preliminary
privilege
procedure
professional
prominent
pronunciation
proprietary
psychology
pursuant
pursue
questionnaire
receive
received
recommend
refer
reference
referral
referred
relevant
relieved
remittance
resistance
responsibility
scarcely
seize
separate
separation
siege
significance
similar

sincerely	tariff	unfortunately
skillful	temporary	until
statutory	tendency	usually
subtle	transfer	valuable
succeed	transference	warehouse
successful	transferred	weird
successfully	transient	wholly
summary	twelfth	withhold
supersede	unconscious	woollen
synonym	underrate	
synonymous	undoubtedly	

Titles and forms of address

PERSONAL TITLES

- Some people have other titles in place of 'Mr', 'Mrs' and so on. They may be a clergyman in which case the addressee is 'The Rev. J. Saunders' and the salutation is 'Dear Mr Saunders' (Note: not 'Dear Rev. Saunders').
- A Bishop is addressed as 'The Right Rev the Lord Bishop of London' or 'The Lord Bishop of London'. The Salutation is 'My Lord Bishop'.
- A Dean is addressed as 'The Very Rev Dean of . . .' and the salutation is 'Very Rev Sir'.
- An Archdeacon is addressed as 'The Venerable the Archdeacon of . . .' and the salutation is 'Venerable Sir'.
- A person who is a doctor is obviously addressed as 'Dr' or 'Doctor Mary Wise', but she may not be a doctor of medicine. She could, for example, be a doctor of philosophy when her qualification could be 'PhD'. It is incorrect to put both 'Dr' **and** 'PhD' in the address, one or the other is fine: 'Dr Mary Wise' or 'Mary Wise PhD'. In the salutation, you would write 'Dear Dr Wise' or 'Dear Doctor Wise'.
- Judges are addressed 'The Hon Mr Justice . . .' and the salutation is 'Sir'. A Judge of a County Court is addressed 'His Honour Judge . . .' and the salutation is 'Sir'.

Other titles such as 'Sir', 'Lady', or 'Lord' are fairly straightforward. When using 'Sir', the salutation usually takes the person's first name rather than surname. For example, if one were writing to Sir Cliff Richard, the salutation would be Dear Sir Cliff, (not Dear Sir Richard). With Lord and Lady, however, the salutation would retain the surname – Dear Lord Callaghan.

For further details of ceremonious forms of address, refer to books such as *Collins Everyday English Usage*.

**See also chapter five concerning
Mr, Esq., Mrs, Miss, Ms, Messrs, Mesdames.**

LETTERS AFTER A NAME

Some people have military or civil honours, qualifications or memberships of professional bodies after their name. The general rule for the order in which they are written is honours before degrees, and degrees before MP, JP and so on. For example:

1 Military honours, for example VC (Victoria Cross) or MC (Military Cross) or DSO
2 Civil honours, for example MBE or OBE

3 Degrees in order of merit, for example PhD MSc BSc (that is, doctorate, master's degree, bachelors degree)

4 Professional qualifications, for example LRAM (Licentiate of the Royal Academy of Music) or ARICS (Associate of the Royal Institute of Chartered Surveyors)

5 Membership of professional bodies, in the order fellowships, memberships, associateships, for example FRSA FIPD MIMgt.

You could perhaps therefore address someone with different categories of letters after their name as Miss Jane Browning OBE PhD MSc FRSA.

We have not dealt with forms of address for royalty, the courts, civil offices (mayors and so on) in this chapter, but have sought to cover the forms of address which are most likely to be encountered when writing business letters.

Answers to the activity on page 114

1 Subject: The grass
  Verb: is
2 Subject: The boy
  Verb: hopped

3 Subject: I
  Verb: went

4 Subject: I
  Verb: Realize

Answers to the activity on page 116

1 lying	2 laying	3 lay
4 laid	5 lay	6 lying

BIBLIOGRAPHY

For further reading and for fuller information on some of the points raised in this chapter, see:

Fowler, H.W., *Dictionary of Modern English Usage*, (2nd edn), Oxford University Press, 1983

Fowler, H.W., and Fowler, F.G., (eds), *The King's English* (3rd edn), Oxford University Press, 1973

Hughes, V., *English Language Skills*, Macmillan, 1990

Nesfield, J.C., *Manual of English Grammar and Composition*, (revised edn), F.T., Wood, Macmillan, 1963

Partridge, E., *Usage and Abusage*, (revised edn) Whitcut, J., Penguin, 1995

---

1 Jesperson, O., *Growth and Structure of the English Language*, Blackwell, 1946

CHAPTER FIVE

Writing Business Letters, Memos and Reports

IN THIS CHAPTER WE WILL LOOK AT THE FOLLOWING AREAS:

- planning, content, style and layout of business letters
- internal memoranda
- formal and informal report writing
- proof-reading documents

Planning, content, style and layout of business letters

Effective letter writing is crucial to the success of your business communication. You can create a professional, helpful, friendly and efficient image through your letters. Business letters are very different in style and content to personal letters, but some people find it hard to adjust their style from one to the other.

Business letters should be as brief as possible, without being curt. Your letters should be courteous and your reader should be able to understand your communication quickly and easily.

There are five basic reasons for writing a letter:

- to inform – tell someone about something;
- to instruct – get someone to do something;
- to influence – persuade someone to do something;
- to interpret – reply to their communication;
- to interest – get someone interested in you or your product.

A letter is a good method of communication when it is important to have a lasting record to which to refer. For this reason, it is a good idea to confirm in writing a verbal conversation which has perhaps been held face-to-face or, even more importantly, on the telephone. Not only do memories play tricks with people, but verbal conversations are sometimes ambiguous and misunderstandings occur because the people involved are talking at 'cross purposes' (see chapter one).

PLANNING YOUR LETTER

In order to keep the letter as clear as possible and to avoid it becoming too wordy and complex (when misunderstandings are likely to occur), it is important to plan the structure.

Things to think about when planning a letter:

- **why** are you writing – your objective/s?
- to **whom** are you writing – your content and style will need to be adjusted according to whether you know the person, their position in the organization, whether it is the first time you have written or whether you are replying to a letter from them . . .?
- **what** do they need to know? – do they know already? do you need to cover?
- **when** are you going to write? – do you have to meet deadlines, are there arrangements to be made before a specific meeting or event . . .?
- **how** are you going to construct your letter and lay it out?

These facts will enable you to establish whether your letter will be formal or informal. Most business letters that you write will be formal, but you can break that down still further:

- people you know;
- people you don't know.

For example: if you are writing a business letter to someone you know as a professional colleague, you are likely to adopt a more personal tone than if you are writing to someone you have never met, or perhaps to an organization where you do not have a person's name at all.

The important thing is that you determine what kind of letter you are going to write before you start. Most difficulties in business letter writing occur because people mix up the styles, adopting the wrong 'tone'.

When you first begin to think about the content of your letter, jot down your thoughts without necessarily putting the points in priority order. You can sort them out later and it is important to get your own thoughts clear before you can hope to get the meaning of your letter clear to anyone else.

**Clarify your thoughts in order to write . . .
don't write in order to clarify your thoughts.**

The style of your letter

> **ABC**
> **A**-ccurate
> **B**-rief
> **C**-lear

Remember that your aim is to communicate your message to your reader so that it may be quickly and easily understood. Think about the person to whom you are writing and empathize (that is, identify with them, 'get into their shoes') with the way they are likely to think and feel as they receive and interpret your message. Do they know your reason for writing and have you conveyed your message clearly and unambiguously?

Formal letters cover official business and need to be short and to the point. Avoid complex sentences full of adjectives and unnecessary words – the old adage: 'Keep it short and simple' applies. For example, if you are writing to someone about a forthcoming lecture which they are to give for you, don't write 'We will make sure there are adequate sound reception facilities'; rather write 'We will make sure everyone will be able to hear you' – you will remember this example from chapter two and it also applies here.

When I first started my working life as a secretary many years ago, it was common practice to write sentences such as 'Thank you for your letter of the 20th ult. and we beg to advise you that . . .' It is rare these days, except occasionally in certain professions such as the legal world, to find the obscure language of 'yesteryear' (a case in point!): phrases such as 'I refer to your letter of the sixth inst. (or ult.)', 'I enclose herewith', 'I remain, sir, your obedient servant' and so on; likewise, words such as 'heretofore', 'hitherto', 'aforesaid' . . . .

Use simple, natural English that you would use if you were communicating with someone verbally. Do not be tempted to go into long-winded jargon. Use short words rather than long words: 'buy' rather than 'purchase', 'expect' rather than 'anticipate'. The modern fashion in business letter writing is undoubtedly simplicity.

Do not get involved in personal issues; stick to the business in hand, say what you want to say and do not elaborate with unnecessary detail. Always be courteous and pleasant; even in letters of complaint, it does not help to be abrasive or aggressive.

STRUCTURING THE LETTER

There is no hard and fast rule for the order of a business letter, but the following is a guide:

- First Paragraph – Opening courtesies Tell the reader why you are writing;

  'Thank you for your letter of 15 June 1996 requesting a price for ten copies of our word processing training manual.'

- Following Paragraphs – State the facts in logical order Give information, the facts of the situation, any problems or difficulties, make requests or suggestions . . .

  These manuals are being reprinted at the moment, but we are expecting to receive a further supply within three weeks.

  The price of a single copy is £7.99, but we would be able to give you a discount of 5 per cent for an order of ten copies, reducing the price to £7.59 per copy.

- Final Paragraph – Confirm and sum up what you have said, clarifying any decisions or action required.

  If you would let us have a firm order, we can guarantee delivery of the books to you not later than 31 July 1997.'

- followed by the relevant close.

If you are writing about several different topics, it is a good idea to write separate letters, because each subject may be dealt with by a different person at the receiving organization.

How should you address the person to whom you are writing?

Where a formal letter is being written and the 'organization' is being addressed, it is correct to use the salutation 'Dear Sirs':

Jo Bloggs & Co
69 Manor Way
SWINDON
Wiltshire
SN1 9KL

Dear Sirs

Thus, you are addressing all the 'Sirs' in the company, as it were! (This is still very sexist, even in this day and age, because we don't write 'Dear

Mesdames' – meaning 'more than one woman' – unless it is very obviously an organization comprising all women.)

If you address your letter to someone using their position in the organization rather than their name, the salutation is 'Dear Sir' or 'Dear Madam'. (If you do not know whether the position is held by a man or woman you can either put 'Dear Sir or Madam' or just 'Dear Sir'.)

If, however, you addressed the letter to the Purchasing Manager by **name**, but did not know the person well enough to write 'Dear Mrs Kahn', you would then use 'Dear Madam':

```
Mrs J Kahn
Purchasing Manager
Jo Bloggs & Co
69 Manor Way
SWINDON
Wiltshire
SN1 9KL


Dear Madam
```

or, if you were writing to a man:

```
Mr J R Hall
Personnel Director
Jo Bloggs & Co
69 Manor Way
SWINDON
Wiltshire
SN1 9KL

Dear Sir
```

People tend to use the person's name as a form of address more than they used to. It is common practice to write Dear Mr Smith, Dear Fred, or, becoming more and more acceptable, Dear Fred Smith. (All these will carry a 'Yours sincerely' close, of course.) Where the letter is to a person you know well, it is common practice to handwrite 'Dear Joan' or ' Dear Joan Morrison'. If you do this, you should also handwrite 'Yours sincerely' at the end of the letter and sign your name without a typed designation. (See below for further details about closing letters.)

People are sometimes confused about the term 'Esquire' (or 'Esq.' as it tends to be abbreviated in letters). This is an old fashioned term that is rarely used today. It might appear in very formal correspondence or in certain traditional professions such as the law or in accountancy. If you do use the term, do not put 'Mr' as well. It is a duplication of title. You would use:

> Joseph Brandenburg Esq.
> Messrs Sydney, Pocock & Brown
> 8A Queen's Crescent
> BRISTOL
> BS2 8JK

Your opening salutation would probably be 'Dear Sir' because it is a formal letter, although it could be 'Dear Mr Brandenburg'.

What about Messrs?

You will notice the term 'Messrs' in the above example. Again, this is tending to go out of use. It used to be included as a courtesy title where a company was not a limited one. When one wrote to Jones & Co Ltd ('Ltd' being an abbreviation of 'Limited') this was considered sufficiently courteous. Where, however, an organization was a partnership or an unlimited company (such as a firm of solicitors), it was considered polite to address them as 'Messrs Sydney, Pocock & Brown', rather than just 'Sydney, Pocock & Brown'. The word 'Messrs' is an abbreviation of 'Messieurs' meaning 'more than one man'. It's use is rare these days and it is quite acceptable to write 'Sydney, Pocock & Brown'. (Note the use of the ampersand (&) in the title of the organization – it is correct to use this abbreviation for 'and' in the name of a company, but not in text within the letter, when 'and' must be used in full.) As well as 'Ltd' these days of course, we use 'plc' (public limited company) where it is relevant following the name of an organization.

The word 'Mesdames' used to address more than one woman equates with 'Messrs' when addressing more than one man. Note, however:

- Messrs Sydney Pocock & Brown = Dear Sirs;
- Mesdames Brown, Silcock & Grove = Dear Mesdames (not Dear Madams).

The term is somewhat archaic, however, and is now rarely used.

The Close

(Also known as the Complimentary Close.)

The way we close business letters has also been simplified. 'Yours truly' is rarely used these days. We are left with just two business-type 'closes' – 'Yours faithfully' and 'Yours sincerely'. People often worry about when to use which, but it really is an easy rule:

> - Dear Sir/s or Dear Madam = Yours faithfully
>   (an impersonal term of address)
> - Dear Mr Smith or Dear Jane = Yours sincerely
>   (the use of a person's name)

There is no variation on this rule, it's as simple as that.

Where the close is 'Yours faithfully', the name of the organization is usually printed directly below and the name and position of the writer is printed with sufficient space allowed for the person to sign the letter (at least five line-spaces):

Yours faithfully
BENTLEY HOLDINGS LTD

Mary Smith
Marketing Manager

It has, in the past, been common practice for a woman to put (Miss), (Mrs) or (Ms) in brackets after her name so that people know how to address her when replying, but again this practice is beginning to be dropped. It is sometimes useful when a woman has a first name which could be of either gender, such as my own: Chris Simons.

Where the letter is addressed by name to a particular person and therefore carries the 'Yours sincerely' close, the name and position is sometimes printed underneath, but sometimes not. If the letter is fairly formal to someone you don't know very well, it is likely that you would print your details (especially if your signature is not easily readable):

Yours sincerely

John Jones
Personnel Manager

If, however, you know the person reasonably well and they would be likely to know your signature, or know who you are by the letter heading you are using, it is acceptable merely to sign your name directly below the 'Yours sincerely'.

Per pro

It is sometimes necessary for a person to sign the letter on behalf of someone else. In this case the person signing should sign their **own** name (you should never sign another person's signature), writing 'pp' (which stands for 'per pro', meaning 'by proxy' or 'on behalf of'), or 'for' to the left of the sender's printed name:

Yours sincerely

John White

ppX Chandra Prakesh
Sales Manager

CHECKING

Re-read your letter before you send it, not only to check it for errors, but also read it as though you were receiving it:

- Could it be put in a clearer way?
- Are misunderstandings likely to occur?
- Are any of your statements ambiguous?
- Is the language likely to be understood by the person receiving it?

This last point is often overlooked. Obviously, if a person speaks a different language, a translation will be necessary, either by the reader or by someone else. However, there are other kinds of language barriers such as 'jargonese' or merely using the kind of vocabulary that your reader may not understand or which may cause offence.

Check any facts contained in the letter: dates, times, places, spelling of names, figures . . .

If it is an important or difficult letter, it is a good idea to 'sleep on it' before you send it, giving you time to reflect on what you have written and amend it later if you feel you can improve on it.

BUSINESS LETTER LAYOUT

Now that more managers have PCs on their desks and are keying-in their own correspondence, less use is being made of secretaries and typing pools It is therefore relevant to spend a little time thinking about letter layout styles.

Business letters should always be typed or word processed. It is not considered professional to handwrite business letters. The intricacies of traditional layout styles have largely disappeared in favour of simplicity and modern uncluttered styles. No longer are people hung up on rules such as 'two spaces after a full stop', whether one should indent the first word of every paragraph, or whether to put the 'Yours faithfully' in the centre of the page or blocked at the left hand side. We are now in a situation where almost anything goes as far as layout style is concerned, as long as it is accurate and legible. Most organizations adopt a 'house style' and staff are expected to follow this with all their correspondence.

Assuming that a business letter is being prepared on a piece of business letter heading which gives details of the sender's organization and address, the following layout is a simple one which can be used. You will note that everything starts at the left hand margin.

Your ref.
*

Our ref.
*

Date
*

Inside address:
Addressee name
Position *(this is optional)*
Name of organization
Address of organization – *(the postal town is written in capital letters)*
County
Postcode – *(Note the postcode may be placed on the same line as the county, or the postal town if a county is not used, but on the envelope the postcode must be on the last line by itself)*
*

Salutation
*

Heading
*

Content
*

Complimentary Close – *(Leave at least five line-spaces to leave room for the signature)*
Sender's name
Job title (designation)
*

PS *(you should avoid the use of postscripts if possible because it suggests that you have not had time to construct your letter properly and have popped in a PS as an afterthought – it suggests a rather casual attitude)*
*

Enc. *(if you have one, see below)*

Line spacing should be consistent; normally two returns where the asterisk (*) mark is placed above and also between paragraphs in the text. Single line-spacing is used elsewhere.

The following is an example of a simple business letter, using the above style:

Your ref. AJ/KT

Our ref. MC/132/HB

1 March 1997

Professor Alfred Jones
The King's School
Severn Thames Street
GLOUCESTER
GL1 8TG

Dear Professor Jones

'COMPUTERS IN BUSINESS' CONFERENCE

Thank you for your letter of 23 February inviting me to speak at your conference on 5 September 1996 on the subject of 'The influence of Information Technology on the publishing industry'. I am delighted to accept your invitation and confirm that my speaking fee for the day will be £600.00 plus expenses and VAT.

I note that you would like me to speak for 1 hour from 10.45 am and to lead two 45 minute workshops at 12.00 noon and 3.00 p.m. I will be in touch with you a little nearer the time to finalize details, but confirm that I will require a slide projector, screen and flip chart.

Perhaps you would be kind enough to arrange hotel accommodation for me for the night before the conference; I shall travel from home by car.

I hope that all the arrangements are going well and look forward to meeting you.

Yours sincerely

Maria Coping
Director

You will see from the above example that everything starts at the left hand margin (we call this 'blocked' style) and that there is no punctuation apart from that which appears in the body of the letter itself. That is, we no longer use punctuation in the date, addressee, salutation, heading or close.

Dates

It is rare to use 'th' 'st' 'dn' or 'rd' within a date (5th March, 2nd June etc) but rather just the number and date (5 March, 2 June). The exception to this rule is when one refers to a date in the text of a letter but does not use the month. For example: 'I notice that your letter is dated 6 March, 1997, but it did not actually reach me until the 23rd'. Dates should always be written out in full. It is incorrect to write 1.3.96 or 14 Sept 96.

Headings

It is helpful to use a heading when writing business letters because the reader can relate immediately to the subject without having to read right through the text to find out what it is about. This can be underlined, typed in boldface, upper case (capital) or lower case (small) letters with initial capitals. There is no hard and fast rule.

Enclosures

You may be enclosing something with the letter and some companies still use the word 'Enclosure/s' or 'Enc/s' at the bottom of their letters. If this is used, it is placed about three lines below the final line of type, which is probably the signatory.

For the attention of . . .

Sometimes, you may write to an organization where the company name is the first line of the inside address and you may use 'For the attention of (this can be a person's name or a position)'. This line is placed either above or below the inside address. (The salutation would be 'Dear Sirs' because you are addressing the first line of the addressee which is the company, not the person whose name or position appears in the 'For the attention of . . .' line.

Special instructions

Words such as **'CONFIDENTIAL', 'PRIVATE', 'URGENT',** and so on should be typed in capital letters and may appear above or below the inside address. Obviously, they should also appear on the envelope.

Routing copies to other people

If you need to send copies of a letter to other people within your organization, as well as keeping a 'hard' file copy for yourself (that is, printed on paper rather than keeping a copy on your computer memory, which would be 'soft' copy), it is usual to mark this at the bottom of the letter. If the person receiving the top copy of the letter (that is, the addressee) needs to know who has received copies, you mark the routing on all copies of the letter. If he does not (which is more usual), you mark the additional copies of the letter only.

Traditionally, we put 'cc' meaning 'carbon copy', although it is rare to find carbon copies these days. The example on the top of page 149 shows routing as it appears following the last line of the letter:

The copy being sent to the Birmingham office would be ticked or marked in some way at the relevant point, similarly the copy being sent to the Edinburgh office and the one being retained for the file. Copies are usually printed on plain paper.

Occasionally, the sender may wish to distribute a copy to someone but not wish others to know the person has received a copy. This is known as a 'blind' carbon copy ('bcc') and the person receiving the blind copy would have their name on their sheet only.

Yours faithfully
JOHNSON & BROWN LTD

J Sellick
Managing Director

Encs

cc　　　Birmingham office
　　　　Edinburgh office
　　　　File

Continuation sheets

If the letter is too long for one sheet of paper, it becomes necessary to use one or more continuation sheet/s. This should be the same colour, quality and size as the first sheet, but will not have the letter heading details. Business letters should be typed on one side of the page only, never on the reverse.

It is incorrect to leave less than two lines of text at the bottom of the first page and the letter should be arranged so that there are at least three or four lines of text at the top of the continuation page. (Incorrect examples of these are known traditionally as **widows** and **orphans**!). It is incorrect to print just the complimentary close and sender's name on a page of its own. It is also incorrect to divide the last word on a page.

It used to be correct practice to put 'Continued' or ' . . .' at the bottom of a page, but this is rarely used now.

Wording at the top of the continuation page for a letter should be in double line-spacing and in the following order:

2	*(page number)*
1 March 1996	*(date)*
Professor Alfred Jones	*(addressee as it appears on the first page of the letter)*

Circular letters

With the advent of computer mail-merge, it has become easier to personalize circular letters. This enables you to merge a one-off prepared letter with a database containing names and addresses etc. It is a tremendous time-saving facility with the potential for hundreds of personalized letters to be prepared in a relatively short time and with minimum labour cost.

The date may appear in three ways on a circular letter:

- 17 October 19—;
- October 19—;
- Date as postmark;

In each case, the words would be typed in the position where the date normally appears.

Sometimes a tear-off slip is included to be used by the person receiving the letter to reply to the sender. This is always placed at the end of the letter and is separated from the rest of the letter by a dotted or dashed line which should go from edge-to-edge of the paper (taking the place of a perforation). There should be a clear line space above and below this line. For example:

Please reserve .... place/s on the training programme to be held on .... in Edinburgh/Leeds*.

* Please delete as appropriate

Name .... Position ....

Company name ....

Address

....

....

Phone .... Fax .... Date ....

Always use double line-spacing where someone has to fill in details. Note that there is a space between the last letter of a word preceding stops used as insertion lines and between the last stop and the first letter of the following word.

Envelopes

Envelopes should always match the letter stationery; the letter should not be folded more than twice (either two horizontal folds or one horizontal and one vertical fold).

'Window' envelopes are sometimes used so that the addressee's name and address show through. These are considered to be suitable for invoices, circulars and so on, but it is better to use a normal envelope for personal letters.

Labels are often used for large mailings where it would be impracticable to print all the envelopes separately, but again it is considered rather discourteous to send a personal letter with a label. Companies sometimes use labels because not all printers will handle envelopes. I personally think it is more personal to handwrite envelopes if this is the case.

The printing of the name and address on an envelope should start about half way down and about a third of the way in from the left hand side. The name and address should be exactly as printed on the letter, with the postal town in capital letters. If possible, each part of the address should start on a separate line and the postcode should always be on the last line on its own. There should be no full stops or commas (except apostrophes where relevant). If an envelope is being used with a flap at one end, the flap should be at the **right** hand side.

The following is an example of a printed envelope:

```
Professor Alfred Jones
The King's School
Severn Thames Street
GLOUCESTER
GL1 8TG
```

Activity

Write the following formal letters, set out in the correct way:

1 to a computer supplier, complaining that the specification of your computer is not what you ordered;

2 to a travel agent, asking for prices and times of an air flight to New Zealand via Bangkok, where you would like to stop over for two nights;

3 to a customer, apologizing for a late delivery of goods and enclosing a discount voucher towards their next order as a gesture of goodwill.

(You may like to compare your results with the examples at the end of this chapter. Although your letters will obviously differ from the examples given, you will be able to judge whether you have set the appropriate tone, included all the necessary detail and laid the letters out correctly.)

Internal Memoranda

Officially 'memorandum' (singular) and 'memoranda' (plural), but more commonly known as 'memos', these are notes sent to others within the organization. They may be formal or informal.

Memos usually follow a fairly standard layout (see below) and have no salutation, no complimentary close and are not signed. If the memo is confidential, it is marked as such and enclosed in an envelope which is addressed to the person concerned and marked 'Confidential'. Otherwise, memos are not usually put into an envelope.

Most organizations have an in-house memo format. The following is an example:

MEMORANDUM

TO: Jane Johnson

FROM: Fred Brighton

DATE: 27 July 1997

SUBJECT: Next sales meeting

Just to remind you that the next sales meeting will be held on Friday 16 August at 10.30 am. I should be grateful if you could bring the southern region figures for the past quarter.

I have asked Jon to organize coffee – could you bring some biscuits?

Memo formats are usually already installed on staff computers and merely need the wording required to be inserted. The memo format for the above example would be:

```
┌─────────────────────────────────────────────────────────────────┐
│  MEMORANDUM                                                       │
│                                                                   │
│  TO:                                                              │
│                                                                   │
│  FROM:                                                            │
│                                                                   │
│  DATE:                                                            │
│                                                                   │
│  SUBJECT:                                                         │
│  _____ │
│                                                                   │
└─────────────────────────────────────────────────────────────────┘
```

Where a memo is being sent to more than one person, each recipient's name appears in the 'TO: line'. Where a copy is sent to someone who is not actually a recipient (for information, for example), the routing procedure is the same as that for letters (see page 148).

Formal and informal report writing

Managers spend a lot of time writing reports and they are an important part of the written communication system within an organization. They can provide a record of actions which have taken place, they can give results of a project which has been undertaken, they can make recommendations to solve a problem or make changes to a current situation, they can put forward proposals, they can be used to present statistics . . . The list is endless. Reports are a way of giving information in writing when a letter is not relevant.

There are times when a formal report layout is necessary and others when a purely informal layout will suffice. It rather depends on the purpose of the report and to whom it is being sent. Sometimes a formal report is called for, at others – usually internal to the organization – an informal one will do.

Many of the aspects covered earlier in this chapter concerning letter writing also apply to reports. Things like keeping it short and simple, the need for accuracy and clarity, your objectives for writing the report, using ordinary, everyday English rather than complex language and technical terms and so on.

There are additional points to be thought about when writing reports, however. For example:

Setting an objective and selecting material

This is somewhat similar to preparation for a presentation which we discussed in chapter two. You are often faced with a mountain of material which could go into your report, but it is necessary to sift and sort this with the **objective** of the report in mind. As with presentation skills, if you try to put in everything you know about the subject of your report, it is likely to be far too long and very boring and difficult for the reader to assimilate. (In fact, they probably won't read it!)

Before you start planning the content of your report, therefore, establish a firm and clear objective and, as always, commit it to paper. Then you will be in a position to reject irrelevant material, simplify your content and make sure that you have the essentials.

When you are writing your objective, think about who you are writing the report for, why they want it, what it is about, and what is required as a result of it. Hopefully, you will be able to answer these questions fairly easily if you were properly briefed before you began the project.

Your objective will provide you with a frame of reference for your report and help you to focus concisely when you write it.

Items such as statistical reports, graphs, costings, research results and so on are best put in an appendix so they do not clutter the main report content and your reader can concentrate on your findings, recommendations and so on. Always quote the sources of any material you use.

Reports are always written in the third person

The layout of a report

A report can be really daunting for the reader, so make it as attractive and appealing as you can. Use double line-spacing and leave wide margins (also useful for people to make notes while reading the report). Each section should ideally begin on a new page.

Organize your material into sections and sub-sections. Each should have headings and sub-headings for easy reference. If it is a very long or formal report, it should have a contents page at the beginning which the reader can use as a route map.

It is not always easy to structure your material into the relevant sections, especially with a formal report containing specific section headings (see below). It is useful to write the report in rough first, putting the right content under the relevant heading. (It is all too easy to find yourself writing about the conclusions you have drawn from your investigation before you have reached the sub-heading 'Conclusions'!) When you have written your first draft, read it through and move any bits which you have placed under the wrong heading.

When I am working with trainee managers on the subject of report writing, I suggest that they make a card for each of the section headings and lay them out side by side on a table as if they were playing Patience. They then write each paragraph from the text of the report, or a number of paragraphs if they appertain to the same idea, onto separate pieces of paper and put them in the correct order under the correct heading. When they have finished this exercise, they sit back and look at them, changing any pieces of paper to another heading if necessary.

Present the report as interestingly as you can. It sometimes helps to bind a report, preferably with a spiral binding so that it opens flat.

WRITING FORMAL REPORTS

Formal reports follow a particular style and the sections of the report are placed in a certain order. The following is a typical example of the layout of a formal report:

Front cover

The title page may itself be a piece of durable, protective material or it may be a piece of clear plastic through which the title page can be seen. It is the first impression of your report the reader receives, so its appearance is important.

The title page itself usually bears the title of the report and the name of the author. The title is a concise indication of the subject of the report, perhaps with a sub-title to give a deeper indication of the subject matter. The title page also shows the month and year of the report.

Acknowledgements

If the report is going to be published, it may be that the author will wish to express appreciation to others, perhaps for help provided, advice given, special co-operation and so on. If so, the acknowledgements page comes immediately after the title page. Even if there are just a few lines, it has a page to itself.

Contents

Next comes the contents page. This gives the headings, an sub-headings of each section, together with the relevant page numbers. Any appendices should be listed by name and itemized (by number or letter) in the order in which they appear in the main text. An example of a contents page might be similar to that shown opposite:

Information about ways to number the sections of a report is given on page 158.

CONTENTS

Terms of Reference

Here you set out (briefly) the reasons why you have undertaken the report together with the objective/s for it, which you have already defined before starting to write your report.

Summary

This comes before the main content of your report and provides a synopsis of its content. You cannot write it, of course, until you have finished the report, but you place it at this point so that your reader can scan the summary and have a good idea of what is included in the report. It is a précis, or if you like, the report in miniature. It summarises all the essentials of the report, including your recommendations. It usually consists of around 200/300 words.

Most people look at the summary of a report first, sometimes in order to decide whether the report is of relevance to them and is therefore worth reading in full.

Introduction

Now you come to the subject of the report itself and first you give an introduction. This is to introduce the reader to what follows and may include points such as:

> - a definition of the problem
> - the background, circumstances and history
> - any assumptions, constraints or limitations on the report
> - an explanation of any terms, abbreviations, jargon etc used in the report (note that if many words are likely to be unfamiliar, it might be useful to include a glossary in your appendices)

Main body of the report

At last, you may be thinking! This is obviously the main proportion of the overall report content. It often starts with an analysis of the current situation (we call it a 'situation analysis').

This is followed by a description of the methods you have undertaken to investigate the situation and the results. (**Note** – if you have research statistics to present, put these in an appendix as noted above. You might also think of presenting them in graphical form – more about this in chapter six.)

The next stage is the analysis of the material you have obtained, followed by a discussion of the implications of possible solutions to the problem or situation. It is important, here, to think about the implications on management, particularly with regard to cost/benefits (do not go into detail at this stage) and the impact on human resources. (**Note** – do not, at this stage, draw any conclusions or make any recommendations. This is very difficult, but you must only discuss pro's and con's at this point.)

Conclusions

Now you draw your conclusions based on the logically reasoned discussion which took place in the last section. Alternatives are considered and evaluated – do not confuse the issue and make any recommendations at this stage. Stick to the deductions you have made.

Recommendations

Having drawn conclusions from the work you have undertaken, you are now in a position to make recommendations for solutions to the problem or put forward proposals to meet the situation as it currently stands.

Statement of costs

If your recommendations were to be implemented, they are likely to have a cost implication. This may be a spend or a save, but either way you need to set out the details at this point in the report.

Appendices

As already stated, any tables, charts, graphs, statistical tables, organization charts, leaflets – in fact any material or evidence which supports or enhances the text of the report – is placed in the appendices. Each piece of information goes into a separate appendix and the appendices appear in the order to which they are referred in the main text. The appendices should be numbered (see numbering a report on page 158) and each should be given a title.

Material should not be put in the appendices merely to supply 'padding'. Only use information which is referred to in the main text and which clarifies understanding or provides further information.

References or bibliography

This may be placed before or after the appendices, but is usually found at the back of the report so that readers may look up references quickly and easily if they wish to consult the original source.

If you have used sources of information such as published material, reference books or reports, you should acknowledge it here by quoting the details of the original material. There are various ways of laying out a bibliography, but the following is a fairly standard one (assuming you had written a report about a project undertaken on hippopotami!):

You will notice that the authors are placed in alphabetical order by surname, followed by the name of the book, publisher and place of publication and year of publication. Where you have placed a reference mark in the text which refers to a specific page number, quote the page number in the bibliography so that your reader could look up the reference if required. Where you are quoting a section covering several pages, use 'pp' (which means between page number 'x' and page number 'y').

BIBLIOGRAPHY

Jones, A.H.A., *Theory Of Snowbound Hippopotami*, Wells & Makepiece London, 1990, Ref 1, p 101

Mainstone, B.A., *Behavioural Study Of The Hippopotamus*, Greenwood, New York, 1986, Ref. 2, pp 23–25

Sharpe, I.P., Hippopotami Examined, IN *A Journal Of Animal Life*, Vol 2, 6 March 1988, Duffle & Spring, Ref. 3, pp 5–9

If you are quoting an article from a journal (as in the latter case in the example), the word 'IN' is written in capital letters and the name of the journal is in italics, followed by the volume and issue number. The date of the issue is given, together with the publisher.

NUMBERING A REPORT

Reports can either be numbered with letters or numbers, or with a decimal system.

Letters and numbers

The following is the standard system, whereby alternate letters and numbers are used to indicate descending order of importance:

I   Main heading ... *then II, III, IV etc*

    A   Chapter heading ... *then B, C, D*

        1   Subject heading ... *then 2, 3, 4*

            (a)   Section heading ... *then (b), (c), (d)*

                (i)   Sub-section heading ... *then (ii), (iii), (iv)*

If you wished, you could omit the large Roman numeral and start with capital letters for the main heading. The chapter headings would then be numbered 1, 2, 3 and the subject headings (a), (b), (c) and so on.

It is important, however, to keep the alternate letter/number sequence.

Decimal system

---

1   Chapter heading . . . *then 2, 3, 4 etc*

    1.1   Subject heading within chapter 1 . . . *then 1.2, 1.3, 1.4*

        1.1.1   Section heading within subject 1.1 . . . *then 1.1.2, 1.1.3, etc*

In Chapter two, subject headings would be 2.1, 2.2, 2.3 , 2.4, etc and Section headings would be 2.1.1, 2.1.2, 2.1.3, etc.

Further divisions are made by adding another digit. For example, a sub-section of section 5 of the 3rd subject of chapter 2 would become 2.3.5.1!

WRITING INFORMAL REPORTS

Informal reports are often written for internal use within an organization. Although they do not require the formal layout above, informal reports still need structuring and presenting in such a way that they appear easy to read, are clear, and are short and to the point. They should still have a summary section at the beginning so that the reader may scan the 'gist' of what follows and they should contain the same kind of material as the main content, conclusions, recommendations and costing implications as a formal report. The formal headings may not appear (such as 'Terms of reference', for example), but the informal report contains much of the same 'meat'.

A Check-list for writing reports[1]

1 **Title** – will readers know what it is about?
2 **List of sections** (Contents page) – does this show the structure and scope of the report?
3 **Summary** – a synopsis of the report contents
4 **By whom**? – who started it?
5 **Why**? – what is it for?
6 **For whom**? – what readers have you in mind?
7 **When**? – did any time constraints affect the report?
8 **In what context**?– is it clear what is already known?
9 **With what constraints**? – time, resource, political, social?
10 **How conducted**? – what methods and techniques were used in the collection and analysis of data?
11 **What happened**? – is it necessary to explain how the way the enquiry was conducted differed from what was originally planned?
12 **What information**? – is the data presented clearly in a suitable format?
13 **Conclusions** – are these logical deductions or partly subjective?

14 **Recommendations** – does the report indicate any action to be taken?
15 **Appendices** – has all voluminous, technical, etc material been suitably segregated?
16 **Sources** – is there a bibliography or list of sources drawn upon?
17 **Checking** – has a friend read the draft?
18 **Index** – is it short enough not to need an index?
19 **Typing** – double line-spacing, on one side, enough copies?
20 **Proof-reading** – has the typing been double-checked?
21 **Distribution list** – is it clear who is to receive it?

Proof-reading documents

A plea on behalf of secretaries (if you have one to help you): it is very easy these days to amend text entered on a word processor and many managers have got into the habit of composing letters and reports in a slipshod way, expecting their secretary to edit it when they re-write it later.

Although it is true that the editing facility on a word processor makes life a great deal easier than the complete re-types which were often necessary in pre-computer days, a great deal of time (and therefore money, not to mention secretaries' frustration) is wasted by executives who automatically expect a re-working of every document and write or dictate accordingly. Amendments should still be the exception rather than the rule.

It is, however, the responsibility of the manager who is signing the letter to proof-read the document before it is sent out (rather than blame the secretary or word processing operator if mistakes are discovered later) and the signs on page 161 are some of the more commonly used conventional proof-reading marks for amending documents:

Sign in margin	Meaning	Mark in the text	
$\wedge$	insert additional matter	$\wedge$	placed where omission occurs
(delete symbol)	delete	/	through words or letter/s
np/or //	start a new paragraph	$\sqsubset$	by first word
run on/	no new paragraph, carry straight on	(run on symbol)	
trs/	transpose letters or words	(transpose symbol)	between words or letters
(indent symbol)	indent	(indent symbol)	by matter to be indented
$\smile$	close up (horizontally)	$\smile$	between words or letters
( )	close up (vertically)	( )	between lines
(insert space symbol)	insert space between lines or paragraphs		at relevant point
(reduce space symbol)	reduce space between lines or paragraphs		at relevant point
(stet symbol – tick in circle)	stet (let it stand, ie type the word/s that have been crossed out and have a dotted line underneath)	- - - -	under words struck out
#	insert a space	$\wedge$	
lc/or =	lower case = small letter	=	under letter
uc/or ≡ or caps	upper case = capital letter	≡	under letter

Examples of letters written in response to the Activity on page 150):

1 To a computer supplier, complaining that the specification of your computer is not what you ordered:

(Assumed letter heading)

16 November 1997

Mr J Smithers
PC Supplies Ltd
16 Worksop Street
BRISTOL
BS1 9RE

Dear Mr Smithers

OUR ORDER NUMBER 1425/JS

With reference to the computer hardware recently delivered against the above order number, we have to advise you that the specification is not as ordered.

Our order calls for 12 Mb RAM whereas you have supplied only 8 Mb. As we need to prepare for a large mailshot which will be sent out next Monday, I should be grateful if you would rectify this error by Friday at the latest.

Please telephone me to let me know when you will be coming.

Yours sincerely

Charles Street
Manager

---

2 To a travel agent, asking for prices and times of an air flight to New Zealand via Bangkok, where you would like to stop over for two nights:

(Assumed letter heading)

5 August 1997

Messrs ABC Travel
The Gregory Centre
HAYES
Middlesex
UB3 8LT

Dear Sirs

AIR FLIGHT TO NEW ZEALAND

I am planning to travel to Auckland in January 1998, via a two-night stopover in Bangkok. I shall be staying in New Zealand for three weeks and flying back directly to London Heathrow.

Would you kindly supply me with prices and times for both weekday and weekend flights, quoting for two different airlines.

Yours faithfully
SIMPLY SPORTS LTD

Jane Smart
Sales Manager

---

3   To a customer, apologizing for a late delivery of goods and enclosing a discount voucher towards their next order as a gesture of goodwill:

(Assumed letter heading)

13 November 1997

Mrs B Wainwright
The Elms
17 Woodhall Street
HUNGERFORD
Berks
RG17 7BA

Dear Mrs Wainwright

THREE PIECE SUITE

Please accept my sincere apology for the late delivery of your three piece suite promised for last Monday.

The reason for the delay is that our lorry was involved in an accident on the M4 while on the way to deliver your goods and the settee was badly damaged.

We are expecting a replacement from the factory to arrive at our warehouse on Friday and will make delivery to you next Monday, 18 November between 2 p.m. and 5 p.m. If this is not convenient for you, perhaps you would telephone to let me know.

We are very sorry for the inconvenience you have been caused and would ask you to accept the £50 voucher which you may use in any of our stores.

Yours sincerely

Bryan Adams
Manager

enc

BIBLIOGRAPHY

For further reading on the subjects in this chapter, see:

Burton, S.H., *Mastering English Grammar*, Macmillan, 1984

Burton, S.H., *Spelling*, Longman's English Guides, 1984

Burton, S.H., *Writing Letters*, Longman's English Guides, 1983

Cooper, B.M., *Writing Technical Reports*, Penguin Books, 1964

Gordon, I., *Punctuation*, Longman's English Guides, 1983

Gowers, Sir E., *The Complete Plain Words*, HMSO, 1954

Turner, B.T., *Technical Writing and Speaking*, Industrial & Commercial Techniques Ltd, 1971

---

1 With acknowledgement to:
  Connors, B., *Undertaking Enquiries, Part 3, Writing a Report*, Social Science: A Third Level Course Public Administration Block III, Part 3 1974, The Open University Press

CHAPTER SIX

More About Written Communication

IN THIS CHAPTER WE WILL LOOK AT THE FOLLOWING AREAS:

- written requirements for meetings
- business documents
- presenting information in graphical form
- personnel issues for line managers
- material for publication

Written requirements for meetings

We have looked at oral communication which takes place in meetings in chapter three. Now it is necessary to cover the various pieces of written documentation which meetings entail.

NOTICE OF MEETING

There is no one way of producing a notice of meeting, but there needs to be an appropriate method of notifying members that a meeting will take place. If it is an in-house meeting, it may be an informal memo informing those who will be attending that the meeting is to take place, but as with any notice of meeting there are certain items which must be included:

- What the meeting is about
- Date
- Time
- Place

Some meetings require formal notice which must be circulated to those invited to attend by a certain date prior to the meeting. Where the meeting is a statutory one, such as a company Annual General Meeting, the amount of notice which must be given to shareholders is written into the constitution of the organization (the Memorandum and Articles of Association).

A typical notice of meeting might look like this:

GREENWOOD ESTATES LTD

Notice of Management Meeting

You are advised that the next Management meeting will be held in the Board Room at the Redhill site on Tuesday 8 October 1997 at 10.00 am.

Josephine Welks Company Secretary 9 September 1997

THE AGENDA

An Agenda is a list of items for attention at the meeting. It is usually sent out prior to the meeting so that members may prepare, and it often accompanies the notice of meeting. If it is an informal meeting, the agenda may appear on the same paper as the notice of meeting.

At the meeting itself, items are usually taken in the sequence they appear on the Agenda unless the Chair agrees to change them for a specific reason. A typical Management meeting Agenda might follow this pattern:

GREENWOOD ESTATES LTD

Management meeting
to be held on Tuesday 8 October 1997 at 10.00 am

AGENDA

1   Apologies for absence
2   Minutes of the previous meeting
3   Matters arising from the minutes
4   Next years' salary review
5   New premises
6   Marketing exhibition
7   Any other business
8   Date of next meeting

MINUTES OF MEETINGS

Whether formal or informal, there should always be a record of what took place at the meeting. Usually, this record is kept in the form of 'Minutes'. The record of what is said at the meeting is kept by someone present, usually the Secretary. That person then prepares a draft set of Minutes, which is usually approved by the Chairperson before it is distributed to members. This distribution sometimes takes place immediately after the meeting, sometimes with the notice and agenda for the next meeting, and occasionally the Minutes are given to members at the next meeting. The latter procedure is not to be recommended, because it does not give members a chance to peruse the Minutes before the meeting in order to prepare. It is a good idea, however, to have spare copies available at the meeting in case members forget to bring their copy with them (this goes for Agendas, too).

Another reason for sending the Minutes to members prior to the next meeting is so that they do not necessarily have to be read out, which saves time. Traditionally, Minutes are read aloud by the Secretary, but these days it is more common for the Chair to announce the Minutes as 'taken as read', and to give the members an opportunity to raise any points of dispute before asking if members approve the Minutes. (This presupposes that member have read the Minutes prior to the meeting.)

Sometimes a verbatim record is kept of what was said (such as court proceedings). Most organizations, however, record decisions and action points only or, more usually, record important discussion, as well as decisions and action to be taken. Just how much is recorded is usually agreed between the Secretary and the Chair.

It is necessary for the Secretary to record who was present at the meeting, together with the names of members who sent apologies for absence. (Minutes should be sent to these people if they regularly attend the meetings so that they are aware of what took place.) If it is a large meeting, members may sign as they come into the room, or an attendance list can be passed round the room for people to sign.

Layout of Minutes

Minutes should be kept in a loose-leaf binder or in a bound book as they provide a permanent record of the proceedings. They should be written up as quickly as possible after the meeting while matters are clear in the Secretary's mind. **Minutes are always written in the third person and in the past tense.**

The '**ABC**' which we spoke of in the last chapter applies here too:

A-ccurate
B-rief
C-lear

The following is an example showing the beginning of a set of Minutes, with a system which uses references in the left hand margin to allow for later reference. This particular system uses a consecutive number followed by the year. There is a right hand column for 'Action' in which the initials of the people responsible are typed. This again makes for easy reference, for members do not have to read right through the Minutes to find out what action they are responsible for.

GREENWOOD ESTATES LTD

Minutes of a management meeting held on Tuesday 8 October 1997 at 10.00 am at the Redhill Site

Present: Sir Richard Greenwood (Chair)
Valerie Ellis
Gunther Feistel
John Greenwood
Augustus Hazelwood (Secretary)
Barbara Williams

Apologies: Jennifer Gresham
Greg Powell

Action

32/96 **Minutes of the previous meeting**
The minutes of the meeting held on Thursday 18 July
1996   were taken as read and approved.

33/96 **Matters Arising**
28/96 Valerie Ellis reported that the staff welfare
committee had met and a report on the new Health
and Safety training programme would be available
for the next management meeting.   VE

34/96 **Next years' salary review**
Following discussion, Gunther Feistel was asked to
prepare a budget for the next financial year based on a
staff salary increase of 7% and it was agreed that the
item should appear on the agenda for the next meeting.   GF

35/96 **New premises**
Sir John Greenwood reported that contracts had been
exchanged on the new Reigate premises and it was hoped
that the commercial department would be able to move
before the end of the year.

Action

36/96 Marketing exhibition

Members were asked to note that the company would
be exhibiting at the Ideal Estates Exhibition to be held
at King's Court from 26–29 July 1997.

Any other business

37/96 Marketing Training

A complaint had been received by Barbara Williams
concerning inadequate study leave from one of her
staff who was undertaking a marketing diploma. After
discussion, it was agreed that the employee be allowed
one day a month for study leave and Barbara Williams
was asked to convey this to her.   BW

There being no other business, the meeting was closed at 12.30 p.m.

Date of next meeting:

Thursday 23 January 1997 at 10.00 am at the Redhill site.

Signed as approved 23 January 1997.................................(Chair)

FORMAL MEETINGS

At a formal meeting, it is essential to record who proposed and seconded a
motion. A motion is the question which is at issue. After discussion, the
Chairperson will ask for someone to 'propose' the motion. If someone agrees
to do this, the Chair will then ask for someone to 'second' the motion. If no-
one is prepared to do this, the motion is dropped. Provided the motion is proposed and seconded, the Chair will ask for a vote of 'those in favour' and
'those against'. If 'those in favour' are in a majority, the motion will be carried. It then becomes a 'resolution'. (Note, if the number of votes is equally
divided, the Chairperson has a 'casting vote'. Otherwise, the Chair does not
vote.)

When preparing the Minutes of a formal meeting, it is necessary for the
Secretary to record the exact wording of the resolution, the names of the people proposing and seconding, and whether the resolution was carried by a
majority or unanimous vote (or whether the motion wasn't carried at all
because the majority were 'against').

OTHER MEETING TERMINOLOGY

You may encounter additional meeting terminology from time to time, such
as:

Ad hoc

This is a meeting which has been arranged for a particular purpose. It is usually a one-off or temporary sub-committee.

Addendum

An addendum adds words to a motion.

Amendment

If an amendment to a motion is put forward, it must be proposed, seconded and put to the members in the usual way. An amendment is a proposal to alter a motion.

Co-option

Committees may have the power to invite people to serve on the committee for a specific reason (for example, they may have specific expertise on a subject under discussion). The majority of the committee members must be in favour of such an invitation.

Ex officio

This means 'by virtue of his office'. A person may be a member of a committee because of the office he holds.

In camera

A meeting which is not open to members of the public.

Lie on the table

When the contents of a letter or document have been discussed at the meeting and it has been decided that no action should result from them, the document is said to 'lie on the table'.

Nem con

Sometimes, not all people present will vote; they will choose to abstain. If all the people who have voted, however, voted in favour of the resolution, it will be said to have been carried 'nem con' (nemine contradicente) – that is, 'no-one contradicting'.

No confidence

If the member of a meeting are not satisfied with the performance of the Chairperson, they may pass a vote of 'no confidence' in the Chair. The Chair must then vacate the position and the members vote someone else into it.

Point of order

No doubt you will have heard this called out in the House of Commons chamber by members questioning the procedure of the debate. It is usually a query relating to whether the discussion is taking place according to the constitution of the meeting.

Proxy

A person who acts on behalf of another, or a document which authorizes a person to attend a meeting and vote on their behalf.

Quorum

A quorum is the minimum number of persons who must be present to hold a meeting. The number is laid down in the constitution of the organization.

Rider

A rider is additional wording added to a resolution after it has been passed (as opposed to an amendment which alters it). A rider must be proposed, seconded and put to the members in the usual way.

Right of Reply

The person who proposes the motion has one opportunity to reply after discussion has taken place before the motion is put to the meeting.

Sine die

This literally means 'without an appointed day' and is usually used when something is postponed indefinitely.

Status quo

A matter in which there is to be no change; as it is now.

Table a document

To 'table a document' is to hand it to members at the meeting, rather than circulate it previously. (It is literally put 'on the table'.)

Ultra vires

This means that a matter is beyond the legal authority or power of a committee or organization.

Business documents

There are many documents used by managers other than those we have discussed in depth. We will review some of these here as a reference guide in case you have to deal with them at any time.

Advice note

An advice note (or delivery note) is packed with the goods on despatch. Strictly speaking, an advice note is included in a parcel dispatched by post or rail, and a delivery note is used by a driver who actually delivers goods and receives a signature from the person who receives them. One copy of the delivery note is given to the recipient and one is retained by the driver as a record for the sender.

Credit note

A credit note is a statement from the selling organization where goods have been returned, an overcharge made, packing materials returned and so on. It is an allowance towards a further order from the purchaser.

Delivery note

See 'Advice note above'.

Goods received note

When an organization receives goods, usually at its 'goods-in' department, a goods received note is issued internally and distributed to the relevant personnel such as purchasing department (to check against order), stores (to initiate stock control), accounts (to check against invoice) and so on.

Invitation to tender

This is also known as 'letter of enquiry' and is used to invite several organizations to quote for their goods or services.

Invoice

An invoice is an account of details and prices of goods sold. It is often printed at the same time as the advice/delivery note and the costs are added.

Purchase order

Most organizations issue a purchase order for goods or services to be supplied. This is an official request and the purchase order number can be matched against a future advice/delivery note and subsequent invoice.

Quotation

In reply to an invitation to tender, or letter of enquiry a supplier will send a quotation supplying full details of goods offered for sale and the conditions of sale.

Requisition order

A requisition order is an internal 'order form' or request for goods or services which is sent to the Purchasing department and stimulates the production of a purchase order to be sent to the supplier.

Statement of account

A statement of account sets out what is owed to an organization by a purchaser and will contain a record of all the invoices issued and payments made since the last statement. It will show the state of the purchaser's balance (either debit or credit) at the date of the statement.

Presenting information in graphical form

Managers are often required to present information, such as statistical reports, sales figures at meetings or in presentations, and so on. Some information can be difficult to communicate effectively, especially if it involves statistics. Such information can be more interesting and more easily understood if it is presented in graphical form. Overhead transparencies or slides used as training aids or in formal presentations, for example, can be produced really professionally using the computer; it is possible to present some stunning displays of information which are much more meaningful to the reader than columns of figures. Not only can pie charts, histograms, bar charts, line graphs and so on be supplied, but they can appear in glorious Technicolor. Colour cannot be shown here, but the following examples will give an idea of the way in which statistics can be presented.

A bar chart

The following chart shows sales figures for the year broken down into four quarters. The figures keyed into the computer were:

	1st qtr	2nd qtr	3rd qtr	4th qtr
North	90	50	65	85
South	50	40	45	70
East	25	30	40	20
West	10	20	30	45

These figures shown on the bar chart give a much more meaningful comparison that merely numbers.

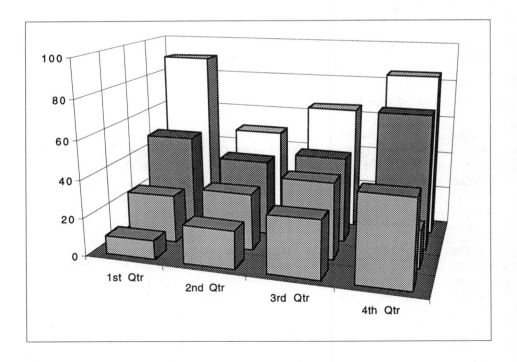

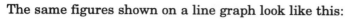

A line graph

The same figures shown on a line graph look like this:

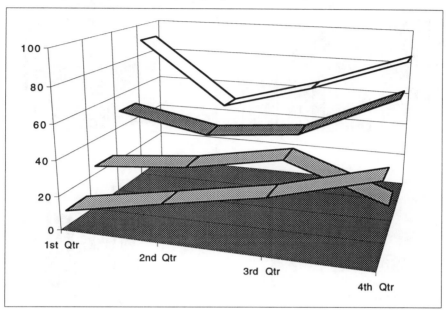

An area graph

The same figures shown as an area graph:

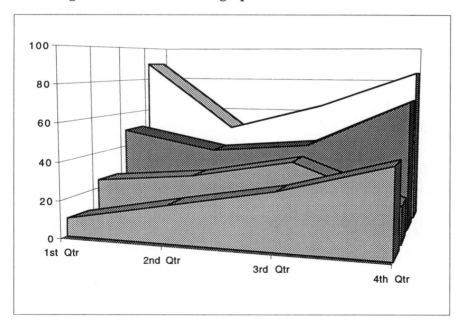

The following charts are all different graphical representations of the same figures:

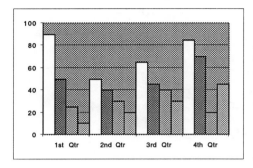

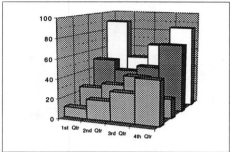

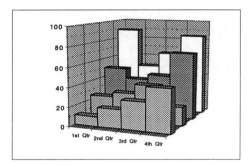

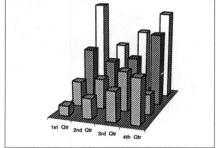

A scattergram

The following chart illustrates how many times John, Mark and Paul jumped distances of 5, 5.5, 6, 6.5 and 7 ft:

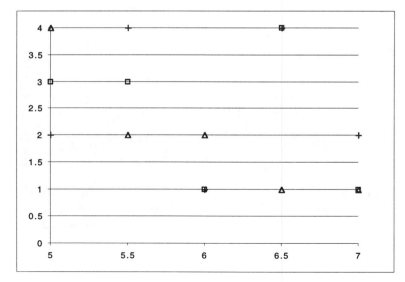

A pie chart

This chart shows the comparison between the percentage of fruit sold, the whole making up the total pie (100%):

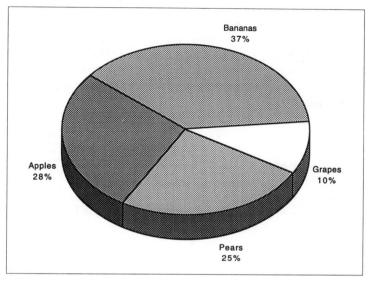

Project management using graphical 'tools'

Most managers are involved in project management, whether it is the kind of project undertaken by the construction industry such as building the Channel Tunnel, or everyday planning and monitoring activities against time, budget and quality.

There are a number of techniques available for helping to plan and monitor projects which are very useful tools for managers. With most projects, the balance between getting the job done at the right time, at the right quality and at the right price is a fine one. If a task is completed just one or two days over the due date, it can cost millions and put the budget completely out of kilter. When a company is planning a large project such as a building programme, for example, workers may be contracted to come in at various stages months beforehand. Many of these tasks are dependent on the completion of a previous stage. For example, the plasterers cannot plaster until the 'brickies' have finished, the painters cannot come in until the plasterers have finished, and so on. If one link in the chain is late, the company has to pay contracted workers even though they are not on the job.

Therefore it is in everyone's interests to efficiently plan and control a project, of whatever size, especially where there are 'dependency links' as described above. Some of the techniques available for this are graphical 'tools'. These vary from simple flow diagrams to complicated charts.

Flow diagrams

Flow charts show something in diagram form which would be difficult to communicate effectively in words and which is much easier to understand graphically.

Before the flow chart can be written, all the data for it must be to hand. The data is broken down into ordered sequence: 'what is the first thing that happens?', 'what happens next?' and so on. Where questions can be answered 'Yes' or 'No', the flow chart divides to show alternative routes. Flow charts can be as complicated as one wants to make them, or they can be very simple. For example, a child's bedtime:

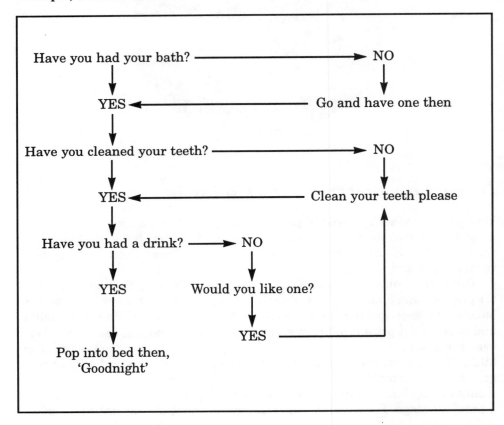

Task breakdown chart

A simple diagram can be used to break down the project into manageable chunks. Supposing the project was to prepare a dinner party for six people. Your task breakdown chart might look something like this:

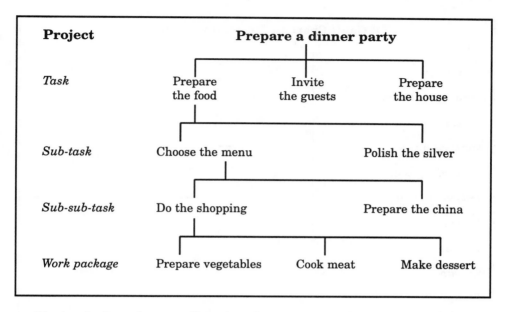

Having broken the overall project down into detailed activities, the next step is to estimate the resources and time you need to complete each one and subsequently the overall project, and to make someone responsible for each step as well as for the project itself. The order in which you undertake each step needs to be thought through so that 'dependence' is assessed. For example, you could not cook your potatoes until you had peeled them, and you could not peel them before you had bought them!

Gantt charts

One of the simple but effective charts used in project management is a Gantt chart, named after Henry L Gantt, an American management guru of around the time of the first World war. He devised a way of showing quite simply the steps needed to undertake a project and the time each step would take. The chart shows the steps in relation to each other over a period of time. A Gantt chart gives an overview of the total project rather than scheduling details.

The example of a Gantt chart on page 182 provides an overview of a project for one person to decorate a room over a period of seven days:

This shows tasks in relation to each other. For example, you obviously cannot paper the walls until you have bought the new wallpaper, therefore wall-papering is dependent on completion of the previous task – that of buying wallpaper. You can, however, buy the new wallpaper before you have stripped the old paper. In fact, buying the wallpaper is not dependent on any other task.

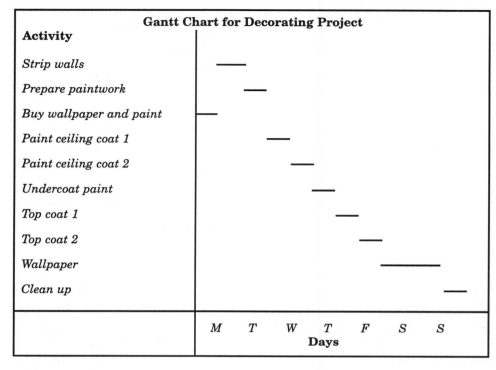

Gantt Chart for Decorating Project

Activity							
Strip walls							
Prepare paintwork							
Buy wallpaper and paint							
Paint ceiling coat 1							
Paint ceiling coat 2							
Undercoat paint							
Top coat 1							
Top coat 2							
Wallpaper							
Clean up							
	M	T	W	T	F	S	S

Days

Activity

Prepare a Gantt chart for the project of preparing a dinner party for six people where the following criteria apply:

Number	Activity	Number of minutes
1	Plan what to have	5
2	Shop	20
3	Prepare potatoes	3
4	Prepare carrots	3
5	Prepare greens	3
6	Prepare meat	3
7	Cook potatoes	20
8	Grill meat	15
9	Cook carrots	12
10	Cook greens	7
11	Make gravy with greens water	3
12	Lay table	3
13	Make mint sauce	2
14	Dish up	3

NB: The activities do not necessarily have to take place in the above order – it is up to you to assess any 'dependencies'.

There is only one person available to do everything – you!

(Answer at end of this chapter)

PERT Chart

I do not propose to go into the subject of Critical Path Analysis in any depth, but recommend that if you are involved in project management you read up on the subject. CPA aims to find out which activities are critical to completing the project within a given time-scale. In order to do this, it sequences the activities, putting down the earliest start times for each activity, depending on the finish time of the previous one. A network diagram is then produced which shows the **critical path** – that is the shortest possible time in which the project can be accomplished, providing at each stage the activity is completed on time.

The following example is a PERT chart, which is CPA in its simplest form. Each **activity** is represented by an **arrow** and a **circle** represents an **event** – that is, the start or finish of an activity. The numbers represent the length of time for each activity on the path (these could be days, weeks, months or minutes). (Note that the critical path is marked with double lines across each activity line.)

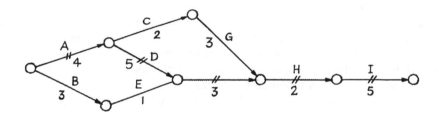

The diagram shows quite clearly that

- activity C is dependent on the completion of activity A
- activity G is dependent on the completion of activities A and C
- activity D is dependent on the completion of activity A (but not on activity C)
- activity B is not dependent on the completion of activity A
- activity E is dependent on the completion of activity B
- activity F is dependent on the completion of activities A, B, D and E
- activity H is dependent on the completion of activities A, B, C, D, E, F and G
- activity I is dependent on the completion of activities A, B, C, D, E, F, G and H

It will be seen from this diagram that the critical path is along activities A, D, F, H and I and that the shortest time in which the project could be completed is 19 (days, weeks, months, or whatever unit of time is being measured).

By being aware which is the **critical** path, a project manager can monitor and control each activity in this sequence, knowing that while he may have leeway on other activities, any delay in those on the critical path could be crucial for the completion of the project.

This section has tried to show how information may be presented in a graphical format to make it more interesting and your communication more easily understood. It has also looked at just a few of the charts and diagrams available to managers to plan, monitor and control projects that they might undertake. There are many more such tools and techniques available, this has been an introduction to them.

Personnel issues for line managers

Although this book is not specifically about personnel matters, it is about communicating with people. Some line managers who are responsible for staff feel that personnel issues are not part of their brief, but most are, thankfully, becoming more aware of their direct responsibility for their staffs' training and development, welfare and personal issues as well as ensuring that they achieve their task objectives. (This is why we looked at coaching and counselling interviews in chapter three.) Kenney and Reid (1986)[1] write ' . . . all managers without exception ought to accept personal responsibility for the training and development of their own staff. This involves taking an active interest in their careers, providing opportunities to improve and extend their abilities, especially by using day-to-day work tasks, and above all, by encouraging them to continue learning.'

Likewise, line managers are, in liaison with personnel managers, becoming more involved in recruiting and selecting staff to meet certain job criteria and therefore in designing and writing documents which until recently were the domain of the personnel department. They are also becoming more involved in issues such as the definition of job descriptions, for after all, who knows more about the job than the manager who is responsible for seeing that the task is completed?

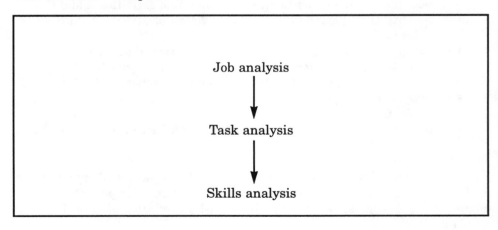

Job analysis

Task analysis

Skills analysis

Job analysis

This is an analysis of a particular job in order to determine exactly what skills are required of the person undertaking it. As with project management, where we have seen that a project is broken down into tasks, sub-tasks and work packages, so with job analysis in that the job is analyzed into a number of tasks. Each task is then examined to see what skills are required.

This enables the manager recruiting new staff to know what the job consists of and what skills she is looking for in a candidate. We talked a little about this in selection interviewing in chapter three. It also enables managers to identify training and development needs where new or existing employees have identified skills which they do not have or which need improvement.

Task analysis

When a job is analyzed and broken down into tasks, some companies use a process known as 'key task analysis'. This means that where a job comprises a large number of tasks, it may not be possible to recruit a person who has the requisite knowledge and skill to cover all of them. Therefore, 'key tasks' are identified in order to prioritise the knowledge and skill requirements, and areas where the person is less able will either be added to a training needs specification, or the tasks may be distributed to other staff.

Job description

From the job analysis, the manager is able to draw up a Job description which is 'a broad statement of the purpose, scope, responsibilities and tasks which constitute a particular job' (Manpower Services Commission 1981). The job description contains:

- the job title;
- the department;
- to whom the job holder is responsible;
- for whom he or she has responsibility;
- the purpose of the job;
- a list of the major tasks;
- a description of any resources for which the employee is accountable (if relevant).

Sometimes, the job description contains hours of working and the place of work (if it is a multi-site organization, for example).

A simple job description might take the following format:

COMPANY NAME

JOB DESCRIPTION

JOB TITLE:

DEPARTMENT:

LINE AUTHORITY TO:

LINE AUTHORITY FOR:

SUMMARY OF PRIMARY FUNCTIONS:

DATE:

JOB SPECIFICATION

From the job description, a Job specification can be written. This is 'a detailed statement, derived from the job analysis, of the knowledge and the physical and mental activities involved in the job and of the environment within which the job is performed' (Manpower Services Commission 1981). Sometimes, the details in the job specification are divided into the two areas 'knowledge' and 'skills', with perhaps a third area of 'attitude' added where it is particularly appropriate – for example, where the employee will meet members of the public. If, for example, the job specification related to a customer service person, the task of answering the telephone would be one which would appear on the specification and the manager would be looking for someone who had the knowledge and skills of using the telephone, together with the interpersonal skills involved in handling sensitive issues and possibly angry customers.

TRAINING SPECIFICATION

Also arising from the job analysis, a Training specification may be drawn up. This is 'a detailed statement of what a trainee needs to learn, based on a comparison between the job specification and the individual's present level of competence' (Manpower Services Commission 1981). National Vocational Qualifications (NVQs) are competency standards for specific jobs and these, too, can provide an opportunity to assess an employee's, or potential employee's competence against a standard laid down by the respective industry's lead body at various levels of ability. Where there is a gap between a person's current level of competence in specific skills or task ability and those required for their job, then a training specification can be drawn up to determine what is required to acquire or improve the person's skills. This often takes place during an appraisal or review interview.

Setting objectives

When a line manager recommends one of their team for a training pro-gramme, objectives should be set both for the trainee and for the organiza-tion. Whether the training programme be internally or externally organized, the trainee should know why they are being given the training and what the expected outcomes are. Only then can the success or otherwise of the train-ing be evaluated. Too many employees are sent on, or choose to go on train-ing courses with no evaluation taking place afterwards (except perhaps a hastily completed feedback questionnaire which no-one reads and which is filed away in a cabinet somewhere, never to be seen again).

In order for the organization to consider whether their investment in a person's training has been worthwhile, they should be evaluating at individ-ual, team and organizational level, that is, evaluating against the business objectives of the organization. This is not just investment in monetary terms, but also in time (time that the trainee is away from the job, time from inter-nal trainers, time in advice and guidance from the line manager and others . . .), knowledge and skills of others involved (trainers, managers . . .) and so on.

Therefore, the line manager should discuss objectives for the training with the trainee prior to the course taking place and the manager should put the objectives **in writing**. As with all objectives, in order to measure the out-comes or results, they should be **SMART** objectives:

S	S-pecific
M	M-easurable
A	A-chievable and agreed
R	R-ealistic
T	T-imebound

It can be seen that an objective to 'go on a word processing course' is not a **SMART** objective. It does not meet the criteria above. It would also be hope-less to evaluate. Yes, one could say that the trainee had attended the course, which would be all that one could measure against this vague objective. It does not, however, indicate that any learning took place, let alone be trans-ferred to the workplace afterwards.

A **SMART** objective for such a programme might be to:

- attend a one-day WordPerfect 6 introductory training programme in order to acquire the basic skills of keying-in, editing, saving and printing on 21 January 1997 at the Holman Institute, Bradwell.

This objective is specific; the outcomes are measurable (did the trainee learn the basic skills of operating WordPerfect 6 or did she not, one can ask and observe from her skill level after the course); the target is achievable and realistic (it would not have been realistic to expect the person to be able to operate the whole WordPerfect 6 at the end of a one-day programme, for example); it is timebound (a one-day programme on 21 January 1997). I have added 'agreed' into the SMART objectives illustration above because it is good to gain the agreement of the trainee to the objective before they undertake the training.

If you as line manager operate such a policy of setting objectives for your staff training and development strategy, you will be in a position to evaluate the outcomes and so contribute to the development of the individual concerned, your department or team, and to the organization as a whole.

You can, of course, operate such a policy for all kinds of operations for which you are responsible, such as personal goals and targets for all your staff, the systems and procedures you introduce – in fact anything for which you can set specific, measurable, achievable, realistic and timebound objectives. In this way, you can continually evaluate performance against objectives and so plan your future strategy to meet the objectives which you have been given for your department.

The important thing to remember is that objectives and their outcomes must be committed to paper to be meaningful in communication terms.

MOTIVATING STAFF

Although not strictly within the remit of written communication, a word about motivation is relevant because whatever communication is taking place with staff, the manager needs to remember that people need to be motivated and will work more effectively and efficiently if they are happy in what they are doing, see the reason for doing it, and feel good about themselves in their work situation.

Simple, thoughtful gestures often help people to feel valued members of a team and go a long way towards achieving maximum potential from staff. The 1996 Daily Telegraph/British Telecom Customer Service Awards gave a Highly Commended award to a pub in Winchester, the manager of which believes that it is important to show consideration towards staff. All 32 of his staff receive written notes with their weekly wage packet. This is an example of positive written communication which really works for the good of everyone concerned. People make business work. Business is there for people. It all happens through communication . . .

Material for Publication

Although not necessarily involved in marketing per se, many managers do find themselves writing material for publication from time to time. You may be one of these, needing perhaps to write news releases, advertisements or articles. Although writing marketing copy is a very specialized technique, some of the basic principles are covered here which you may find helpful if you are communicating through the media.

SOME BASIC PRINCIPLES

Marketing is all about letting your potential marketplace know that your products or services exist. It is not just about selling, as some people believe, for it involves activities such as market research, costing and pricing, packaging policies, public relations, promotion, distribution outlets, after sales service – to name but a few.

When considering publicized material, it is important to realize that we are talking about promotion, that is communicating with customers and potential customers over distance and time in order to raise awareness about our business. We may be reaching a totally new audience, or we may be communicating with those who already know something about our products or services, but there is more that we would like them to know. The more the message can be repeated, the more it will be reinforced. Where companies spend a lot of money on advertising, together with press releases, editorials, mailshots and so on, the more the communication is likely to be received and understood by those receiving it.

Defining the target customer

One of the most important things about preparing material for publicity is to first identify the target customer. Rather than attempt to reach the whole world with your publicity (which is probably impossible), home in on the audience you are targeting.

How do you decide who your target customers are? The first thing is to define which industry your organization belongs to. This may sound obvious, but it is not always so. Parker pens are a case in point here. For a long time, this company identified their marketplace as the communications industry, but having carried out a major piece of research, they changed their thinking. People were asked questions such as 'Do you have a Parker pen?' If the answer was 'Yes' they were asked 'How did you acquire it?' In the vast majority of cases the response was that it had been a gift. Parker pens are relatively expensive and most people buying a pen for themselves aim for a cheaper pen. The organization therefore changed their promotional strategy to target the **gift** market rather than the communications market.

This illustrates my point that to define the industry your company is in is not always as straightforward as you might think.

Having defined your industry, the next step is to identify which **segment** of the industry you are targeting. If you think of your industry as an orange, it can be seen as made up of many segments. For example, I am a management development trainer. I have therefore identified my 'industry' as that of training and education. However, there are many segments of this industry that I have nothing to do with at all: school teaching, further and higher education, non-vocational training, and so on. My market segment is that of training, but I can narrow it down much more than this to adult vocational training in management development.

Within my market segment, I next need to consider my **position** in the marketplace and place that position in my potential customer's mind. I am the managing consultant of a private training consultancy; I do not work for a large consultancy organization, nor do I work for a college or university. I therefore communicate with my clients on a very personal level, which appeals to a certain kind of customer who needs a flexible, tailor-made service.

Can you see that gradually I am able to home in on a specific target marketplace? I can now begin to identify my target customer as:

- an individual who requires training in management skills

  or

- an individual within an organization who has authority to contract my services for a fee, either for themselves or for others

---

What might these individuals be like? They are managers, which tells me something about them. For example, they are likely to be over 25, they may be male or female, their income is likely to be £20,000 plus and so on. I can now begin to build up a picture of a typical target customer and I will keep this person in my mind all the time I am preparing my material for publicity.

Goods and services are bought by different people for different reasons and you need to identify those reasons before you can begin to plan the writing of your publicity material.

Consider, for example, the two products Porsche and Volvo. What words do you think of when you think of a Porsche? (Perhaps 'expensive', 'fast', 'flashy', 'sports car' etc.) Using very general majority terms, what kind of person would own a Porsche? (Probably a middle or upper-class male between 25 and 40 in a high income bracket.)

And now think of words which describe a Volvo? ('expensive', 'stable', 'safe', 'rural', 'reliable', 'family car' etc). What kind of person is likely to own a Volvo? (Possibly a middle-class, family man of between 30 and 55 in a middle to high income bracket.)

Admittedly, these are subjective generalizations, but they give you an idea of target marketing. Both products are relatively expensive, up-market cars but with entirely different marketplaces. Therefore, the promoted message of these two products is likely to be quite different. Questions need to be asked such as 'Where and how can we promote to reach our potential customers? What do they read? How do they spend their leisure time?' and so on. Thus, one sees advertisements for Porsche in sports car and fashionable male magazines, broadsheet newspapers etc, with the relevant image being communicated in the promotional message. Volvo advertise in journals which are likely to be read by potential customers such as 'Country Life' and 'Horse and Hound', as well as family magazines and broadsheet newspapers.

Write to one person

When preparing publicity material, write it for this one typical target customer as if you were writing to them directly. This will get the tone of your communication right. Many of the general points that have already been made in this chapter apply here too:

- Who are you writing to?
- What are you writing for? (It is essential to set **SMART** objectives for any piece of promotion that you undertake)
- What are you trying to achieve as a result?
- Be accurate
- Be brief
- Be clear
- Be simple
- Be direct
- Be friendly but not too informal

There is, however, a major difference between this type of communication and others we have considered. That is that publicity is a **one-way** communication process – an impersonal communication. How much more, therefore, is it necessary to ensure that our message is going to be understood.

Corporate image

In any publicity promotion, it is essential that you convey the right corporate image to **your target customer**. (Think of the example above about the difference in corporate image of Volvo and Porsche.) An organization's image shows its 'personality' and includes both the external and internal faces of the business. An organization needs to make some policy decisions about the way in which it would like to be seen by its customers and this needs to be conveyed across all aspects of promotion, including logos, stationery (colour themes, quality of paper, typestyles etc), advertising, brochures, facia signs, work clothes, business gifts, vehicles (not just what make they are, but quality of any promotional lettering and cleanliness) and so on.

When writing publicity material, this corporate image must always be borne in mind so that choices such as the style of writing, vocabulary, and the media used, match the image and relate to **the organization's target customer.**

Features and benefits

What do you talk about in publicity material? Probably, what is being offered and why people should respond to the offer. When you know a lot about a product or service (which presumably you do, otherwise you would not be writing about it in the first place), there is an easy trap to fall into and one which needs to be avoided. You may be tempted to extol the virtues of the **features** – that is, what your product or service **is**. However, people do not buy the features of a product (for example, lots of small pieces of wood, each with a piece of sulphur on the end, laid out neatly in a box), they buy what the product or service does, that is the **benefits** (they buy the flame that the match produces).

One of the features of my car is that it is a five-door hatchback. That in itself does not make me buy it – it is the space which the feature allows which attracts me – the fact that I can carry around large objects such as projector screens which I need for my work.

There is an old sales adage 'Sell the sizzle and not the sausage'. It is not always easy, however, to separate features from benefits, but one way of doing it is to define a feature (for example, the oven has 'x' cu ft capacity) and ask yourself 'so what?' (it is big enough to take a 16 lbs turkey) which leads you to the benefit to the customer.

There will, of course, be many benefits of your product or service, but when you are writing publicity material, remember the one typical person for whom you are writing, for what reason (objectives) and therefore which particular benefit/s you are going to write about.

Advertising with AIDA

Aida is a mnemonic which comes in useful at all sorts of times, but perhaps most of all in marketing.

A	–	**A**-ttention
I	–	**I**-nterest
D	–	**D**-esire
A	–	**A**-ction

Attention

The first thing your publicity needs to do is capture the attention of . . . who? Yes, your target customer. You do not need to worry about capturing the attention of anyone else.

Activity

Before you read on, open a newspaper or magazine and note the advertisements which capture your attention immediately. Look at them again and try to analyze **why** you noticed them. Then compare your thoughts with the points over the page.

Things which capture a reader's attention include:

- colour
- graphics (the most effective way of getting attention, especially photographs which attract 25 per cent more attention than line drawings)
- headlines (see below)
- size of advertisement, size of print
- border around the advertisement
- white space

A word about **headlines**:

- on average only one person in five reads further than the headline, so use it effectively
- don't waste it on your firm's name (unless it catches attention itself, such as 'Harrods'). 'Blackford Ltd' is, in itself, hardly an attention getter!
- if you can, include the three most important headline words: **NEW**, **YOU**, **FREE**
- write the headline with your target customer in mind
- mention the target customer if you can and a key benefit to them
- use questions where you can and try to arouse curiosity
- put news into your headline if you have any
- if you are using an illustration, put the headline below it; people's eyes go to the graphic first and they tend to read down rather than up.

An example of a good headline is:

A quiet word to the hard of hearing

It has curiosity value, mentions the target customer and promises benefits.

Another is:

Expand your small business with free expert advice

Interest and Desire

Once you have the attention of your **target customer** (it doesn't matter whether anyone else has paid attention to your advertisement – you are interested only in the attention of potential customers), you aim to hold their interest so that they read the rest of the advertisement, and create an overwhelming desire for your product or service!

This is done through the wording in the main body of advertising text:

- write about **benefits**
- be enthusiastic
- persuade

Be careful about the amount of wording you use in relation to the size of the advertisement. People are less likely to read a mass of dense text than short paragraphs with lots of sub-headings (research shows that this increases readership by up to 12 per cent). Use short, factual sentences. Don't use jargon or get technical!

Action

Having persuaded readers that they would like to buy your product or service, attend your meeting, or whatever your advertisement is about, make it easy for them to do so. Sometimes the obvious is missed completely. I recently saw a poster advertising a play; it was beautifully produced but there was no venue shown! Check that you have details such as contact name, address, telephone, fax, Email address, relevant places, dates and times and so on. It may be pertinent to offer free coupons, free brochures, free advice, a response coupon or whatever to encourage urgent action (if people don't respond immediately, a large proportion will lose the desire you have created and will take no action).

One of the best advertising leaflets I have ever seen was a folded card, the front of which was in colour and showed a bare foot, under the arch of which was a circular, vaguely brown blob. The caption was:

What's underfoot could be overwhelming

My **attention** aroused, I opened the card and was faced with quite dense text which took a bit of reading (which in itself added to the intrigue and created **interest**). There was also a diagram of some kind of floor space and I was fascinated to find out what was being advertised: 'Was it carpeting?' I wondered. Eventually, I discovered that the objective of the advertisement was office space and what was 'underfoot' was a set of air tickets for a holiday trek in the Himalayas which were placed under one of the carpet tiles (a ruse to create **desire**). The reader was encouraged to visit these new offices and place a business card on one of the carpet tiles still free. (These last two words were clever, too, because they suggested that urgent action was needed to have a chance of winning.)

Only on the back of the card, in small print, were the details of the estate agent concerned (for **action**).

The object of this excellent piece of advertising was indirectly to sell office space of course, but initially to persuade managers to visit the new offices – no more than that.

BROCHURES AND LEAFLETS

Much of the above also applies to the preparation of copy for brochures and leaflets. Personally, I would advise the use of a designer/copywriter if you can afford it, because to write the text for brochures is a very specific art and most of us do not have what it takes. (The same goes for advertisement copy; if you cannot, don't try – use an advertising agency.)

When you are preparing leaflets and brochures, continually bear in mind for whom you are writing it (your target customer), and why you are writing it (your objectives). For example, I once led a workshop on the subject for small businesses and I remember a plumber who designed what I considered to be an excellent leaflet. His objective was to deliver an inexpensive 'flyer' to households so that, in the event that they should need a plumber, they could put their hands on his telephone number quickly. His was not the kind of business where his leaflet was likely to gain an immediate response. However, when people need a plumber they usually need one urgently!

He chose to use a fairly cheap, but durable, coloured paper. (People do not expect plumbers to use good quality paper – they would probably think they were charging too much for their services to be able to afford such elegance, whereas a management consultant, for example, probably would need to use a better quality paper. These are the kinds of things that need to be thought about under the heading of 'image'.) He had one fold in his leaflet and all he put on the outside, (to capture Attention), in letters about 2" high and on both sides of the fold was:

DON'T THROW ME AWAY!

These leaflets were designed to be put through letterboxes, and a person picking up a leaflet, whichever way up it fell, would see that headline. Because of the curiosity value, most people would have at least opened the leaflet (which was all the headline was intended to do – create **Interest** to read on).

Inside the leaflet were the words:

KEEP THIS LEAFLET HANDY FOR WHEN YOU NEED A PLUMBER

(that is the **Desire** for such a person which would arise in an emergency) followed by his name, telephone number (24 hour service) and professional quality assurance stamp (how to **Action** a need for his services). In this instance, no address was necessary because the target of the leaflet was people requiring urgent plumbing assistance, therefore a 'phone number was sufficient.

This illustrates and reinforces the essential point of setting an objective for your publicity material and aiming it at a specific target customer, including the image you are trying to convey, the type of leaflet or brochure chosen, the text itself, the way in which it is to be distributed (does the brochure fit a standard size envelope for mailing purposes, for example), whether graphics should be included, and the cost/benefit ratio.

News releases

Another kind of copywriting that you may be involved in is that of writing news releases for the trade or general press, radio or television. Editorials often attract more readership than advertisements, and radio and television reports provide excellent publicity. (Notice the term '**News**' release rather than '**Press**' release, which fails to include radio and television.)

News releases are written quite differently to advertising copy. Editors receive hundreds of news releases, so you need to make sure they at least read yours in order to persuade them to use it. Obviously, one of the main criteria is

• keep it short and simple

(Where have we heard that before?!) You do not need to compose clever headlines or write the kind of persuasive copy that we discussed when looking at advertising composition.

Copy is still written according to AIDA, however, but this time your target customer has changed to a busy, possibly harassed editor who is intent on meeting deadlines, and who is looking for interesting articles to fill his paper and capture **his** customers' interest. Therefore, you are providing newsworthy copy and at the same time making your company and its products or services known. Make sure that you provide a contact name, the company's name, address, 'phone and fax, the subject of the news release, together with brief details about the content (the editor can always ask for more detail if interested).

News releases should be typed, ideally on one side of A4, using double linespacing with wide margins. As with advertisement copy, use short sentences, short paragraphs, but it is not necessary to use sub-headings unless the news release is a long one. Write in the third person and avoid over-punctuating (for example, full stops in company names, the use of exclamation marks and so on).

If you are sending photographs with your news release copy, put the company's name and address on the back and cross reference to the text (in case the photographs become separated from the copy).

Send your news release to a named person rather than to a newspaper. (A quick 'phone call will produce the name of the right person.)

This section has looked at some of the basic principles involved in writing publicity material, but further specific reading is encouraged if you are to be involved in this function to any great degree.

Answer to Gantt chart activity on page 182

Your Gantt chart may not look exactly like this one because your thinking on dependencies may be different.

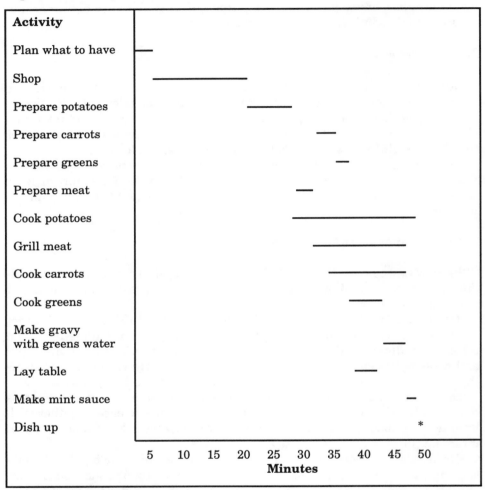

Rationale for answer

1 I first planned what to have for the meal (5 minutes);
2 I then went shopping (20 minutes);
3 I prepared the potatoes as soon as I returned from shopping because they would take longest to cook (20–28 minutes);
4 I put them on to cook as soon as they were prepared (28–49 minutes);
5 I then prepared the meat as that had the second longest cooking time (29–31 minutes);
6 I put the meat on to cook (31–47 minutes);

7   Next I prepared the carrots (32–34 minutes);

8   And I cooked them (34–47 minutes);

9   I then prepared the greens (35–37 minutes;

10 And I cooked them (37–43 minutes);

11 As soon as the greens were on, I laid the table (38–42 minutes);

12 As soon as the greens were cooked, I made the gravy with the greens water (43–47 minutes);

13 I made the mint sauce (47–49 minutes).

14 AND AT 50 MINUTES I DISHED UP!

BIBLIOGRAPHY

For further reading:

Adcock, D., Bradfield, R., Halborg, A., & Ross, C., *Marketing Principles And Practice*, Pitman Publishing, 1993

Armstrong, M. & Baron, A., *The Job Evaluation Handbook*, Institute of Personnel & Development, 1995

Forsyth, P., *Making Meetings Work*, Institute of Personnel & Development, 1996

Foster, D., *Mastering Marketing*, 2nd Edn, Macmillan, 1984

Fowler, A., *Negotiating, Persuading And Influencing*, Institute of Personnel & Development, 1995

Kenney, J., & Reid, M., *Training Interventions*, Institute of Personnel & Development, 1986

Marchington, M., & Wilkinson, A., Core Personnel And Development, Institute of Personnel & Development, 1996

Maxwell, R.G.I., *Marketing*, Macmillan, 1989

---

1 Kenny, J. and Reid, M., *Training Interventions*, Institute of Personal Management, 1986

PART THREE

HOW WE COMMUNICATE THE MESSAGE THROUGH INFORMATION TECHNOLOGY

CHAPTER SEVEN

Computers at Work

IN THIS CHAPTER WE WILL LOOK AT THE FOLLOWING AREAS:

- What are computers?
- A closer look at the computer as a tool
- What do computers consist of?
- How do computers work?
- What do computers do for managers?

This is the start of a new section about communicating through Information Technology – often referred to as 'IT'. IT is technology that helps you control, process, produce and send information as text, data, images or sound – or perhaps a mix of any of these. Computers, telephones and the links between them, are important parts of IT.

More businesses than ever invest heavily in computers and now depend on them. That's why it's important that you and your staff use them effectively and to do this you need a basic understanding of what a computer is and what it can do *for* you – and *through* you – for the business. You need a small amount of specific knowledge to get you started on the road to using IT for effective communication – and if the thought of 'computers' turns you off, all the more reason for you to read on.

You can catch up on the basics in this chapter and then Chapters 8 and 9 build on the basics to present you with ideas that could be beyond your wildest dreams – but possibly at your fingertips!

The topic of 'computers and communication' is a large one and the extent to which it can be covered in these chapters is limited – but sufficient to get you off to a good start. Along the way you will cover some of the most commonly used jargon words and phrases. To help you further, there is a Glossary of Computer Terms at the end of Part Three

As a supervisor you need to know enough about computers and what they can do for you and your department, to use them effectively. This chapter covers some of the basic questions you may have:

- What are computers?
- What do computers consist of?
- How do computers work?
- What do computers do for managers?

What are computers?

Computers, like cars, are tools that help us survive in the age we live in. Here are a few comparisons showing how they fit into some people's lives:

The car	The computer
The car is a tool that enables me to get from a to b, quicker and more conveniently than walking or any other form of land based transport.	The computer is a tool that enables me to produce professional looking documents or presentations and analyze information more quickly and conveniently.
Before learning to drive I already had the skills for getting from a to b: I walked or 'cycled, or took whatever public transport it needed to get me there. However, now that I can drive and own a car, I usually get from a to b much faster.	Before using the computer I already had administrative skills. I could type letters, make calculations, sort lists from a card index and so on. Now that I use a computer I can carry out these tasks much more quickly and accurately.
It's more convenient, especially if I'm carrying luggage or a computer in my boot.	It is more convenient, especially if I base a letter, or document, or calculations on something I've already done. I simply access the existing work and change it to meet my new needs.
It also gives me flexibility because I can come and go as I please.	Instead of waiting for someone else to do the work or access information, I can do it myself, immediately.
Also, on some journeys it can save me money.	Using a computer makes me more efficient and cost effective.
There are some occasions where it's better to use alternative transport – for example in London I would use the tube or get a taxi.	There are some situations where it makes sense to ask a personal assistant or a typing pool to do the work, for example, dictated letters on tape, or long reports.

The car	The computer
The car is not a tool for every transport requirement – for example I would not use it to get to the top of a multi-storey building (unless it was a multi-storey car park). Depending on the circumstances I might use other tools such as the stairs, lift, ladder, crane or helicopter.	The computer is not the answer to every business problem. It needs to be used appropriately along with other business tools.
The car doesn't suit everyone's lifestyle. Some people have never learnt to drive for a various number of reasons and others know how to drive but don't drive anyway.	The computer doesn't suit everyone's work. Some people have never learnt to use a computer for a various number of reasons and others know how to use computers but don't need them for their work.

A closer look at the computer as a tool

Take a closer look at what sort of tool the computer is:

First, you enter information into the computer, typically via the keyboard.

This is called **input**.

The computer takes the information and does something with it, according to the instructions you give it. For example, it organizes text on a page according to your instructions – or it turns a list of figures into a bar chart – or it calculates your month end figures.

In other words, it **processes** your information.

The computer shows the information to you in a format you can understand. You can view the information on the screen or print it on paper.

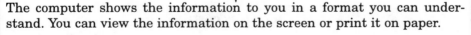

This is called **output**.

The computer needs to be able to store these facts, and figures or results, so that you can access them. You might want to refer back to them, or change or print them. So, computers have the ability to store your information as **files**.

A file in computer terms is a collection of data stored in the computer and you give this collection a name. When you give the command to the computer to store a file, it is called **saving**. So for example, you can **save** the collection of words which make up a letter – as a file. You can **save** the sales figures you entered – as a file. And so on . . .

Once you have saved a file, you can retrieve it time and again by name. This is called **opening** a file. When you **open** a file you can look at it on the computer, a screenful at a time. This is equivalent to looking at a file in a filing cabinet by taking it out and viewing the sheets of paper in it. Alternatively, you can print it out so that you have it easily available on paper.

So, a computer is a **processing tool**. It takes your input and processes it according to your instructions. It can also store your input as files so that you can look at it or print it when you need it.

THE COMPUTER AS A PROCESSING TOOL

As the computer is only a **processing tool** for processing and sorting information, it is not the answer to all business problems. Also, like any tool the computer is only as good as the **user** – the person who uses it. It takes instructions very literally – and therefore if the user is careless the results will be wrong.

Most computer users already have the skills to do what they want to do, but the fast and accurate processing power of the computer gives added advantages. It means you can do what you normally do:

Faster;

With less work or re-work;

With fewer errors;

For less cost.

Activity

Example of computer use	Tick the advantages (The first one is done for you)
1 Sarah is pleased she has at last been given a computer to replace her typewriter. One chore it will help her with is the weekly letter to departmental heads. Instead of typing eight different letters she is going to type a master letter, which the computer will copy and automatically insert each individual's name, job title and department.	☑ a) Faster ☑ b) With less work or re-work ☐ c) With fewer errors ☑ d) For less cost
2 Brian's main worry when producing reports is his spelling. Now he has a computer he uses the spell checking facility.	☐ a) Faster ☐ b) With less work or re-work ☐ c) With fewer errors ☐ d) For less cost
3. In the past Anya had to calculate columns of figures using a calculator – but often found that she got three different results for the same column. With her new computer she can now automatically add columns of figures and know that the results are right first time.	☐ a) Faster ☐ b) With less work or re-work ☐ c) With fewer errors ☐ d) For less cost
4. One of Rudi's responsibilities is to get the company newsletters out. With the new computer and printer it's possible to get an exciting layout and a professional looking result without having to cut and paste pieces of paper onto card, using scalpels and spray mount.	☐ a) Faster ☐ b) With less work or re-work ☐ c) With fewer errors ☐ d) For less cost

For all the above examples, the benefits include improved efficiency and this means that there is a cost saving. However, apart from the last example, where the software saves on materials, it is not directly money in the bank.

So, a computer is basically a processing tool that has the potential to get you from a to b quicker in your job. It doesn't replace you, take over your job, or your work. Like any tool, it still needs your expertize behind it. Hopefully, it allows you to do what you know best, efficiently. By helping you become efficient it gives you time to do more things – or the same things as before, but better.

What do computers consist of?

Computers consist of:

- Hardware;
- Software;
- System software.

HARDWARE

Hardware refers to the parts of the computer you can touch – or 'kick', though I don't recommend the latter. The type of computer you will normally find on your desk is a Personal Computer, 'P.C.' for short. These often look like a box (the system unit) placed under or on your desk, with a screen (monitor) and keyboard. You can see a couple of variations in the illustration. A computer is made up of some or all of this hardware:

In order for input, process, output and file storage to occur you need these components.

Keyboard – The keyboard is usually a standard QWERTY keyboard – like a typewriter. It is what you use to input information – for example, type text and give commands. It is therefore your main means of communicating with the computer. You would normally have a full size keyboard unless you use a portable.

Mouse – The mouse is another means of communicating with the computer. There is a ball under the mouse. You drag it across the surface of your desk and the computer processes the movement of the ball. So, as the mouse moves you see an arrow, often referred to as the mouse pointer, move on the screen. You usually position the mouse pointer to point to the command or option you want. Then you press the left mouse button to select that command or option. It is normal for a mouse to have two buttons – a left and right button. However, you might occasionally come across a three-button mouse or other variations such as a roller ball or joy stick.

System Unit – This is the box that holds the electrical components of your computer and the brain of your computer – the Central Processing Unit, 'CPU' for short. It can either take the form of a tower unit – a vertical unit usually placed on the floor under your desk; or it can take the form of a desk top unit that sits on your desk and serves as a useful stand for your monitor.

Hard disk drive – The hard disk drive is part of the system unit. It is called the 'hard' disk drive because the storage consists of a stack of hard, rigid disks, with a small gap of about a quarter of an inch between each one. You can usually see the blank panel covering the hard disk at the front of the system unit. You would never remove the drive or the disks in it yourself – unless you are a computer technician replacing one that has gone wrong.

The computer uses the hard disk drive to store your files. Some people find it better security or easier to carry a separate hard drive that they can plug into any compatible computer, but this is not common practice.

Floppy disk drive – The floppy disk drive is built into the system unit. You see it as a slot in the system unit into which you gently push the floppy you want to use. Floppy disks used to be more delicate, were about 5.25' and also called 'five and a quarter inch floppy discs'. These are now out of date – though you may still come across them. They have been superseded by the slightly hardier 3.50' ('three and a half inch floppy discs'), about the size of a drinks mat – but don't be tempted to use one for your mug of coffee! Some computers accommodate both sizes – but these days computers are more likely to have a 3.50' floppy drive and a CD-ROM drive.

The disk can hold information for your computer – so the slot is a way in for information you want to send into your computer, and store permanently on the hard drive. You can also save onto the disk, take the disk out and away with you, to use the same files on another computer – so it is a good way out for information too.

CD-ROM drive – The CD (Compact Disk) drive is also built into the system unit. You are probably familiar with the CD as an alternative to records or tapes for music. However, it has also been used as a means of holding computer data for quite a while now. You often see it as a slot in which you insert a CD-ROM in a caddie, or there may be an eject button you press so that you can insert the CD-ROM on a platform that you then press in. Lately, the majority of PC sales in business are for computers with at least one CD-drive if not two. Many manufacturers now fit them as standard. Usually you can only read files from a CD or listen to music on it! It is still quite rare to have drives that enable you to save your work to a CD, although it is probably only a matter of time for this to become common practice.

Monitor – The monitor displays your current computer activity on the screen. Newer machines are usually supplied with a colour monitor, although as many companies still print in black and white, colour might seem a bit superfluous. However, more people are using their computers for colour presentations and for running training from CD-ROM drives where colour adds an important dimension.

Printer – The printer enables you to print out documents from the computer. There are many different types.

Activity

> **Use the information you have read so far to answer these questions:**
>
> - Which parts of the computer enable you to input information?
> - Which parts of the computer process the information?
> - Which parts of the computer do you use to view the output?
> - Where do you store your files on the computer?

- Input is usually by using the keyboard. Alternatively you may have seen shop assistants use different devices to read bar codes on goods. An input device is any piece of equipment used to put information into the computer.
- Processing takes place in the CPU, inside the system unit;
- The output you get from the computer can be visual output from the screen, or printout from the printer;

- Files are stored on hard disks or floppy disks. The data is written on to them in the disk drives.

Portable computers

It is quite common these days for business executives to be given portable computers for business use. The powerful ones are still quite weighty but they are more compact and easier to transport than a larger PC. Lighter weight ones are on their way.

Peripherals

Another term you might come across when you're working with hardware is **peripherals**. Anything that is not in the system unit, is outside it, on the periphery – hence the name **peripheral devices**, usually referred to colloquially as 'peripherals'. Typical examples of peripherals I have already mentioned are the mouse and the keyboard.

Activity

Use the information you have read so far to answer these questions:

Which of these computer parts are usually built into the computer?

- Keyboard;
- mouse;
- system unit;
- hard disk drive;
- floppy disk drive;
- CD-ROM drive;
- keyboard;
- mouse.

Which of these computer parts are usually peripherals?

- Keyboard;
- mouse;
- system unit;
- hard disk drive;
- floppy disk drive;
- CD-ROM drive;
- keyboard;
- mouse.

Ports

The way you connect your peripherals to the system unit is through a port. This is the point in the back of the computer where you plug in a peripheral. There are different ports for each peripheral. Sometimes they are labelled. Usually it is not possible to plug a piece of equipment into the wrong port because each one varies in size and shape. So for example, when you need to connect your computer to a printer, you do so with a cable from the printer that you plug into a port at the back of your computer.

What next?

So you switch hardware on and it does something – right? Wrong. Unfortunately hardware is like a body with no life in it – incapable of any action whatsoever. You make it come to life, and turn it into a useful working tool, using software . . .

SOFTWARE

When you use a computer you are totally dependent on software. When you tell the computer what to do its software instructs the computer how to do it.
   If you hear someone using any of these terms:

- **Program;**
- **Software;**
- **Application;**
- **Packages.**

or a combination of them:

- **Software application;**
- **Applications program;**
- **Application package;**
- **Software package.**

– remember – that they mean the same thing. They all refer to the software you run on the computer to carry out your tasks.

   Many people relate the word **computer** to the word **program** and think that they have to literally learn how to be a programmer to use a computer – if you are one of these people, put your mind at ease. A computer program is a set of instructions that the computer follows in a set sequence. An application usually consists of several of these programs that make whatever you are doing possible. However you never actually see a program and you certainly don't need to be a programmer to use an application package.

'Software' is a general term that applies to any computer program, or group of programs. A 'package' or 'application' is software with a name and purpose. For example, Word is the name of a software package, and its purpose is word-processing.

Widely used purposes for applications are:

- **Word-processing** – to enable you type professional-looking documents;
- **Database** – to enable you to store records such as client names and addresses;
- **Spreadsheet** – to enable you to quickly carry out calculations automatically and create charts of information.

These general applications suit many different types of organization.

Software companies program the software and put it on the market for you to buy. For example, you might hear the package Word, referred to as 'Microsoft Word'. Microsoft is the name of the software company. Word is the name of the package.

Some software is designed with specific company departments, or business functions, in mind. For example:

- **Accounting** packages – suit accounts departments, since they are usually divided into ledgers, and accountants are more likely to understand their record structures better than anyone else;
- **Stock control** packages – are designed to help staff handle stock inventories. The system checks your entry for minimum stock levels required against your entry for current stock levels and alerts you when you need to order more.

Some software companies produce applications for specific needs such as **Hotel, Dental Practice** or **Doctor's Surgery Management**.

Software development

Software companies strive to make software more helpful, easier and faster to use. When they have made significant improvements to an application they launch a new version of it. You might see the name of the software written as 'Microsoft Word v 6' implying that this is the sixth version of the software. Sometimes one version works in a similar way to the previous one, but with a few extra features added. On other occasions a new version of the software can be so different to use it's like a totally new package. Hopefully, if your organization updates a package with a new version, they will train you to cope with the changes. However, as applications are becoming easier to use with each new version, don't panic about updates, they are for the best.

Tailor made software

A company may have software tailor-made for it, especially if its work is done by few other companies, or it uses different methods from most. It will have cost your organization more to have the software tailor-made than to buy an existing application – and therefore it's important to use the application effectively, as it was designed to be used. Don't expect more from it than it was designed to do.

Activity

Find out the names and other details of up to five applications used in your organization and for each one complete the table below:			
Software company	**Name of application**	**Version**	**Purpose**
e.g. Microsoft	e.g. Word	e.g. v 6	e.g. Word-processing

What next?

So, you switch the computer on, with the application in it and it starts up, ready to use. Right? Wrong. In order for any application to be loaded onto the computer and work, it needs **system software** . . .

SYSTEM SOFTWARE

System software consists of operating systems and operating environments. The operating system is what enables both you and your application to communicate with the computer. Here are some examples of what an operating system does:

What the operating system does	For instance ...
It starts up the computer	
It runs your application	
It acts as a translator between the hardware and software.	... it tells the computer what the application software wants it to do.
It helps you manage the computer.	... if you give the command to save a file or open an existing file, it is the operating system that does it.
It tells the computer how to control the peripherals.	... how to control the read-write heads in the hard disk drive when they read from or write to a disk.
It reports back to you about what you are doing.	... if you give the command to print a document, the messages you get about the printing activity, such as what is being printed, are from the operating system.
It reports faults to you	... if it has tried to print but there is no paper in the printer, it will tell you

The parts of your operating system that helps you do your computer housekeeping are called **utilities**. This includes common tasks like deleting files, sorting files, finding files, setting the date and time, preparing a floppy disk for use – called 'formatting a disk'. You can also buy separate utilities applications with further computer 'housekeeping' options, besides those supplied with your operating system. For example, if you use literally hundreds of graphics in the type of work you do, you can find packages that will help you organize them so that you can find what you want quickly.

Your organization will have received the operating system with the computers they ordered. The computer supplier usually loads it, but will also supply operating system disks in case it ever needs to be reloaded.

The software manufacturer updates the operating system, like any other software, on a regular basis. If your organization wants the new version they will ask the dealer that gave them the operating system originally, for a new set of disks.

DOS – an acronym for Disk Operating system – has been around for many years. Several versions later it is the major operating system for PCs. Different companies license it and so you may sometimes hear of it referred to under different names, for example, PC DOS or MS-DOS. These are all DOS and they all work very similarly – they may be different in small ways, but in general they are the same.

First-time computer users still find DOS technical, unfriendly and off-putting. For example, to clear a file from the system from DOS you would type DEL followed by the filename. First time users find this sort of thing daunting because the spacing and punctuation – known as the syntax – have to be exactly right or things could go wrong.

A few years ago Apple Macintosh reacted to the problem by developing software that was more user friendly – it used pictures called **icons** instead of words. So, for example, instead of entering code words, such as DEL or CD\ or DIR, for some of the management tasks you manipulate pictures or make choices from a menu. For example, to delete a file you could use the mouse to drag the file icon (a little picture of a file with the file name) to the wastebasket. The wastebasket became fatter as a result so you could see something was inside it! – or select **empty wastebasket** from the menu. In either case you don't have to worry about typing correctly. This was the start of what is called 'the operating **environment**'.

As operating environments use icons and menus to replace keyboard commands you may hear them described as a Graphical User Interface – GUI – pronounced 'gooey'. However, do remember that even if you use a GUI – you may still have an operating system.

The software company Microsoft followed Apple's lead and brought out their version of an operating environment called Windows. Currently this is the most popular operating environment for PCs. It uses pictures and icons to represent things like applications and disk drives, but working in the background, doing all the things I listed earlier, is the operating system called DOS.

It is worth mentioning here that when you buy an application package you need to specify what operating system or environment it will work in. For example if you have the DOS operating system, not Windows, you need to specify that it is a DOS application. If you have an operating environment you want to use, such as Windows, you need to specify that you want a Windows application.

A DOS application . . .	A Windows application . . .
starts up in DOS. It can also be set up to run from Windows but will not look like a typical Windows application, e.g. 'WordPerfect for DOS'.	cannot be run from DOS, has to run in Windows, e.g. 'Word for Windows'.
usually expects you to give keyboard commands or menu choices using the keyboard.	allows you to give commands by clicking on icon or menu options with the mouse. You can also give keyboard commands which are the quickest method once you have learnt them
usually vary considerably in the way they look and the way you do things in them.	look very similar to other Windows applications. This helps if you have to learn a new package, as you will recognize many options and therefore learn new packages quicker.
as the package runs directly from DOS you will normally find there is a fast response from the computer.	Windows uses DOS in the background. Windows slows applications down – more powerful computers are needed to cope.

Activity

Find out what **system** software your organization uses (remember system software means operating systems and environments). You will probably find you only fill one row with this information; however if your organization has different operating systems in different departments, note some further examples.

Operating system	Operating environment
e.g. DOS	e.g. Windows

The term platform refers to your mix of CPU and operating system or environment. There are two major platforms used in business:

- PCs – favoured across the business spectrum for a wide range of uses.
- Macintosh (often referred to as 'Macs') – favoured particularly by designers.

The leading manufacturer of PCs is IBM and when they first made the IBM PC they allowed other manufacturers to make imitations. So other manufacturers make 'copies' of the IBM PCs using the same parts, the operating system and software. You might hear these copies referred to as 'IBM compatibles' – since they are compatible with equivalent IBM computers, though usually cheaper.

Software that works on one platform will not work on another – in other words, they are not compatible – so departments tend to opt for one platform and stick to it.

- **PC software only runs on PCs**

For PCs you can get DOS applications or Windows applications. DOS existed long before Windows so some companies still continue to use DOS applications. They take up less RAM and often work faster than Windows equivalents. However, applications designed to work specifically with Windows tend to be easier to use once you know the features of the package. All Windows applications look and feel similar because they are based on Windows guidelines. This means that once you learn one, you will find another quick to learn. As computers increase in power many organizations are upgrading their PCs and switching from DOS to Windows applications. You might also come across the IBM operating system O/S2, and of course you need the relevant software to run with it.

- **Macintosh software only runs on Macs.**

This situation is changing as I write as it is possible to buy computers that can cope with both PC and Mac software, but most organizations find these computers expensive.

Some platforms go with particular uses better than others. For example, Marketing or Design departments, or complete organizations dedicated to this type of work, often opt for Macs.

All organizations should have a computer policy that suggests a platform to stick to, so that all the equipment and software are 'compatible'. It makes sense because then everyone can share the software. When an organization wants to share software between several computers they buy a site licence from the software manufacturer – otherwise they should use one set of software disks per computer.

Activity

Find out what platform or different platforms your organization uses.		
Which of these platforms does your organization use?	Yes	No
PC made by IBM or other various manufacturers		
Macintosh ('Mac') made by Apple		
Others?		

What next?

'So, your organization buys hardware to match its policy?'
'Yes, ideally.'
'The dealers or organization technicians put the system software onto the hardware?'
'Yes.'
'The organization buys software to go with the existing platform (hardware and system software)?'
'Yes, that's right.'
'OK. So how does it all work?'
'Read on . . .'

How do computers work?

Just as you can drive a car without knowing how the engine works, so you can use a computer without knowing the details of what's happening inside it. However, understanding a few important facts can help you understand your computer better and therefore use it better.

To help you understand how computers work I am going to tell you about:

- **Your computer and its memory**

Then see how this topic affects your experience of using the computer in:

- **Your computer switched on**

YOUR COMPUTER AND ITS MEMORY

A computer has two types of memory – permanent and temporary. Here is a comparison:

Permanent memory . . .	Temporary memory . . .
is called 'Read Only Memory' or ROM for short.	is called 'Random Access Memory' or RAM for short.
stores data written in the factory where the memory was produced.	is the CPU's short term memory. When you switch on, the computer loads DOS into this part of the memory so that your computer can work. When you select an application you will find you have to wait while the computer loads the application into temporary memory so you can use it.
it is 'Read Only' because the computer can only read it, you cannot ask the computer to change or add to it.	it is 'Random Access' because the computer accesses it randomly, based on what you do, since everything you do sits in RAM, e.g. when you start on your piece of work, create a new file or open an existing one and edit it.
is a bit like the subconscious part of your brain that carries out instructions for you to breathe, digest food and so on – without you being aware that it is doing so. For example it enables the computer to read the information you type by scanning switches connected to the underside of keys on the keyboard – as a result the characters you type are displayed on the screen.	is like your conscious brain, e.g. whatever skills you need for your current activity become available in your brain. For example, if you are driving, your driving skills come to the fore. Similarly with RAM, if you decide to wordprocess, the tools you need to do the job are fed into RAM and accessed by the computer as you need them for your current activity.

Permanent memory . . .	Temporary memory . . .
is still in the same place when you switch off the computer. You can never empty ROM.	does not store anything while the computer is off. By switching the computer off you empty its RAM Therefore to ensure your work can be retrieved again you must save your work as files on floppy or hard disk.

YOUR COMPUTER SWITCHED ON

As PCs using DOS and Windows applications are the most popular computers in business to date this is what I use for my example below. However, these computers can be set up in so many different ways, that your own experience of 'logging on' and selecting an 'application' could be completely different. Keep this in mind as you read about a typical day in the life of a PC . . .

 First, you switch the computer on and what happens?

The mains switch is on. You sit down at the computer and switch on the computer power and the monitor. The power lights on both pieces of equipment shine bright immediately. Meanwhile, inside the computer, the CPU looks to the ROM, the permanent memory, for instructions and as a result, DOS starts itself up and copies itself from the hard disk into RAM – this is known as 'booting up'. You can actually hear the drive spin as the computer reads information from it and passes it on to RAM.

 Second, you select an application and what happens?

What you eventually see on your screen depends on how the supplier or your organization's technicians have set up the computer.
 You might see a DOS prompt which looks like this:

c : \

It is called a **DOS prompt**, because you give a **DOS command** at this point and like the Prompt sitting behind the wings at a theatre it is waiting for you to deliver your words – in this case by typing a command.

Alternatively, as companies are becoming more security conscious your computer might prompt you for a Login code:

```
c:LOGIN\>
```

and you type your user identity and password before you can access any applications or files.

Once in the system, you may want to start a DOS application such as WordPerfect by typing WP. Alternatively you might want to open your Windows operating environment by typing w or win. Let's say you are going to use a Windows application. You wait several seconds while Windows loads into RAM. You see the Windows title screen appear and then you see what is called the Windows desktop. This a screen that shows all the applications available to you as pictures called 'icons'. It helps to think of it like an organized desk where there are tools for doing your job that you can open up and use.

You want to type a letter so you are going to use a word-processing application, for example, Word. To open up an application you double click on its icon. As a result the computer loads it from the hard drive into RAM – you may have a bit of wait while this happens, but eventually you see it on the screen ready for you to use. The application opens on-screen in its own frame or border called a 'window'.

Once in the application you can give the command to open an existing file and do some more work on it, or start a new piece of work. You open the file you have been working on and it appears inside the application window – in its own window.

When you have several files open in an application, each file in its own window, you can 'switch' between these windows; for example, you can copy standard paragraphs from one letter to another.

    Third, you do your work and what happens?

The CPU, the computer's processor chip, processes the information you enter using the keyboard or the mouse, and presents it to you on the screen.

The computer takes the content of what you do, for example, your letter, and automatically stores it in RAM – but this is a dangerous place for your work to be. You could lose all your work if someone trips over your mains cable, inadvertently unplugs your machine, turns off the mains switch or the computer power switch, or there is a power cut (all these things have been known to happen).

Fourth, you decide to save your file and what happens?

To ensure your **work** is in a safe place, where you can access it easily whenever you want, you need to save it onto hard or floppy disk on a regular basis – every 10 minutes or so. (You can set your computer to do this for you automatically.)

There is no need to worry about saving your **application** – the computer copied it into RAM from the hard disk and it will still be on hard disk when you switch off. Also the supplier or technicians probably originally loaded it from floppy disks and these must be in safe-keeping somewhere; so relax, you can close your application in the knowledge that it is safe.

 Fifth, you decide to make a backup copy on floppy disk and what happens?

Many organizations require their staff to make another copy of their day's work before they go home – and this is called a 'backup copy' or simply a 'backup'. Many organizations take the precautions of putting the disks holding backup copies in a fire-proof cabinet at the end of each day. This means that if some disaster destroys your office or computer, the organization can carry on business as usual because you have backed up the latest business information.

To make this backup copy you need a floppy disk. These disks are usually blank when you buy them. Before you can store files on them you must format them, which means you create something like storage boxes on the disk to store data in.

Some disk manufacturers now sell pre-formatted disks – and they print the word 'formatted' clearly on the disk label. Obviously if you have one of these there is no need to go through the formatting process. If you don't then it's a good idea to format several disks in one sitting and label them 'formatted' – so that whenever you want to save information on a floppy, the disk is immediately ready – rather than having to go through the formatting process before you can save your backup.

The best place to organize formatting disks and copying files is in File Manager, an application that comes with Windows that enables you to organize your files. Instead of having to remember the DOS commands for deleting, copying, creating new directories for files, renaming files or performing other file management tasks you can work within the graphical environment where all the options available to you are visible – so there is no need to memorize commands.

When you save your work onto floppy disks the computer writes your files onto the disk. The computer uses the outside edge of the disk as a directory where it stores information on which 'storage box' it has used for your file.

Sixth, you have a spare half-hour, so you decide to take a tour round your system, and what do you find?

If you have some spare time there are many features in Windows you might like to explore:

Control Panel	to Personalize the way your PC interface looks – for example, by changing the colour scheme of your screen.
Calendar or appointment option	to use as a diary to schedule meetings and other appointments.
Calculator	to use like a hand-held calculator, but instead of pressing numbers you click on them using the mouse.
Games	to fill in a spare five minutes and improve your mouse skills.
and more . . .	

 Finally, you decide you have done enough work for the day, you switch off and what happens?

If you work in a security-conscious organization you always log off when you have finished doing your work or when you are about to leave the machine **unattended**. You don't want unauthorized staff accessing information through your Login code while you are not there. This might mean that you log on and off several times in a day.

As computers use such a small amount of electricity it is normal to keep them switched on all day, and then switch them off before going home at night. When you switch off, the work you were doing and the application you used to do it disappear from RAM. Remember you cannot keep anything in RAM on a long term basis – once you switch off (purposely or by mistake) its contents have gone. RAM is now empty for when you next switch on. But remember, you have not lost your work, you have saved it as a file that is now sitting on your hard disk. It is sitting there, waiting for you to retrieve at any time, in the same way that a paper file sits in a filing cabinet.

What do computers do for managers?

A BUSINESS TOOL

Early on in this chapter you saw that:

- Computers are just another **business tool**, like the telephone or the calculator
- The computer is a **processing tool**.

You saw examples where, by using computers, managers or their staff can carry out work:

- Faster, so time is saved
- With less work or re-work, or repetition
- With fewer errors
- For less cost

Also, important for you as a manager, is the ability to manage more effectively through more timely and better information – and this is what your computer can give you. You have learnt that an application changes your computer into a specific tool. So for example, you can get applications that turn your computer into a tool for:

- **Word-processing** – comprises a host of features to help you create professional looking documents, fast.
- **Spreadsheet** – enables you to fill a grid with your numeric data, and gives you the tools to analyze the information fast, even if it's constantly changing.
- **Database** – gives you the facilities to enter your data in an organized way, then re-organize and sort it in different ways to give you the information you need.
- **Communication** – enables you to use your computer to talk to other computers (More about this in Chapter 9), usually by a phone line. You might use this facility to get information from the mainframe (large computer) at head office, such as the latest stock report figures.

Alternatively, instead of buying the above as separate applications your organization might have chosen a more cost-effective option of an integrated package.

- **Integrated** – combines word-processing, spreadsheet and database, and often communications, for the price of one package but sacrificing some of the useful features that you get in the larger, separate applications.

Other packages used in business include:

- **Graphics** – a drawing tool, giving you the capability to produce logos, illustrations and diagrams to use on their own or insert into your documents.
- **Desktop publishing** – gives you the ability to create professional looking documents from the view point of a graphic designer.
- **Presentations** – allows you to select appropriate backgrounds and enter text to create slides. Once you have created your slides you can add notes to make support materials for courses or presentations.
- **Financial** – enables you to balance your incomings and outgoings, create an accounting system, dotax returns and other tasks related to keeping track of finances.
- **Education and training** – used by staff as a training tool, or for reference, to learn business skills such as management techniques and software skills.

This isn't an exhaustive list. There are a wide variety of software applications and they don't all fit into the above categories. New programs are being created all the time for business and for home use. For example, there are more applications for specialist requirements like hotel receptionists' applications, Sales and Marketing for keeping records of clients and orders, Computer Aided Design for Engineers and Architects. If you are in a specialist business, look out for applications that might specifically suit your organization.

It is now common practice for managers to have their own computer on their desk or at least, to have access to one that they use to:

- **Type in their own letters** – using a word-processing application.
- **Refer to, update, collate and retrieve information** – for example, customer names and addresses – using a database package.
- **Make calculations to help with decision making** – for example projected sales figures or project costs – using a spreadsheet package.
- **Update calculations** – for example, to check project progress or expenditure, or produce project statistics – using a spreadsheet package.
- **Present information in a more meaningful way** – for example progress reports to senior management or steering committees – using a presentation package.
- **Send and receive information** – using a communications package *(See Chapter 9).*
- **And more** . . .

Activity

Browse through some computer magazines. For PCs try *Personal ComputerWorld*, *PC Pro*, *PC Direct* or *PC Magazine*. For Macs try *Mac Format*, *MacWorld* or *Mac Power*. These will help to give you an idea of the types of software available. Have a think about what *is* currently used in your organization and what *would be* useful to you and your team.

CHAPTER EIGHT

Information Storage and Retrieval

IN THIS CHAPTER WE WILL LOOK AT THE FOLLOWING AREAS:

- Our concept of information
- Communication systems
- Information storage and retrieval systems
- The direction of information

Our concept of information

INFORMATION IS NOT JUST FACTS AND FIGURES

Working in an office, dealing with numbers, names, addresses, dates and other facts and figures, it is easy to forget the many forms that information can take.

Think about how, as a human being with a variety of senses, you take information in:

Sensors:	Information:
Eyes	Light intensity, colour, contrast, distance, quantity, movement, speed, size. Also the facts, figures, ideas and emotions conveyed by text, video.
Ears	Sound, vibration, movement, balance. Also pictures, ideas and emotions conveyed by voice, music and lyrics.

Sensors:	Information:
Nose	Smell and scents. You may not think that this is anything to do with business – but organizations involved in health, beauty and catering depend on this form of information to communicate to their clients.
Mouth	Taste, texture, temperature.
Touch	Texture, temperature, movement, pressure.
Lifting	Weight.
Combination of senses	**The more senses you involve in communication, the more powerful the message.**

Any other senses? Can you add to this list?

Activity

Look at the list of information in the above table. Is there any type of information that, in your opinion, you think could not be 'sensed' and processed by computerized equipment of some sort?

- You might think that the taste and smell aspects of information would be difficult to analyze and store. Yet computers already exist that can analyze and duplicate tastes or diagnose health problems by smelling a patient's breath;
- You might think that touch is difficult for a computer, yet the science of robotics simulates touch and enables machines to lift, handle and manipulate a variety of objects;
- You might think that sensing temperature is difficult for a machine, yet computers with heat sensors have been controlling the heat build-up in manufacturing processes for decades.

So it seems that most of the information we can sense can be recognized and processed by computers too. The developments that are going to affect communication in the majority of organizations, are technologies which allow us to enter, send, receive, compare, store, access and change:

- Text;
- Sound;

- Images in the form of still colour pictures, animation and video, including simulations;
- Larger quantities of the above.

Read on to find out about some of the most important tools available for communicating information in many of its various forms – and managing it.

Communication systems

TELEPHONE SYSTEMS

Once an organization reaches a certain size management usually decide they need a telephone switchboard. These are electronic devices which organize incoming and outgoing telephone calls. Just like a PC there is a microprocessor chip inside, processing information, in this case, telephone calls. Management employs a telephone operator or receptionist to use the switchboard in order to route incoming calls to the various extensions. The switchboard itself automatically processes internal calls: those made from one member of staff to another within the organization.

Features that help the switchboard operator manage calls and messages include:

- **Queuing** – If several callers ring your organization at the same time they are placed in a queue on the line, so that the operator can respond to each customer in order. This is often accompanied by a message to the caller to say that they are in the queue and their call will be dealt with shortly;
- **Music** – The switchboard plays a recording of music to callers while they wait to be connected to their extension. On some systems this is combined with the queuing system so that callers have music while they wait;
- **Call logging** – The switchboard logs every call made in the company. When you make an outgoing call the number, date and time of the call are printed out. This helps your organization assess telephone expenditure;
- **Tannoy or paging** – Some organizations have loudspeakers located through the organization and in other cases, the speakers on telephones are used to convey organization-wide announcements which are spoken at the switchboard by the operator. In an office environment too frequent use can be distracting and intrusive. In other environments it can be very useful. If as part of your job you tend to be paged in this way regularly, make sure you know the telephone buttons to press for a quick response.

Activity

Find out what it is like for a customer calling your organization:

- Talk to the switchboard and find out whether they have any of the above features, or any extra ones I haven't mentioned;
- Make a call from outside, to a colleague in your organization, and experience how the call is managed.

Queuing   Yes ☐   No ☐

Music   Yes ☐   No ☐

Call logging   Yes ☐   No ☐

Tannoy or paging   Yes ☐   No ☐

Other (list below)

For you the switchboard means you can:

- Use your 'phone to contact people internally, using a short three or four digit number;
- Use your 'phone to contact people externally via the switchboard or directly from any of the extensions, often by dialling nine first.

Most of us are quite comfortable using the 'phone. (If you are not then refer to Chapter 3). We usually all learn at an early age how to dial a number and the difference between a ringing tone and an engaged signal. Then at work most of us manage to learn how to transfer a call to another 'phone. Does that sum up your total use of the 'phone? If so, take another look – it has developed into a multi-function communication tool with a whole host of features to help you save time and communicate more effectively.

Telephone features you should look for to improve your effectiveness include:

- **Redial** – A memory stores the last number you dialled. This means that if you want to redial because the line has been engaged you don't have to punch out all the numbers again, just press the redial button;

- **Hotline** – Your telephone can be programmed to automatically ring a number when you lift your handset and do not dial within a few seconds;
- **Automatic or speed dialling** – You press a single button or combination of buttons to instruct the system to dial automatically for you from your list of numbers you use the most, which you have entered into the system;
- **Ring back** – If the extension you have been trying to get has been engaged, you press a button and put down the receiver. Your 'phone will ring once the number is free and when you pick up your receiver you will hear the ringing tone;
- **Reminder call** – Your extension is automatically called at a time you set to remind you to attend a meeting;
- **Liquid Crystal Display (LCD)** – This is a panel on your telephone which shows the time, date, and internal or external number called. If you have stored that number in the 'phone's memory, the name of the caller is also displayed.

Telephone features to help you handle enquiries or calls from customers:

- **Secrecy button** – If you have an enquiry which you need to discuss with a colleague in the same office as you, covering the mouthpiece is no longer a guarantee that the caller will not hear your conversation. Inform the caller you have to make an enquiry, then press the secrecy button and they hear pleasant music, not the confidential conversation you are having about them or their problem;
- **Hold or enquire** – The call is held while your ring another extension to make an enquiry. Once you have obtained the information you can continue with the original call.

Some of the features involve your colleagues, so you need to ask for their approval before you put these into practice:

- **Pick-up groups** – You can program your 'phone to pick up and answer a call to another 'phone. Then when one of these extensions rings you lift your handset, type a pickup code, and you can take the call from your desk – instead of having to rush round to someone else's. This is especially useful in open plan offices;
- **Call divert** – Calls to your own telephone are diverted to other members of your department or team, so that you can be left undisturbed, or to ensure your calls are taken while you are on holiday;
- **Conferencing** – If you know a call is coming in and several colleagues need to be involved in the discussion, by dialling a code on the extensions involved several people can have a discussion at the same time. Usually one or two external callers can be involved with one or more internal users, depending on your system.

Useful features for managing calls coming in to you:

- **Automatic answering** – You leave a message on the system, so that if you are not available to answer the call within a certain number of rings, your message is played to the caller who can leave a message which is stored in your Voice Mail box. You can listen to your Voice Mail messages when it suits you.

Your Voice Mail message should include:

- **A greeting**;
- **Your name** – and possibly the name of your organization if the caller will have called you directly, without involving the reception;
- **How to leave a message** – 'Please leave your name, number and message after the tone';
- **How to get back to the switchboard** – 'To return to the switchboard please remain silent. Your call will be automatically transferred after a few seconds.'

- **Remote access** – Allows you to operate your answer machine away from the building it is in. This is useful if your job involves a lot of travelling and you need to handle your own calls personally.

All the features listed above might have different names on your telephone system – they do vary. Alternatively, some might not exist on your system. If they are there, do make the most of them.

Activity

- Find out what features are available on the telephone system at work;

- Find a user guide and pick four or five features that will help you become more effective;

- **If there is** someone in your organization whose remit is to teach telephone skills – ask them to teach you to use the functions you have listed;

- **If not**, teach yourself one function a week and so you don't forget – write this training plan in your diary now.

PAGERS

A pager is a small device the size of a small calculator, you can clip onto an article of clothing or put in a pocket, in and outside the office. It is sometimes called a 'bleeper' because its function is to 'bleep' at you when someone calls you on the 'phone – and in this way it alerts you to the fact that someone needs to talk to you or you are needed at a different location. They are cheaper than mobile phones, which is why many organizations still use them.

Britain is divided up into paging zones – which are literally geographical regions within which messages can be sent and received. Your organization selects and pays for the number of zones they need from a providers such as BT or Mercury. The whole point of a paging system is that it can be linked to your organization's telephone system so that each telephone can act as a paging terminal. This means that when the telephone rings the pager linked to the telephone, bleeps, wherever the pager and its owner happen to be (as long as they are within the zones the organization pays for).

Different types of pager are available:

- **A tone pager** – Has up to four different tones and these could each mean something different such as, call the office, call the supply depot, call your manager, call your secretary;
- **A numeric pager** – Can only display numbers, typically, telephone numbers;
- **A message pager** – Can display messages up to 90 characters long, including numbers.

Say you are the owner of a pager. When someone rings your extension the pager bleeps. You might be sitting in the staff canteen, or watching television at home. Wherever you are you know you must get to the nearest telephone to ring the number indicated by your pager. Alternatively, depending on the system your company use, you might call your voice mail box to hear a message that has been left for you by the caller.

Activity

Does anyone in your organization have a pager?

- If they do, list the reasons why;
- If they don't list reasons why some jobs don't need pagers.

MOBILE TELEPHONES

These days just walking up and down the street you see people talking to their mobile 'phones. There are also cordless 'phones which enable you to be more mobile in your workplace as you talk on the 'phone. Both these types are known as 'mobile 'phones'.

Companies like Cellnet (owned by BT and Securicor) and Vodaphone – have set up 'cells' which are areas with their own transmitters called base stations. These cells are set up all over the country so that you can make a call from any cell to any cell in 98 per cent of the UK. The telephones used for this type of contact are 'cellular' 'phones. You can use them to call another cellular 'phone or an ordinary one because the base stations link you to the public telephone network. You can also receive calls from either.

There are three types of cellular 'phone:

- **Car 'phone** – permanently installed in a vehicle such as your car, or company delivery vans. It is powered by car battery and enables you to make calls as you drive without holding a handset;
- **Transportable** – can be used in or out of your car or van. Designed for lengthy use outside, you recharge it in your vehicle;
- **Hand portable** – small enough for a pocket, handbag or briefcase, these need to be recharged regularly.

These telephones come with various features such as:

- **Any key answering** – When the 'phone rings you press any key to answer;
- **Number memory** – You can store numbers you use frequently for automatic dialling;
- **Automatic redialling** – It will automatically redial the last number you tried;
- **Illuminated keypad** – Enables you to see the keypad, making it easier to make night time calls from your car.

FAX MACHINES

The term Fax is short for 'facsimile' which means: 'Copying, imitation', also 'An exact copy, counterpart or representation' (*The Shorter Oxford English Dictionary, Third Edition*). So, the wonderful thing about fax machines is that they send a replica of any form of printed, typed, hand-written or drawn material. For example, you can send, letters, reports, drawings or photographs, or a combination of these down the line and the recipient gets a good copy at the other end, no matter how far the information has to travel, providing they have similar equipment.

However, it can be quite time consuming to send several pages – so if for example, your fax message is over ten pages long – you might consider other alternatives such as emailing the document so that it gets there the same day, or posting a floppy disc, which can get to most destinations in the UK by the following day.

Organizations usually have standards related to faxes that go out – for example, a standard header sheet that becomes the first page of the document. It usually states this information:

- Name of sender;
- the sender's organization;
- telephone number;
- fax number;

- Time;
- day;
- date;

- Name of recipient;
- their job title;
- address;
- telephone number;
- fax number.

Most word processing packages give you a template for a fax header sheet. You open a new document, specify the fax header sheet layout you want, enter the information listed above and print it out – as simple as that.

To send a fax:

- You put your header sheet on top of the other pages you want to send;
- At the Fax machine, first you position the sheets of paper containing your message. On more basic machines you have to feed one sheet at a time and so you would position your header sheet first, face down. At a more sophisticated model you place all your sheets face down, ready for the machine to automatically feed them through one at a time, once you give the go ahead;
- When you send pictures, check whether your fax machine has a **shades of grey** setting – the higher this setting, the better the quality of transmission for your pictures;
- You give a start command by pressing one or two keys, typing in the fax number, which is like telephone number and pressing a send key;
- Different makes will vary to some degree, so do check with someone who knows how to use the fax machine if you are about to use one for the first time.

It is normal practice when you send a fax to send a following letter that contains the pages you originally faxed because fax paper discolours with time. If you are the recipient of a fax and the header page does not tell you whether the originals are in the post or not, it is best to photocopy it for the same reason.

The benefits of using fax machines are:

- They are quick and easy to use, therefore particularly useful for information you want to send fast. For example, if you fax advertizement text or a press release to a paper they receive your information within a few seconds;
- They send hand-written order documents with complete accuracy – nobody has to type them and check them;
- They can print out messages 24 hours a day, provided you keep your machine switched on and loaded with paper. If you expect a fax from a far away place such as Australia, they can send messages when it suits them. The caretakers might have locked your office and you could be at home asleep at the time. You can read the message the next day when you come in to work;
- They make it easier to communicate in a foreign language. A translator can type the message you want to send, in the foreign language. Similarly when you receive a written a message you can get it translated. This is a lot easier than trying to work out meaning over the telephone;
- They can get orders to you quicker than by post. You can also combine the use of BT's Business Choices services so that customers can use an 0800 or 0345 fax number to send their written order or message to you, free (Freefone) or for a local (Lo-call) charge.

If you don't have to have a fax machine, or it is out of order, and you want to send a fax there are three alternative ways I know of (you may know of others) They usually charge a fixed rate per page:

- **BT Messaging Services** – This is a BT run service that you use by telephoning your message to the BT bureau. Your message can be transmitted via computer, telex and fax;
- **Business bureaux, telecottages and telecentres** – These are businesses whose work is to support other businesses. Although the work of Telecottages and Telecentres can vary, they often send faxes as well as type letters, photocopy and so on. You can find them through local papers and Yellow Pages;
- **Faxpost** – This is the Post Office's fax service for the transmission of documents available at a few selected branches. Get the list of centres from your local post office.

If you have large distributions to send, your company could subscribe to a service such as BT's Feature Fax. You fax your document to them and they will fax it out to up to 24,000 different organizations for you.

You can find out fax numbers that fax owners have registered with BT on the Directory Enquiries service by ringing 192, or 153 for overseas numbers. There is no fax directory at the time of writing, although one is being compiled.

Activity

- Approximately how many fax machines do you think there are in your organization?
- What types of document do departments send on these machines? Orders? Invoices? Reports? Diagrams or illustrations of some kind? Technical specifications?
- If you do not know of a fax machine in your organization – do you think one could be usefully employed? Where and why?

TELEX SERVICE

Telex is a BT service that your organization can subscribe to. It involves hiring the line to the telex exchange and the rental of a piece of equipment called a teleprinter, plus the charge for each telex sent. The teleprinter itself looks very much like a PC with a monitor, keyboard and printer attached. In fact it is a computer with some RAM and two purposes – to receive and send telexes. Some models can be used as a word processor. Once your organization is a subscriber it can contact its other branches or other companies who are also subscribers and who also have teleprinters.

Say for example that your organization wants to send a client their written confirmation of actions to be taken on a particular project. The client organization is also a telex subscriber and so you decide to send the confirmation using telex.

- At your end the teleprinter operator types the confirmation document on the teleprinter machine, in much the same way as you would type it using a word-processing application on a computer;
- The teleprinter operator then sends the contents of that document down the line to the client company and other destinations if required;
- The sending and receiving teleprinters print out the message;
- If any of the numbers called are engaged the teleprinter will try again until it sends the message successfully.

The advantages of the teleprinter are:

- The operator can type and edit messages to go out while other messages come in;
- The message is reliable because it is typed at your organization, not at some outside agency;
- The message is clear, which is particularly useful for technical, legal or accounting documents such as orders and invoices. However, if you send orders and invoices to your telex service as hand-written documents, there is room for error when the telex operator types them. You need to check the details before they are sent.

There is a Telex Book which lists the numbers of BT telex customers. You can also make Telex directory enquiries on 192 and 153 for international contacts, but you must state that you want a Telex number.

Activity

Does your organization send Telex messages? – List the reasons why;

OR

If your organization doesn't send them – List the reasons why not.

CONFERENCE CALLS

Audioconferencing is a BT service for meetings and conferences held on the telephone. The telephone conferencing facility at work might allow you to conference on the internal telephone network, and perhaps include one or two external callers. However, the Conference Call bureau can link three or more organizations or locations in the UK or internationally. The audioconference can be used within 30 minutes of your request and a BT receptionist is on hand for assistance.

VIDEOCONFERENCING

It is amazing how important these things are to human communication:

- Body language, especially facial expression;
- The ability to show products close at hand;
- The tools to create diagrams and drawings.

Nowadays, you can cut out travel stress, travel time, and expensive nights away from this type of communication by using videoconferencing facilities. Facilities range from a single PC to a video studio set-up:

- **Video phone** – a multimedia PC with a small video camera perched on the top of the monitor and a 'phone attached. It is suitable for one or two people;
- **Visual communication system** – looks like a television on an expensive stand, but recognizable by the rectangular panel above the screen which hides the cameras. It is suitable for up to eight people;
- **Videoconferencing suite** – video studio with control panels for setting the views and camera angles. It is suitable for eight people or more. British Telecom has two videoconferencing centres available in London which can be hired to link with other video conferencing facilities in the UK.

Some techniques for preparing for a video conference session include:

- **Assign a chairman** before the meeting, whose prime role is to ensure that those involved cover all the necessary topics in the time allowed;
- **Assign someone who has done this before** to adjust the cameras to give the views you want;
- **Prepare fully** what topics you need to cover before you go into a video conferencing suite;
- **Be prepared** to only take up the time you have booked the suite for as usually there are others booked in to take it up after you leave. It is a good idea to set a time limit for each topic you want to discuss;
- **Have to hand** any visuals you want to show;
- **Organize** your papers or other references so that you don't have to spend time looking for information during the meeting.

When you go into the video conferencing suite you will see control panels to adjust cameras. Usually you can organize the picture to show several different locations at once. Check on the monitors and with all involved to ensure that everyone can see each other. Allow for adjustment time when you plan your meeting.

Activity

Consider the experience below, from someone who, out of necessity, used a video conferencing suite and then answer the questions.

Paula was someone the company had brought in on a tightly scheduled interior design contract. The only way she could talk to the two experts she needed on the same day, one in Birmingham, one in Carlisle – was to grab them for two hours using the company's video conferencing suite. Both had other important meetings to attend that day – she was the only one available to travel about and so she joined Tom at the Birmingham office.

Tom and Paula prepared for meeting prior to going in to the conference suite. They ended up with a set list of technical construction questions they needed to ask Pat, the structural engineer in Carlisle. They went into the video conferencing suite, adjusted the cameras, and then started. On about the tenth topic in a list of twenty, Tom began to dominate the meeting. He went round-and-round in circles for about half-an-hour, despite the fact that Paula tried to get him back on track.

There was a knock on the door – the next party who had booked the suite were ready to come in. Paula looked at Tom aghast. Instead of getting directly to the point he had made Pat and herself sit there for ages listening to a single issue. He was the senior project manager, he knew that only a couple of sentences would have conveyed the changes he wanted her to make, but, instead, he had chosen to take up over a quarter of their precious conference time on this one item. Paula turned to him and responded explosively, and when she looked back at the monitor she could see Pat's shocked face, and body language exhibiting great surprise, conveyed in good detail all the way from Carlisle. The camera angle was just right. The remaining necessary points had to be covered over the telephone in Tom's office and this was difficult as most of the discussion was centred around Paula's drawings.

- What did the people involved in this meeting do right?
- What did the people involved in this meeting do wrong?
- What steps could they have taken to ensure the meeting went better?

BUSINESS TELEVISION

Business Television is a service provided by BT. This is a private satellite-based network that enables your company to broadcast a message or presentation to a specific audience anywhere in the world. What you transmit can be pre-recorded. BT can make up professional programmes for your organization, and this package includes an operating crew and equipment. Your company could transmit a live event to people at work – possibly to several different locations. They could also organize a live response from the audience.

Typical uses for Business Television are:

- **Training and staff briefings** – To ensure everyone in the company receives the same standard of training and exactly the same information;
- **Company announcements** – To give a personal touch to company announcements from the director or board, and in a large national or international company it puts faces to people who are otherwise just names;
- **Product launches** – To link up to client companies interested in seeing your organization's products or services.

The advantages of this form of communication are:

- It cuts out travel expenses;
- It is a way of contacting many people at several different locations at the same time;
- It ensures a consistent message is sent out and received;
- It gives your organization technical credibility and kudos.

Activity

Has your organization ever used video conferencing? Or has your organization done something similar – for example sent out a video to all branches at Christmas for managers throughout the company to show at the same time?

If so, do you think the method of communication was more personal and effective than a letter on a notice board or a brochure, or a speech from the chairman read out by your departmental manager?

If you are not aware of your company ever having used such a service – do you think it should? For what reasons and in what circumstances?

Information storage and retrieval systems

Information, in all its various forms, face to face as well as written and broadcast is more prolific than ever before. We have to find media to help us store, organize and manage it. This part of the chapter covers:

- **Microfiche**
- **Video**
- **CD-ROM**

MICROFICHE

You've been on holiday and you get your photographs developed. The friends you went with want copies of some of them. You have to look at the negatives that are on strips of film, and they're very small so it's often difficult to make out what's on them. If you wanted to see a photograph in detail, for example, to see the name of pub on a sign in the distance, you would have to use a special viewer to enlarge the images.

Microfiche works on this basis. It is information photographed onto film, and stored on a material very much like your negatives – but instead of being in small strips, it is a sheet of film, approximately postcard size, with several images stored in a grid format.

Each image on a microfiche has a reference. As the information is so small you read it using a special viewer to search through the images until you find the one you want. Libraries, including technical libraries in specialist subjects, use this technique to store reference material. They pay a subscription to an information supplier who renew the microfiches as they update the information on them.

Some organizations like to make and store their own microfiches, because they take up much less space than paper. So, for example, an Engineering office, that has completed a job but does not want to keep all the large plans, takes a picture of each plan using a special camera, develops the film as a microfiche and then throws out the unwieldy paper originals.

You may still come across microfiche, but in most cases organizations tend to use more floppy disks (described in the previous chapter) and CD-ROM (which you can read about below).

VIDEO

Video film – the video tape that you are used to recording films on – is a way of storing all sorts of information. You need a video camera with tripod and video tape which slots into the camera. Modern cameras adjust the lighting for you so that there is no need to set up special lighting. Here are a few examples of the sort of information organizations find it useful to store on video:

- **Events** – The chairman's annual speech to employees, training that has been given, a lecture for future reference and so on;
- **Places** – Showing people environments that would otherwise be difficult or costly for them to visit. For example, on a company induction course, you might want to show them activities at the Denver, USA plant and the Carlisle, UK factory. It would be costly and time

consuming to visit both – but quick and cost effective to show a
video;

- **Procedures** – Video is also a good way to show company procedures, such as safety procedures, without putting employees at risk
of anything going wrong. For example, if you want to show people
how to use a fire extinguisher – it can be shown very well on video
without the mess and need for fire extinguisher maintenance that a
live demonstration would involve;
- **Useful television programmes** – Many organizations whose businesses include education and training services, record educational
or informative programs, relevant to the company, which are shown
on television, so that group or individual viewings can be organized;
- **Video Training** – There are some very good training programmes
available on video.

CD-ROM AND MULTIMEDIA PCs

CD (Compact Disc) technology that Philips and Sony created for digital sound
has transformed the PC. Music CDs were launched in the early 1980s– you
know the things – light plastic discs with a mirror-like finish. The companies
who developed them, soon realized that they could store **any** digital data on
them – not just 75 minutes of stereo sound. In computer storage terms this is
equivalent to:

- About 660 megabytes of data, which is equivalent to a typed script
containing 660 million text characters – you know, a, b, c, etc.;
- Or a shelf full of hefty books such as computer manuals, or ency-
clopaedias, or telephone directories;
- Or about 1,000 floppy disks;
- Or one hour of video.

This means that a CD-ROM can store and enables you to access other
types of information, which take up far greater amounts of memory than text,
such as pictures, animation, sound and video. In other words, a CD-ROM
gives you multimedia – which opens up a whole new exciting world of communication possibilities.

There are several different formats of CD for use on a computer and the
range and possibilities are changing all the time. Here are a few examples,
available at the time of writing:

- **Audio CD** – You are already familiar with these – and in some cases
the CD-ROM drive on your computer can be used to play them! I
have been in less formal organizations where staff tune into music
to help them concentrate while at work, providing they use headphones – and I notice many students prefer to work like this too. On
CD drives the earphone jack is often at the front of the CD drive so

that it is easy to plug them in. This may help your staff concentrate on their work better, particularly in open plan offices. Perhaps producing in-company audio CDs could be a way of disseminating factual or procedural information to staff about the organization or their work within it. However some multimedia computers do not accept this format of CD;

- **CD-ROM** – (pronounced 'see-dee-rom' and in full: Compact Disk – Read Only Memory). The computer can only **read** from the disk not **write** to it. You see this type of CD attached to computer magazines, or you receive your computer applications on them, or you run training from them, or you get information from them. You cannot change the contents of this type of disk – and they are quite hardy;

- **CD-R** – (Compact Disk – Recordable). This is a CD you can record on but currently you need a special piece of equipment called a CD-writer to do this. Once you have recorded on one of these you cannot wipe the information off, or re-record over what you have already put on it. Do handle them carefully – a thumb print on the mirror finish can stop them from working;

- **CD-E** – (Compact Disk – Erasable). This is a CD you can store files on, also erase files, then use again for storing other information. Handle a CD-E with the same care as a CD-R;

- **Kodak Photo-CD** – Now, when you take snaps you can go to the film developer, such as Boots, and ask them to put your photographs on to a Photo-CD. Each of these CDs can hold over 100 photographs, and as you complete a film you can ask for the developer to add to the contents until the Photo-CD is full. Slot the Photo-CD into your CD drive and you can access the photograph you want, perhaps calling it into a graphics package to touch it up. Once you are happy with the picture you could save it on your hard drive as a file. Then you might want to use the image in a piece of work, for example marketing literature, a company newsletter or financial report you are developing using a word-processing package or desktop publishing package. Or perhaps use it as an illustration in a presentation you are developing using a presentation software. Alternatively, if you are making your own CD-ROM, you are probably using 'authoring software'. Stills (a word in media used for non-moving images) from a Photo-CD can liven up your presentation. You can use a still as a background to text, as a main illustration beside text, or create a collage of several stills;

- **CD-I** – (Compact Disk – Interactive) This is a format devised by Philips. Training organizations and departments or home users buy this format. You need a CD-I player attached to a television to run it, not a PC with a monitor.

You need a multimedia computer to use CD-ROMs, CD-R and CD-E. A multimedia computer could be a multimedia PC (sometimes referred to as an

MPC) or it could be a multimedia Mac, or another platform with multimedia facilities. You can use Kodak-CDs on both multimedia computers and CD-I players.

Multimedia computers are built in the factory, to ensure that all the parts work together, to enable you to use multimedia technology. You can recognize them by the built in CD drive, or drives. Sometimes these drives are separate, but plugged in to the appropriate port at the back of your computer. Quite often in an office situation you will see them with headphones plugged in so that the user can hear the stereo sound without disturbing others. If you see a multimedia computer in a public area such as foyer or exhibition, used for information or marketing purposes, you will either see a pair of good stereo speakers attached, or more likely these days, speakers built into the monitor.

On the inside of most computer system units, there are **expansion slots**. The supplier, or a technician, slots in **cards** or **boards** which hold the appropriate chips for additional things you want your computer to do. Every slot is already connected to the CPU which remains in control of whatever is happening in the computer. At the end of each board are the ports you need to attach specific equipment to – and as you will have already noticed these ports stick out at the back of your computer.

In a multimedia computer some expansion slots have been filled at the factory with cards for specific purposes, including:

- **A sound card** – which enables you to play CD sound;
- **A video card** – which enables you to play video.

The ports on these cards enable you to plug in equipment like headphones and speakers.

If you are going to make multimedia you need additional cards which will supply ports for microphones, video cameras and video players enabling you to create files of sounds, still and moving images – a range of different types of information. You will also need video editing and sound editing software, plus additional programming software or authorware to write your multimedia program.

So what sort of information management tool have we got here? A multimedia computer looks like and works like a PC; the only difference is that it has the added ability to handle multimedia. As a result, it's a tool that changes the face of information management in a variety of areas:

- Information storage and reference;
- Applications;
- Training;
- Information tailored to your company needs.

Information storage and reference

The CD-ROM's enormous capacity means that a single CD can replace vast amounts of paper or microfiches. So for example, instead of receiving several microfiches on the latest Architectural legal requirements, you may get one CD-ROM. Or a library that used to keep hundreds of back copies of newspapers now subscribes to receive CD-ROMs containing several months' worth of back copies. These types of CD-ROMs, also contain software to enable you to search through the information and quickly find what you want.

John wanted to find out about Internet and what it could do for his company. He went to the local library where they have newspaper CD-ROMs. The librarian asked him to sit down at the computer, accessed the CD-ROM for John and showed him how to type in the keyword and search for relevant articles. When John typed in the word 'Internet', he had to wait a few seconds while the computer searched, then a message appeared telling John that 600 articles were available on that subject. John pressed the space bar to see the titles and the list of articles appeared. He scanned the resulting list using the cursor movement keys. A couple of articles caught his eye. He used the cursor movement key to move to one of them. He pressed the Enter key on the keyboard to see the article. There was just text, no diagrams or photographs, but John could see at a glance that it contained the sort of information he wanted. He pressed P to print the article, so that he had a copy of the information he could refer to. The type of interface John used was friendly. By entering a key word he could quickly find the information he wanted.

Information is quickly accessible providing the interface has been well designed. It can be much quicker than searching through papers or microfiches. More reference CD-ROMs are becoming available. The information on them can include the full range of multimedia, for example, sound recordings and video footage.

Applications

You or your technical department may receive your software applications on one CD-ROM instead of a number of disks.

Training

You can be in the middle of doing something at your computer, for example word-processing, and suddenly realize you need to learn a new skill. If the appropriate CD-ROM is available it is just a matter of inserting it into the CD drive and you can access the training you need.

Jo had been newly trained in the company's word-processing package. She was typing a report and needed to create a table in it. She remembered there was a facility for drawing lines – but felt there must be quicker way to create a grid for the information she needed to enter.

She asked Mary if she could borrow the training CD-ROM for the software she was using. She inserted the CD-ROM into the drive, it loaded up in a few seconds, and she selected the lesson on creating tables.

She worked through the lesson at her own pace. It was very easy. She exited the training program and was then able to get on with her work.

CD-ROMs that contain training are very popular in a wide variety of organizations because users:

- Can work through the training at a pace that suits their own needs;
- Can go over the same information as many times as necessary – the computer will never get bored or cross;
- Receive consistent information – its memory does not change and it does not run out of time (although the user might);
- Can usually check their understanding through exercises.

CD-ROM training cannot replace a human trainer – but can be used to support training activities. There are training CD-ROMs available for a wide variety of business skills. Some of these make learning fun and as a result you may hear them referred to as 'edutainment'. Some managers and trainers disapprove of this 'enjoyment factor' – but perhaps this stems from a puritanical view of the work environment rather than an understanding of the way the human brain works and of human nature. Obviously it is important that business training products do not become 'gimmicks'. However, our minds are more receptive if the training experience is a relaxing and enjoyable one, rather than inciting tension or boredom. If you are ever in a position to assess the content of a training CD-ROM, put your personal tastes and preferences aside and view it in the context in which your staff or customers will use it. If the product trains people to do something that their organization needs them to do and it makes learning an interesting and enjoyable experience, then that can only be good.

Information tailored to your company needs

It is now relatively easy to make your own Multimedia – but it is important not to underestimate the amount of work and project management involved.

Avril rang up the local further education college to see if there was anyone she could talk to about multimedia. The receptionist suggested she talk to their training support department that was involved in making multimedia – particularly Mary Mayhew who project managed these products. Avril set up a meeting with Mary and then visited the college.

Avril told Mary that their company had updated their hardware and everyone now had multimedia PCs on their desk. She felt that her company should be developing tailor made products to keep staff and customers informed of available products and services. She herself was an experienced computer user – but not a programmer.

Mary told Avril a bit about herself – how she had worked for a couple of multimedia companies before joining the college. She explained that a good multimedia product involves a variety of experts: script writers, film teams, sound experts, voice artists, actors, graphic artists, photographers, musicians and others. She said that where she used to work they had programmers working in a language called C++. They put in hundreds of programming hours to bring all the resulting multimedia elements together to make marketing or training CD-ROMs. She explained that now at the college they did not use programmers, but instead trained college staff to use 'authoring software'. She said that this enabled just about anyone with average intelligence, with the time and patience, to produce relatively quickly what only a programmer could do before.

She explained to Avril that there were about four different options she could take if she wanted to develop CD-ROMs:

- Buying existing products would be much cheaper than developing their own – but it looked as though what she wanted needed to be tailor-made;
- The college had the tools to develop CD-ROM and that they could develop a product for Avril's company;
- Alternatively, they could help Avril learn the software and project manage the product herself.

Mary warned, 'If you decide to develop it yourself you will need to be trained in the authoring software and you will find the learning curve a steep one. Also once you start developing your product you will find it time consuming.'

Avril went away very enthusiastic saying she would have a chat with her manager about the best way to proceed.

Further education colleges and universities are now using and in some cases developing multimedia. There are also multimedia development companies who have been developing this type of product for a while. You could ask any of them for a quote once you have a product specification. Many companies ask for project proposals and bids before choosing the company with whom they want to develop multimedia.

The types of multimedia products you might think about are for training, information or marketing. Multimedia gives an attention-grabbing energy to these forms of communication.

Activity

- Are there any multimedia computers in your organization?
- What are they used for?

The direction of information

A couple of decades ago, most business communication consisted of voice or text. It was relatively time consuming to create charts such as bar or pie charts – so these might have appeared in reports where there was more time or money spent in their preparation, for example, annual reports, or life insurance marketing leaflets.

Now, as we have seen a much wider range of information is available in multimedia. Here are some of the directions that multimedia is going:

- The hardware used to play CD-ROM has now dropped dramatically in price, since 1993, making it more accessible to many different sizes of organization and home users;
- CD-ROMs are now an accepted media for storing programs or data and people now **expect them**;
- The number of software CDs is going to rise, so more applications will arrive on CDs;
- The number of training CDs is going to rise. This means that staff can sit at self-paced interactive training in the topics they need at their own desks;
- A number of reference CDs are already available and will rise;
- Video CDs are already available and will be used more;
- The power of multimedia computers is increasing so that video plays more smoothly and information is accessible faster;
- As it becomes cheaper to buy and use equipment to write on to CDs people will use them very much like floppy disks, with the advantage that they can store far greater amounts of information on them;
- People will come to expect instant access to information in the form of multimedia.

Major developments in the way consumers and businesses view information now include:

- Types of communication that used to be created by specialists have become available as more friendly equipment or software. In place of camera crews we have home video cameras. Instead of typesetters we have word-processing or desk top publishing. Instead of multi-media programmers we have authoring software. (However, note the tools are limited compared to what the specialists with their skills and equipment can achieve.);
- With our ability to create, store and manipulate pictorial information and moving images better – businesses now convey more information by these means than ever before. As 'a picture speaks a thousand words' this makes sense;
- Technical improvements in computers such as faster processors, to enable us to manage sound, video and graphics effectively, are ongoing. It means that you will be able to store and manipulate an increasing amount of this type of information in the future;
- Probably due to the experiences of marketing on television everyone is more aware of the subconscious elements of communications, from colour and texture in backgrounds, to sound effects and music that creates moods. These elements that affect us at subconscious levels will be used (knowingly or unknowingly) in a greater range of communication.

Activity

At the start of this chapter I said that 'The more senses you involve in communication the more powerful the message.' On this basis, which are the most powerful communication tools described in this chapter?

Where and how could these tools be effectively employed in any organization – or particularly in your own organization?

REFERENCES

PC Videophone – Where Minds Meet, British Telecommunications plc., 1994

Factfile No 3 BT Products and Service, BT Education service, British Telecommunications plc., 1993

In Touch – Your Guide To The Products And Services That Fit Your Life – Winter/Spring 1995, British Telecommunications plc, 1996

In Touch – Your Guide To The Products And Services That Fit Your Life – Winter/Spring 1996, British Telecommunications plc, 1996

The Business Catalogue Summer 1994, British Telecommunications plc, 1994.

Visual Communications Portfolio, British Telecommunications plc, 1994

Secretrial Duties, 9th Edn, John Harrison, Pitman Publishing, 1994

All You Need To Know About CD-ROM, Damien Noonan, Future Publishing Limited, 1995.

Multimedia: Making It Work, 2nd Edn, Tay Vaughan, Osborne McGraw-Hill, 1994

The Business Week Guide to Multimedia Presentations, Robert L Lindstrom, Osborne Mc-Graw Hill, 1994

CHAPTER NINE

Making the Most of IT

IN THIS CHAPTER WE WILL LOOK AT THE FOLLOWING AREAS:

- Networking systems;
- The future for communication;
- Networking people;
- Where do you go from here?

In this final chapter I take a look at the potential of linking computers and the whole new dimension this gives to communication at work. First the chapter introduces computer networks, and then it looks at how these communication tools revolutionize people networks. It covers these topics:

- Networking systems:

This covers, computer links at work, telecommunications, Email, Internet and the future of communication.

- Networking people:

This covers, telecottages and teleworking, and where you go from here.

Networking systems

LOCAL AREA NETWORKS

A Local Area Network, called a LAN for short, is a way of linking several computers and peripherals, usually on the same site, for example, spread throughout an office block.

The reasons an organization might set up a LAN are that they want staff to be able to share facilities more freely, for example:

- Use Email (see below), and thereby cut down meetings and the aggravation of 'telephone tennis';
- Make the most of expensive resources such as printers and plotters.
- Share expensive software;
- Share the organization's database and resources such as, staff names, departments, project numbers, budget numbers, invoices, sales figures, standard documents, procedures and more;
- Share links to outside services such as commercial databases to get information.

The way a network is organized is called the 'network topology', and for LANs there are several types, here are some examples:

- The star network;
- The switch network;
- The ring network;
- The bus network.

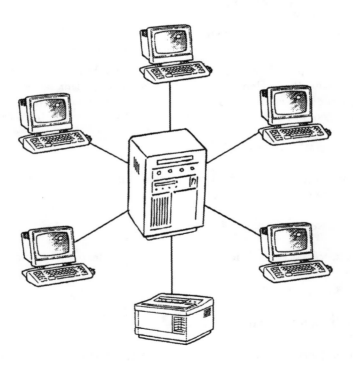

Star network

This is probably one of the most popular arrangements for a LAN:

- A powerful computer controls the network – sometimes referred to as the 'network controller', 'host computer' or 'server'. This stores the files users access from their computers;
- A network operating system like UNIX or Novell, allows all the individual computers to talk to each other and to the server itself;
- A network card in each computer enables them to talk to each other;
- Cables link the computers and file server. The information passing from one machine to other goes down these cables;
- Technicians or support services manage the server, ensure that it works, back up files on a regular basis, make company-wide information such as databases, policies and procedures available, and ensure data security.

For you, using one of the computers in a star network is very similar to using a stand alone computer. However, you might notice small differences:

- Perhaps a slightly longer wait for your software to load, because it comes from the server;
- The ability to send documents from one terminal to another;
- You access your files in the same way as before, but instead of coming from hard disk, they usually come from the server;
- You don't need to keep to one particular computer, you can access your files from the server at any machine on the network;
- If you want a paper copy of a file, you can print it on a printer you share with others on the network.

You cannot access anything and everything on the server. Users on networks are usually given different levels of access depending on who they are and what information they need. For example:

- Top management will be able to retrieve important financial information and the applications they need to do their work;
- The accounting department will be able to access accounting as well as various other applications;
- Personnel will have access to personnel details and other applications;
- Other employees might have access to specific applications – but not to financial information, accounts or personnel details.

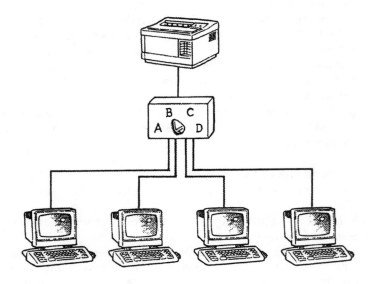

Switch Network

This type of network usually applies to a small area such as an open plan office. It is normally set up in a department when several computers need to share a single resource such as a printer, or a plotter. A switch system (literally a box with switches on it) is attached to the resource you want to share, such as a printer. Then, every computer that needs to have access to that resource is linked to the switch system. Each switch on the system relates to one computer. So for example, if you are sitting at a computer and want to print the report you have been working on, you walk over to the switching device and push the correct switch to enable your computer to connect to the printer. On some switch systems the switching is automatic. As you need to walk over to the printer to collect your printout anyway, this does not save you much effort – although it could save you time if you print several documents in quick succession.

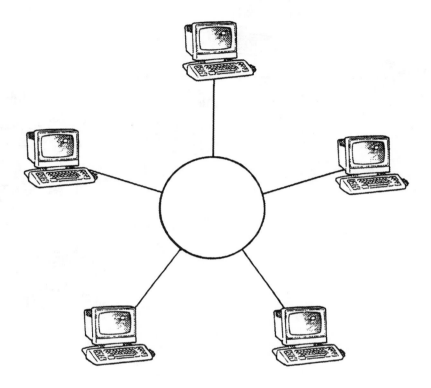

Ring Network
This type of network does not rely on any one computer as a server. The messages passed throughout the network are passed from computer to computer (node to node). Unfortunately this limits the number of messages in the network at any one time. Information and system security cannot be centralized as there is no central server.

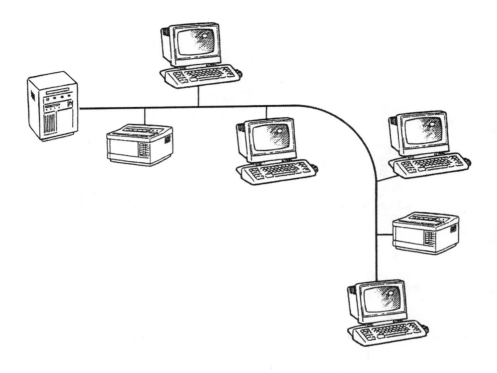

Bus network
Thi bus network uses a simple, single cable, to carry information to and from the computers and peripherals involved. There can be a central computer which holds the files. The cable on this type of network is like a narrow country lane where cars have to drive carefully – otherwise suffer serious head on-crashes. There have to be special rules in the system set-up called 'protocols' to ensure the data does not collide.

Security is something that has to be thought about carefully on all networks. For example:

- Staff can be issued passwords and their access limited to whatever is appropriate for their role in the company;
- Regular backups can be organized by the technical support staff;
- Virus checks can be set up to occur automatically, or virus checking software is made available to staff, so that when they use disks, viruses cannot be introduced to the system.

Activity

- Find out whether you have a LAN in your organization;
- If so, what is its topology?

The networks we have talked about so far can be mixed to form a hybrid network. For example, a switch network, could be part of a star network. They all work well if your computers are within a few hundred feet of each other. If your organization is widespread, it might have a Wide Area Network.

WIDE AREA NETWORKS

In a Wide Area Network or WAN there can be several miles of land or sea between computers. A large company might have a manufacturing plant, a distribution centre, shops all over the country and abroad and these could all be connected to their national headquarters. So for example, the computers might be used to collect data from the company's outlets, distributors and manufacturing plant at the end of each working day. The system processes this data overnight, and next day management have up to date information on which to base their decisions, such as the quantity they need to manufacture during the week to meet orders.

There are three good reasons for setting up a WAN:

- Management data can be collected and collated even though company sites are several miles apart;
- Staff can communicate directly to all the other sites, no matter how geographically spread out they are using their computers;
- The speed of communication over long distances means the raw data is processed very fast, the resulting information is transmitted very fast and the information is immediately relevant, enabling management to make decisions based on the latest information, and enabling staff to chase up queries, and find answers to problems quickly.

Many different businesses depend on information that comes from long distances and as a result they are totally dependent on their WANs – travel and banking are just two examples.

WANs are much more complex than LANs, because they:

- Are spread over a large geographical area;
- Are used for many different requirements;
- Cope with a lot more information for a lot more people.

This complexity means they can be organized in many different ways. One term you may hear mentioned is a 'hierarchical' network. This describes the system which has large mainframe computer in the company headquarters which communicates with small but powerful minicomputers lower down in the hierarchy. Attached to this middle level are the microcomputers at the bottom of the hierarchy.

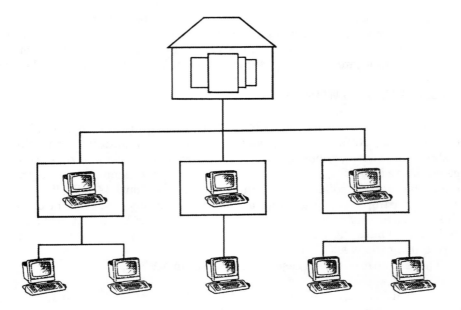

Hierarchical Networks

Alternatively you may hear the term 'Distributed Networks' or 'Distributed Data Processing Networks'. This describes any system which has groups of computers working at regional sites. So a 'hierarchical network' is also a 'distributed network'. The advantage is that the data for the headquarters can be sent out, and data relevant locally is not sent out.

The disadvantages of both LANs and WANs are:

- They need maintenance and upkeep, which can be expensive;
- Staff need to be trained how to use them, if they are to add to the efficiency of the organization;
- Very occasionally the network 'goes down' (fails). The information is not normally at risk because it is backed up. However business can suffer because information and software people depend on to carry out their work are not available.

Activity

Find out whether you have a WAN at work, and if so, what different regions or countries does your company communicate with?

The links that connect different sites in a WAN can be privately owned, or over long distances they are more likely to belong to telecommunications companies who charge for their use. So have a look at telecommunications links and what they enable an organization to do . . .

TELECOMMUNICATIONS

The prefix 'Tele' means far off, or remote. The word 'communications' has traditionally meant telephone lines. The complete word refers to **sending data down telephone lines**. The data can be sound, text, pictures, even video and it can be sent down cable, optical fibre, or radio waves.

Cable connections vary:

- **Twisted pair cable** – is made of copper wires twisted together and insulated and it is used for short or long distance communication;
- **Coaxial cable** – is made of copper or aluminium wires, well insulated so that the data travelling down the cable is not spoilt by noise or static interference. It is used for short, and long distance and also laid underwater;
- **Flat or ribbon cable** – is made up of several insulated wires running in parallel to form a flat ribbon of cable. It should only be used for short distances and data can suffer from static interference;
- **Optical fibre** – These days is often used instead of coaxial cable. The fibre is made of thin glass or plastic filaments and each fibre is coated with cladding. Information is carried down optical fibre in the form of high frequency laser pulses – in other word laser light.

There are two types of radio links:

- **Microwave** – This consists of high frequency radio waves which only travel over a short distance, such as 50 miles. The signals are received by antenna usually placed on the top of tall buildings, mountains and hills. When an organization is considering using a radio connection over a relatively short distance, on a fine day you will see members of the project team on the roof, binoculars in hand and looking across the roofs to the building they want to connect to. They are checking that the 'line of sight', literally the view from one antenna to another, is clear. As microwaves travel in straight lines any interruptions, such as a church spire between antennae will spoil the transmission;

- **Radio waves** – This consists of low frequency waves that can also be used for long distance satellite transmission. There are about 100 privately owned communication satellites in orbit around planet Earth. Organizations that want long distance, line of sight communication, buy into the services offered by these communications companies.

In the rest of this section I refer to the connections as lines even though as you have seen, some of the connection options are invisible, and some of them are underground and underwater. The information that goes down lines now is a mixture of voice (travelling in waves) and data from computers (travelling as digital signals in the form of 0's (off) and 1's (on). The 0's and 1's of digital communication are called bits – and it take 8 bits to communicate a text character such as the letter 'a' or the number '1' – so you can imagine the vast quantity of signals travelling down the lines just to communicate a report.

The speed that the information travels down the line is called the 'baud' rate. There are other settings too, that affect the way information is transmitted down the line. The format that the information takes on the line is called the 'protocol'. Some systems are automatically set up with the right settings. Alternatively you may need to change the settings using your communications software.

The two types of information, data and voice, are treated differently on a standard telephone line designed for voice transmission. The computer's digital signals are turned into sound. For example, on a low speed telephone line, a '1' bit is translated into a low-pitched sound and a '0' bit is translated into a high-pitched sound. New cables being laid, whether they are optical fibre or copper wire carry digital information only and they are used for voice and computer bits. We are undergoing a period of change in the way transmission occurs.

To sum up the situation:

- **There are two types of data for transmission – analogue and digital;**
- **There are also two ways of transmitting data on the line – analogue and digitally;**
- **Older lines tend to be analogue;**
- **Newer lines tend to be digital.**

The piece of equipment which converts the signals from your computer into signals which match the characteristics of the line is called a 'modem'. The name is an acronym for 'modulator-demodulator'. The name describes what a modem does, as it 'modulates' the signals from the computer before they go down the telephone line, and at the other end of the line it 'demodulates' the signals so that they are acceptable to the receiving computer.

There are two types of modem which you plug directly into a telephone jack. If you work on a network, this will already be done for you, it's not something you do each time you send an Email message. An **internal modem** is on a card that fits into one of the expansion slots inside a computer. This card provides the port where you plug your computer to the telephone line. These are the most commonly used type of modem now. An **external modem** sits beside your computer, and looks like a small box, which connects to the computer on one side to a telephone line on the other.

> [1]The modem . . . is the transducer you need to send digital information from a computer over an old fashioned analogue communications system like the phone network. One day modems will be a quaint curiosity, a relic from a bygone age, together with the tape cassette.

Currently, it is having a modem and communications software that enables you to send Email.

EMAIL

Email is an abbreviation for 'electronic mail'. Its function is to enable you to send messages and receive them inside an organization, but also to other organizations, even in other countries. So, it does not matter whether you have a stand alone computer, a LAN or a WAN, you can still contact anyone, even in another organization in another country, using Email.

Many organizations have Email now. In order to get to that point, they will have:

- Set up modems to link internal computers to the telephone network;
- Contacted a service provider, such as CompuServe, Demon, Pegasus or Telecom Gold. There are several of these;
- Paid a subscription to the service provider;
- Set up the communications software to enable you to send Email.

This means you can send and receive information, such as your word-processed documents, spreadsheet, or database reports, to anyone over telephone lines, or internally over your organization's network. If your organization has Email you will know, because each member of staff will have an Email address which enables them to send and receive messages. Some organizations have departmental addresses, rather than individual ones. Internally, these addresses are quite short – perhaps only five or six letters such as TECHBN. If you are sending an Email to someone outside your organization the address is longer and the format depends on their service provider. It could be something like this: PMLOND@MEGADOC. DEMON.CO.UK. Here the service provider is Demon.

The advantages of Email are that:

- If you have a computer available you can make contact the moment you need to– whether it is to find information, or pass it on;
- You can attach files, such as reports, or copies of letters, spread-sheets and charts to the Email message. This saves time and postage, particularly for large documents. If you do this, ensure the recipient has compatible application software so that they can retrieve the document successfully;
- Sending messages takes a few seconds, or perhaps a few minutes if the message is going across the world. You can send a message to a pre-defined address list, of perhaps 50 or even 100 people, and it still only takes a few seconds, or minutes. Whereas internal post within your office building, by the time it collected, sorted into pigeon holes or delivered, can take a day or two;
- Messages wait to be read at a convenient moment, unlike a phone call, which can be intrusive;
- It improves accuracy of communication. Telephone messages left with someone else can work like Chinese whispers or never get there;
- It is less expensive because it does not necessarily involve paper or postage. The recipient can print out the message to get a hard copy of it – but that is not necessary – they can refer to the message on the screen as often as they want.

To send an Email message you would normally access your Email software and then:

1 Enter the Email address of the person you are sending the Email to.
2 Enter a heading for your message.
3 Type the message you want to send.
4 Perhaps 'attach' existing computer files which relate to your message, for example, word-processed documents, spreadsheets, databases, graphics, or a mix, such as documents containing graphics, pictures and charts.
5 Perhaps edit your message, there are basic editing features available, similar to those of standard word-processing packages.
6 Click the Send button.
7 If the message is sent successfully you do not receive any feedback from the computer. If there is a problem with your message, you will see a note on the screen telling you what the problem is – and perhaps (depending on the problem) it might be worth trying to send it again.

ADDRESS] PMLOND@MEGADOC.DEMON.CO.UK.
SUBJECT] Info on Internet
COPIES]

>Peter,

>It was good to hear from you so soon after our meeting.
>Yes I can give you that information.
>You can find it in the file I'm attaching to this message.
>Speak to you soon.

>Belinda.

As most of my messages tend to be to people I know, I start with their first name, then begin the rest of the message on the next line. I finish off with my first name if they know me well, or first and surname if I seldom see them. Other European countries tend to be more formal, and often approach sending an Email like sending a letter. If your messages are to foreign business contacts, you might wish to be more formal – starting with 'Dear Mr Ledbetter,' and finishing 'Regards' or 'Best Regards'.

Once you send an Email it is held in memory at the recipient's address until the they read it and choose to delete it. They can store a copy of the text of the Email message itself on hard or floppy disk, or print it out to be filed. They can also do the same with any 'attached' files that they have 'extracted'. If their printer is different from yours, or they do not have compatible software, they may have difficulty accessing, viewing or printing the files. On the whole, it is friendly and easy to use.

Email is not only fast, accessible and easy to use, it also creates a freedom of communication. In many companies there is a healthy of use of Email to get business done quickly and effectively, but it also creates whole new social possibilities. Yes, staff send messages about company activities, procedures, sources of information, management decisions – but they also send party invitations, adverts to sell cars and more, occurring on a social level.

Activity

Sue Evans, is a supervisor who does well at her job, often staying till late to make sure work meets deadlines. In her spare time Sue is the proud breeder of pedigree Siamese cats and has 5 kittens to sell. In her lunch hour she decides to send out an Email message to everyone in her department:

- 'Siamese kittens for sale – £20 each. Contact Sue Evans x 5167'.

Bill, Sue's manager, says 'Sue, you're using the Email for your own personal communications again, aren't you?'

Sue replies, 'Yes, I sent a one line message to 40 people. But if I stop and chat at the same number of desks for five minutes in order to pass on the same message – it would take me half a day. This only took a few seconds out of my lunch hour. In fact, its taking longer to explain it to you than it did to type it and send it out to several people at the same time!'

- Is it right that Email in companies should be used for 'social' communication – not just business communication?
- What are the pros and cons?
- If you have Email in your organization what is the policy for its use?
- What do you think Bill's response should be?

Email is one level of communication you can get from service providers. They also provide a gateway to the Internet . . .

INTERNET

Internet is an abbreviation for 'internetwork' – which means a network of computer networks – which is exactly what it is.

---

[2]Statistics about the Internet are legion . . . it currently comprises around 50,000 networks, with more than two million computers and perhaps 10–15 million users in many countries around the world. Nobody really knows what the numbers are, because one of the fundamentally outrageous and fascinating things about the Internet is that nobody is in charge.

You cannot avoid hearing about Internet, also referred to as the web, World Wide Web or W3, cyberspace, the information superhighway and so on. However, according to Dr John M Taylor, Director, Hewlett Packard Laboratories, Europe, 'Far from building information motorways, we are just about to begin building B roads and a few A roads' This is his account of how Internet started:

'The Internet started life over 25 years ago as the ARPA net, an experimental computer communications network sponsored by the Advanced Research Projects Agency of the US Department of Defence. It was a very far sighted project which invented and demonstrated many key new concepts and technologies, and I was personally quite closely involved with it in the early days. It gradually grew to link many of the university and industry research labs in the defence research community in the US; it became linked to Europe and gradually spread widely beyond the defence community, particularly as people realized how powerful electronic mail could be in helping research groups in many different organizations, disciplines and countries to communicate and co-operate.

Then quite suddenly, two things happened. Firstly, a group in CERN in Geneva and elsewhere, showed how a word in a document in one computer connected to the Internet (say a name in a telephone list or a reference to the title of an article in a scientific journal) could be linked electronically to a previously unrelated document (say the photograph of the person, or a copy of the article itself) which was stored on a totally separate computer on the Internet, often in a different country. Many people spent long hours putting millions of these hypertext links in place for a wide range of different kinds of information in which various groups of researchers happened to be interested. So was born the 'World Wide Web' because they have created an incredible web of linkages across the globe between an already huge collection of information and items on databases.

The second thing that happened was that the Internet discovered informal information. Until then it had been a classical 'keyboard and data' kind of world, specialized to computer experts and indeed rather jealously guarded by them for all sorts of reasons. Then some of them started putting pictures on the Net, so that when you clicked on a name like 'Hubble', you could find your way, not just to a table of data about the Space Telescope, but also get on your screen the latest full colour images coming from space direct from the computers of the NASA research labs who were running the experiments.'

The services you can get on Internet come from the service providers who enable you to access a vast array of major information resources. Special software gives you graphic and text based screens that help you navigate your way through all the different servers that make up the Internet. Information which business organizations world wide might be interested in include:

financial services and financial market information, newspapers, research papers, news, business tips, legal topics, booking services, direct hotel and travel booking, weather information.

There are also plenty of other tempting resources: Sports news, electronic shopping malls, games, recipes, special interest clubs, software resources, medical resources, graphics resources, education references such as courses available and qualifications required for entry to college courses, tuition and much more.

If your team need to use Internet make sure that they know it costs money. On the one hand your organization pays a fixed monthly subscription fee for the use of the service, so it is important for them to get their money's worth. On the other hand what does your management feel about staff 'browsing' at the organization's expense? Using Internet is equivalent to sitting chatting on the 'phone. Your organization pays a connection charge, plus more for the amount of computer time used.

To keep your organization's Internet costs down it is a good idea to ask staff to:

- Use Internet when the lines are less busy – probably during non-business hours. With use staff will find out the peak times to avoid, and the best times for faster access to information;
- Print information from Internet by saving the information to a file, closing Internet, then printing the file. This is quicker than printing straight from Internet;
- Leave Internet if they are not using it, rather than clocking up time on the line.

Terms you may hear in relation to the Internet are:

- **Web server** – a computer used to display information about your company or related services. This server is usually separate from your company's computer network, so that users of Internet cannot find their way into your computer files, or sensitive company information;
- **Web pages** – screens of information stored on web servers. These are pages that Internet users all over the world can look at and 'browse';
- **Web browser** – the software you use to 'browse' other people's web pages. Netscape Navigator is currently a popular one, with a wealth of different features. Not all web browsers have the same search facilities;
- **Home page** – used to refer to the page your company put at the front of the web browser, as many companies used to put their own information here. Now the term is used more to refer to the first page of a series of web pages;

- **Web site** – a collection of web pages of which the home page is the first;
- **Intranet** – an organization's internal documents on the web server, which are only for internal use and can only be accessed internally. This is useful for policy documents, quality assurance procedures, staff lists, and any other information the company can benefit from sharing;
- **HTML** – stands for HyperText Markup Language. It consists of codes to standardize the text in all web pages, which make the text readable to all web browsers. As an Internet user, when you look at a page, you do not see the codes, they are converted by the web browser, which can then display the page as you see it;
- **URL** – stands for Uniform Resource Locator, literally the address where the web pages are located. A typical address might be something like:

http://www.zoo.com

- If it is longer it will be because you have been given a file address so that you go directly to a particular file on the web server:

http://www.zoo.com/camel/humps.html

- **http://** – the letters stand for HyperText Transfer Protocol. It is one of the transfer methods used in the web for sending web pages from one place to another, for example, from the web server where the page originated to your computer.

The growth rate in the use of the Internet has been phenomenal.

> [3]There are now (1994) over 21,000 commercial 'domains' registered on the Internet, (the rough equivalent of a shop front in the High Street) through which companies offer facilities to browse electronic catalogues and order goods and services via the Net, compared to 9,000 in 1991.

Activity

> Many organizations are worried about the effect that Internet will have in the workplace on productivity. It is bound to have effects on the way people work and their approach to work:
>
> - If they normally used to buy a paper to read in the lunch hour, but now read it on Internet instead – is that OK?
> - With all the amazing information and leisure resources on Internet – will people find excuses to explore and shop from Internet during working hours?
> - If they do, could it be to the organization's advantage?
> - What is your organization's policy on the use of Internet?

Internet is in its early stages, so what sort of future can we look forward to . . .

The future for communication

Technology has moved so fast in the area of communication that we currently have more exciting possibilities than many people ever imagined say, ten, or even five, years ago. IT is moving in directions that continue to change the way we communicate and you can see some of the latest trends in the table below:

- **Equipment integration** – For example, where before there were two separate machines, one to send a fax, another to type the fax, now a microcomputer can do both. Also whereas before there were two types of screen, a television and a VDU, there is now a monitor that is both;
- **Links between equipment** – Computer terminals, faxes, photocopiers and other pieces of equipment can be linked to each other to form a network, so that messages can be passed with great speed from one machine to the other;
- **Reduced size of equipment** – Portable computers and mobile telephones;
- **Increased power and durability for less money** – More businesses and individuals own computers;
- **Increased speed** – You can produce better quality documents quicker. Also, the links between machines means that communication can be faster than ever before. The speed with which information is carried is increasing and this means that the type of information we can convey can now include pictures, charts and even animation and video;
- **Easier to use and more inviting** – Computer interfaces are more attractive, are designed better, and with the introduction of GUIs have become more standard, making computers much easier to use;
- **More pervasive** – Computers affect more aspects of our lives – for example at work more people are getting PCs to work on, and at home more people buy them for budget planning, communication, education and entertainment. The Internet has given another dimension to computer use, bringing home shopping and other services into the office and home via computer;
- **Changing content** – Expectations about the nature of information has changed. More coloured images, still and moving are used, than ever before. Communications can include more than text or the spoken word – you can include pictures, animation, video and colour;

- **Higher quality expectations** – It is easier to make changes therefore there are high expectations with regard to quality and accuracy. Also it is easier than ever before to create visually attractive messages, and with the sophistication of the images that surround us in our everyday lives, people expect visual quality. This affects every type of communication, from letters and reports to sales presentations, proposals and so on;
- **Changing materials** – Information can be sent directly down lines avoiding the need to send paper. Also, standard formats like the glossy brochure are being replaced by demonstration CD-ROMs and Internet bulletin boards.

'It is my belief that within the next five years . . . quite new forms of information appliance will start to become commonplace and will move us on from today's PC's, printers, fax machines, photocopiers and so on, and that as a result we will be discovering:

- **New ways of doing existing activities,** like catalogue shopping and travelling;
- **New ways of getting existing information objects,** like books, films, magazines, photos, images, videos and music, by converting them to electronic form and sending them across a network;
- **New kinds of activity,** that become possible, such as living-room to living-room multimedia conferencing, and virtual reality visualization of places and environments;
- **New kinds of information 'stuff',** that we can create and use, that have their primary existence inside electronic systems rather than as discrete, physical objects, and which indeed cannot be accessed or viewed without an electronic system . . ..

For example:

- The electronic Christmas Parcel which you send over the net to your daughter and contains: the latest chart video album of her favourite pop group, tickets for a video-on-demand movie, an Internet Saver train ticket to come home for Christmas, a video greetings card from Mum, some photos of the family which can be printed on the colour printer in her hi-fi stack, and a subscription to an interactive training course she needs for her college course.

And:

- Millions of cameras on the Internet allow you to wander around your house (did I leave the saucepan on the gas?), around your office (is Ruth at her desk?), and around the country and the world (what's the traffic like on the M32 at the moment?).

Activity

> Do you think any of these communication trends are going to affect:
>
> - The way you communicate?
> - Your work environment?

Larger organizations are quick to take on the latest technology and smaller companies are following their lead. The changes don't just affect **how** you communicate, but also the **places** you communicate from and to. The sales-person in a hotel bedroom, with a portable computer, can check stock at the warehouse 300 miles away, or even in another country. The project manager can download the latest database details onto his portable to prepare for a meeting 70 miles down the M4. For someone else video conferencing may mean less need to drive or fly; or for another person fast and accurate com-munications networks may enable them to work from home; which brings me on to the next section and the topic of Telecottages and teleworking . . .

Networking People

TELECOTTAGES AND TELEWORKING

In the past two sorts of businesses have been able to organize their life so that they work from home:

- Crafts businesses;
- Professional services: writers, designers, accountants, consultants, technical authors, translators and others.

With the recession we have suffered in the late eighties and early nineties, there are many more of these types of business running from home than ever before. But also, the recession, causing greater competition, has forced large businesses to restructure, cut down their overheads, and invest in better technology to make themselves more efficient. It is these trends which have brought about a new group of people working from home at all sorts of levels, but particularly:

- Lower paid, clerical jobs.

Communications technology has also resulted in the Telecottage move-ment, where government funding has been used to support the creation of Telecottages. The word 'Telecottages' indicates what these are – offices usu-ally supplied with the latest information technology sited in rural areas on the whole – but some exist in towns too. Their purpose is to bring new tech-nology to businesses running from home or a long way from town services.

You can usually find your local Telecottage in Yellow Pages. The services they provide depend on their particular interests, local needs and local skills. Some may provide business services you are looking for. Others may be able to provide support services to your team of teleworkers. The Telecottage Association represents teleworkers in this country – and many unions, for example banking unions are also aware of the special needs of teleworkers.

From your organization's point of view the advantage of having telework-ers is that the services or business you offer can expand without the need for additional premises and all the overheads that come with more premises such as furniture, heating and lighting. Alternatively, existing overheads can be reduced. Teleworkers who work mainly from home but who need to visit the organization occasionally can share an office desk and terminal, some-times referred to as 'hot desking', thus still keeping office overheads to the minimum.

Teleworking, sometimes also called 'flexible' working or 'telecommuting', can be organized in many different ways. Organizations tend to employ tele-workers on temporary or fixed term contracts, which means the workforce is more flexible, it can be shrunk or enlarged to suit the current market needs.

If as a supervisor, you are asked to oversee a team of teleworkers, you will find that it involves different techniques to managing a team that is right under your nose. If you have the opportunity to offer teleworking to staff in your department, then you need to choose someone who you know will be self-motivated. If you have the task of supervising a team of teleworkers you need to understand what it is really like working from home – there are advan-tages and disadvantages:

Advantages	Disadvantages
They waste less time, if any, on commuting.	Less contact with the working environment can result in feelings of 'not belonging' or lack of status and as a result, isolation.
They can have increased quality of life, including more time with friends or family.	Their home life can interfere with work, possibly causing stress for the family. Similarly, work commitments can interfere with family time.
They can make better use of their own time.	Social life can interfere with work, as friends and neighbours drop in.

Advantages	Disadvantages
Home is possibly a more comfortable place to work in.	They need to organize dedicated office space which is difficult as standard houses are not designed for work. Also they need increased security at home if your organization is supplying expensive computer equipment.
If they are self-employed with a mortgage, the interest they pay on their 'office room' can be counted as a tax deductible business expense.	If they plan to use a room as an office, or build an office onto the house, there could be planning conditions which need approval from the local authority planning department and tax disadvantages, which an accountant should advise them about.
They can market their home-based business, for example by advertising in the local press, if they are offering a general service on their own equipment.	Their activities in the house must be in keeping with the requirements of the deeds or rent agreement they have signed. There are quite often restrictions in these relating to the type and quantity of vehicles parked outside for example. If restrictions need to be altered to take account of their teleworking activity, they must inform the planning department.

It might be easier for you to start with a small team of a couple of teleworkers, and when you feel that you have ironed out the issues of this new way of working and learnt from the experience, then go ahead and organize a bigger team.

When I was involved in the Telecottages in the South West, we talked about some of the different issues of supporting Teleworkers and what sort of mechanisms the Telecottages could put in place, for example to support a team of teleworkers working for a bank. These are some of the topics we considered and which you will need to think about and understand too:

- **How will you give moral support**? – Working on your own, small problems can get out of proportion. Being able to talk over worries or problems, or just receiving a call from someone asking if everything is going well can make a world of difference. Are you just going to provide this support over the telephone or using Email, or are you going to provide video conferencing facilities to all your teleworkers? Depending on what the teleworker is doing for the company, you may find you have less control over the way the job is done or the time taken to do it;

- **How will you provide technical support**? – Is the company going to supply the equipment, or ask people to use their own computer and telephone? If people are to meet deadlines and do a good job there must be procedures or support on call to ensure that equipment which goes down can be sorted out;

- **How will you ensure health and safety procedures are being followed**? – Is your organization going to supply teleworkers with a fire extinguisher in case there is an electrical fire caused by the equipment? How will you ensure that teleworkers know about how to avoid getting repetitive strain injury and eye strain? Training will help;

- **How can you give a teleworker a sense of belonging to a team**? – A self-employed or sub-contracted teleworker probably will not feel the need to be a part of your organization. However, if you have given existing employees the opportunity to become teleworkers it is important that a few weeks into their new role they do not feel that they have 'lost out' on possibilities for promotion and better earning. Also, teleworkers that used to be full time staff should still be involved in all the office events, departmental meetings, parties, leaving 'do's' and so on. Self-employed or sub-contracted teleworkers might not expect to be involved, but might appreciate being invited.

Activity

> - Two members of the clerical staff you supervise have decided to take the opportunity to become teleworkers. They have said they want to know what disadvantages there are to this decision.
> - List what the disadvantages are to teleworking and describe how you and your organization would try to overcome them.

These issues that surround teleworkers highlight the fact that although technology has enabled this way of working, the most important element is 'people' – they are the core of everything you do. In all your communications with teleworkers the elements that people look for everyday in their working communications, and from an organization as a whole, like trust, commitment, ongoing training and development, feedback on how to do the job better in the future and gratitude for a job well done are equally important. However, these things do not come naturally because of the distance between supervisor and teleworker – you will need to be aware of this and work at it.

Where do you go from here?

We hope this book has given you:

- Skills to communicate more effectively;
- The ability to come to terms with technology that is vital for modern communication;
- Prepared you for the inevitable changes in the way we communicate.

Good communication has plenty of benefits for your organization as it helps everyone in it to:

- Work more efficiently.
- Reduce errors and the need for re-work caused by misunderstandings;
- Feel happier because they are clear on what is expected of them and what they have to do;
- Make better decisions because they are well-informed;
- Know where and how to store information;
- Know where and how to find information quickly;
- Use the best tools for communicating in different situations.

There are also knock-on effects such as good customer relations – because all these things enable the organization to meet customer needs and enquiries better.

However, as a supervisor you are going to find that the new technologies also bring changes, not only in the type of tools you have, but how they are used:

- First, with the greater potential for communication, more people are pushing information at us. You will find information coming at you from all directions: from the post, television, the computer network, sample CD-ROMs and so on. The skills you need to develop from now on are those that will help you assess, sort, manage and find information – as well as communicate it;
- Second, the clear-cut division between a home life and a working life are being eroded by the flexible working and also the ability to bring Internet's leisure facilities into the working environment;
- Third, new communication technologies are more about freedom of access, than control. You may have less control over how, where or when staff do their work.

Some of the answers you need for the future are in this book – but you might want to develop your communication skills even further. If any of the topics have particularly interested you, find out more by reading and speaking to experts from professional bodies as well as colleagues. Keep polishing those communication skills you acquire along the way because they will never lose their value.

Activity

> • What skills do you and your staff need in order to become more effective communicators?
> • Note them down and then talk to your manager about setting up some training.

References

Information Technology – For First Year Degree Students, First Year Study Guides, BPP Publishing Ltd, 1993.

Rowe II, S.H., *Telecommunications for Managers*, 3rd Edn, Prentice Hall, 1995.

Gray, M., Hodson, N., Gordon, G., *Teleworking Explained*, John Wiley & Sons Ltd, 1993.

Kent, P., *10 Minute Guide To The Internet*, Que Corporation, 1994.

Randall, N., *Using HTML*, Que Corporation, 1996.

ISDN International: What It Does; Where It Links; What It Costs, British Telecommunications plc., 1993

Factfile No 6 Telecommunications Today, BT Education Service, British Telecommunications plc., 1993.

Factfile No 8 IT In BT, BT Education Service, British Telecommunications plc., 1994.

Factfile No 10 ISDN – Integrated Services Digital Network, BT Education Service, British Telecommunications plc., 1995.

---

1   Taylor, J.M., The Networked Home: Domestication of Information, Third Biennial RSA/BCS Lecture, RSA, London, 7 December, 1994
2   *ibid*
3   *ibid*
4   *ibid*

Glossary

Term	Pronunciation /usage	Definition
3½ inch disc.	Three-and-a-half inch disc	A round floppy disc enclosed in a hard square plastic case which is never removed. Available in two capacities: 720K and 1.44Mb.
Application	Also called 'application program' or 'application software'	A program, usually purchased by the computer owner, to carry out a specific function, such as word-processing, accounting or database management.
AUTOEXEC.BAT	AUTOEXEC DOT BAT or AUTOEXEC BAT	A file that DOS runs when you start the computer, which tells the computer where your files can be found etc.
Backing storage		An extension to the main store of a computer, the most common being magnetic disc.
Backup		A copy of data or programs that you make on a regular basis, to ensure that if the original files are damaged or disappear for whatever reason, you still have the latest version available.
Batch file		A file which contains a series of DOS commands – for example – a file that starts up an application when you type the name of the batch file at the DOS prompt.
Bit		An abbreviation of Binary digit. A unit of information. Eight bits equals one byte – See Bytes.
Board		A printed circuit board that can be slotted into an expansion slot inside the system unit. Also called a card.

Term	Pronunciation /usage	Definition
Boot up	Or simply, boot	To boot up or boot is the process the computer goes through when you switch on which involves loading the operating system into RAM so that the computer can carry out your commands. This computer activity of loading the operating system is called 'booting up' or 'booting the computer' – and as a result, DOS starts loading from the hard disk into the RAM. apparently coined from the phrase 'pulling yourself up by your own bootstraps'. (No, I had never heard of such a phrase before either.) The point is that the computer manages to start itself up.
Business Television		A service provided by BT. This is a private satellite-based network that enables your company to broadcast a message or presentation to a specific audience anywhere in the world.
Byte		This is a unit of information, equal to a character such as a letter, number, symbol or space. When you type an **a** it takes up 1 byte. 1 byte consists of 8 bits – *See* Kbytes.
CAD		Computer Aided Design
Capacity		This is term used about disk storage to indicate how much information it can store. The capacity is measured in kilobytes (K) or Megabytes (Mb).
Card		*See* Board
CD-ROM	See-dee-rom	Compact Disk – Read Only Memory – a format of CD, which can hold multimedia.
Central Processing Unit		*See* CPU
click		To press and release the mouse button.

Term	Pronunciation /usage	Definition
Clipboard		A temporary part of computer memory that holds whatever you cut or copy. It only holds one item at a time, so for example if you cut one thing with a view to pasting it, then cut something else, you will have lost the first item you cut, but the second item will still be in memory ready to paste.
Command		An instruction to the computer. You issue a command when using the disk operating system, an application or a programming language.
Communications programs		Applications software that enables you to communicate with other computers by transferring information from one computer to another.
Compiled programs		You won't be able to read or change your application programs because they will have been compiled, that is, translated into a machine language which your computer can understand, but you can't.
CONFIG.SYS	Pronounced: CONFIG DOT SYS or CONFIG SYS	This is a special file that sets configuration settings on your computer for different parts of your computer and peripherals when you switch it on. Some applications require special commands in this file to enable the application to work.
CPU		Central Processing Unit. The brain of the computer consisting of a storage, arithmetic unit and control unit – these days taking up no more than a silicon chip called a microprocessor mounted on a circuit board. The processing speed of the CPU has a bearing on how fast your computer is. The higher the number the faster the computer probably is, for example, a 80486 is faster than an 80386.

Term	Pronunciation /usage	Definition
Cursor		A marker on your screen, usually flashing, which tells you where you are on the screen. The cursor can be a different shape or colour depending on what application you are using – but it is usually either a small vertical bar or square.
Data		Facts fed into the computer – which when processed give information. The term data implies that the information is coded or organized so that it is easy to process, sort or interpret.
Database		An application used to store and retrieve related information stored in a structured records – such as client names and addresses, or a stock inventory.
Density		A description of the amount of information you can store on a floppy disk. Double density disks store 360K or 720K of data. High density disks store 1.2M or 1.44Mb of data.
Desktop publishing application		An application combining text and graphic layout facilities enabling users to create professional looking documents such as brochures and newsletters and illustrated reports.
Dialog box	Dialogue box	An on-screen window that displays options. It is the means by which you carry on a dialogue with the computer – hence the name. Often a dialog box reminds you of the results of your command and asks you to confirm that you want to complete this action – the dialog box offers you the opportunity to Cancel if you gave the command by mistake.

Term	Pronunciation /usage	Definition
Directory		A directory is an area of computer memory where you store files. A computer is like a filing cabinet — and just as you may label different filing cabinet drawers, so there is the facility on the computer to divide up the memory into directories which you can use to help you organize your files in to subject matter groups.
Disc		The principal storage medium used by the PC. *See* floppy disk and hard disk.
Disc drive		The device used to read and write on floppy disks and hard disks. As the disk spins a read-write head moves over the disk leaving ('writing') or locating ('reading') magnetic signals on the disk.
DOS	doss	An acronym for Disk Operating System. DOS carries out the commands you give to the computer — for example, when you save a file in a particular directory, DOS organizes the file according to your instructions.
DOS prompt	doss prompt	The mixture of symbols and letters that tells you that DOS is waiting for you to give a command. For example: C:\>
DOS screen	doss screen	The screen in which you give your DOS commands, and where you see the DOS prompt.
Double clicking		Pressing the mouse button twice in quick succession.
Drag		Using the mouse to point at an item, then holding down the mouse button and dragging the mouse so that the item moves on the screen.

Term	Pronunciation /usage	Definition
Email		An abbreviation for 'electronic mail'. Its function is to enable you to send messages and receive them inside an organization, but also to other organizations, even in other countries.
Extension	File extension	The extension to a file name which follows a dot. For example in the file name LETTER1.DOC – the extension is DOC. Here is a list of common extensions and their meanings: **BAK** – backup file **BAT** – batch file **COM** – program file **EXE** – executable file (usually a program that starts up an application) **WKS** – a worksheet file (usually the extension added to the end of your filename when you have been working on a spreadsheet).
External modem		A small box which sits beside your computer and connects to the computer on one side and to a telephone line on the other. Its purpose is to translate signals from the computer into a format acceptable to a telephone line.
Fax machine		A machine that sends a replica of any form of printed, typed, handwritten or drawn material.
File		The computer work you do, whether its a report, memo, database, or chart etc., is stored as a file on hard or floppy disk so that you can refer to it again in the future.
File name		The name you assign to a file when you store it to disk. A file name consists of two parts, the name and the extension. The name itself can be up to eight characters, but no punctuation, mathematical characters, or

Term	Pronunciation /usage	Definition

File name (*contd*)

spaces. It is followed by a full stop and a three character extension – which can be optional. For example letter1.doc is a valid file name. letter1 is the name of the file, doc is its extension. You can type the file name in most applications in upper or lower case or a mixture – it does not normally make any difference. In order for the computer to recognize file names there are few rules for them. Each file in a directory must have a different name – otherwise what will happen is that one file replaces the other – as the computer can't tell the difference between them. The file name consists of two parts – the first part is the name which can consist of up to eight letters of the alpha or numeric characters (letters or numbers) – but no punctuation, spaces or mathematical characters. LETTER1.DOC is a valid filename. If you use an application you save your file within that application before you close it down. It is often best to give your file a name up to eight characters long – without using an extension. This is because the application you are using will often add a meaningful extension to your file name. For example, if you are working in the Microsoft Word Word-processing package, each file you save is given the extension.doc on the end. This tells you it is a document file which you created in Word.

Floppy disk

Used for storing files on a permanent basis. Floppy disks can be bought in two different sizes: 3½ and 5¼. There are two densities, double density and high density. 5¼ disks can come in two capacities – 360 K or 1.2 Mb. 3½ disks can store either 720 K or 1.4 Mb.

Term	Pronunciation /usage	Definition
Floppy disk drive		A device, usually built in to the system unit. It is used to write to the disk in order to store files. It is also used to read the disk in order to retrieve files.
Format		There are two typical situations in which the word format is used. If you want to use a floppy disk it has to be formatted before you can use it – to format a disk is to prepare it for use. Format is also used about a document where you might use various commands in a format menu which will allow you to do things like choose a border for your text, underline text and so on.
Function keys		At the top of your keyboard you see keys: F1, F2, F3 and so on, to F10 or F12. Different applications use each function key differently.
Generation		First generation computer: Computers built in 50s and early 60s using valve circuitry. Second generation computers: Computers built in the early or mid 60s using transistors instead of valves. Third generation computers: Computers built in the mid 60s onwards using micro chip technology.
Gigabyte	gigabyte	One billion bytes. Abbreviated to G or Gig.
GUI	gooey	Graphical User Interface. A computer environment that uses pictures and symbols to make the computer more easy to use or 'intuitive'. Microsoft Windows is an example.

Term	Pronunciation /usage	Definition
Hard disk		Used for storing files on a permanent basis. Hard disks vary in size from 20Mb to over 155Mb. Some are built in to the computer, others can be attached to the computer by a cable so that they are portable.
Hardware		The physical parts of the computer, inside and out, that you can touch and see. For example, the system unit, screen, mouse, printer and so on.
Icon	eye-con	A picture that represents an application, a file or other elements within Microsoft Windows.
Information		Information itself is the meaning that comes from data.
Input		Data or instructions is sent into the computer via an input device such as a keyboard.
Integrated software		A collection of two or more programs that operate independently but are also compatible so that they can share information. Typically you get word-processing, spreadsheet, database and communications in one package.
Internal modem		A card that fits into one of the expansion slots inside a computer which provides the port where you plug your computer to the telephone line. Its purpose is to translate signals from the computer into a format acceptable to a telephone line. These are the most commonly used type of modem now.
Internet		An abbreviation for 'internetwork' – which means a network of computer networks. These networks supply a phenomenal array of business and leisure resources.

Term	Pronunciation /usage	Definition
Kilobytes (sometimes abbreviated to Kbytes or K)	Kill-o-bites, kay-bites or kay	Kilobytes = 1024 bytes. Used to measure the memory capacity of a computer RAM or disk drive e.g. (TO COMPLETE)
Keyboard		An input device. You give commands to the computer by typing on the keyboard.
Light pen		A pen-like instrument used for inputting information, for example, in supermarkets light pens are dragged across bar codes to enter the price on the article onto the system.
Local Area Network or LAN	lan (as in 'land' without the 'd' at the end)	A Local Area Network, called a LAN for short, is a way of linking several computers and peripherals, usually on the same site, for example, spread throughout an office block.
Magnetic storage		Disks or tapes which have a magnetic coating and information is stored magnetically.
Megabyte	megga-bite	1 megabyte = 1 million bytes
Memory		The part of the computer that stores information. PCs have two types of memory, RAM which empties each time the computer is switched off, and ROM which contains the same data all the time – it cannot be added to.
Menu		A list of commands or options displayed on the computer screen.
Microchip		Sometimes referred to as a silicon chip because it was made of a sliver of silicon, perhaps up to an eighth of an inch square, layered with alternate insulating and semiconducting materials, on which an electric circuit, in miniature, is etched.

Term	Pronunciation /usage	Definition
Microprocessor		The central processing unit or CPU.
Modem		A box like piece of equipment that stands next to your computer, or a board inside it, enabling your computer to be attached to other computers via the telephone lines.
Monitor		An output device and a piece of hardware, like a television screen, that displays computer options and your data.
Mouse		An input device and a piece of hardware, pulled or pushed along a flat surface by the user to move a pointer on the screen, in order make selections and give commands.
Mouse pointer		The on-screen symbol that moves as the user moves the mouse. The pointer changes shape depending on the task, for example it becomes an arrow when pointing and clicking on buttons, but is displayed as an I-bar when used to point at word-processed text.
MPC		Multimedia PC – an IBM compatible computer that can deliver multimedia (text, sound, video, animation).
Multimedia		A few years ago, the term multimedia referred to the mix of information including text, sound, pictures and video you could store on a CD-ROM. It was not multimedia unless CD-ROM is the storage media. Now the term seems to have changed in meaning again, because people are referring to the mix of information – text, sound, pictures, video, animation – as multimedia. Whether this has been accessed from hard disk, Internet, CD-ROM does not seem to come into the definition.

Term	Pronunciation /usage	Definition
Output		Data that is sent from the computer to an output device such as the monitor or printer.
Pager		A pager is a small device the size of a small calculator, you can clip onto an article of clothing or put in a pocket, in and outside the office. It is sometimes called a 'bleeper' because its function is to 'bleep' at you when someone calls you on the 'phone – and in this way it alerts you to the fact that someone needs to talk to you or you are needed at a different location.
Path		The route from the root directory to the file. For example, c:\sales\letters\com1.doc. Here, c: is the drive, \ is the root directory, sales is the directory, letters is the sub-directory, and com1.doc is the file name.
Peripheral		A piece of hardware, attached to your computer, not part of your computer. A printer is peripheral.
Port		A plug at the back of the system unit that you use to connect a peripheral. It acts as a gateway through which the data is transmitted from the computer to the peripheral. So for example you use a port to attach your mouse, monitor and printer to the computer.
Program		A list of sequential instructions for the computer. An application is normally made up of several programs. Software is the collective term for programs or applications.
Programmer		A person who writes programs.

Term	Pronunciation /usage	Definition
RAM	ram	Random Access Memory – a temporary storage area in the computer which is emptied when the computer is switched off.
Resolution		A measurement of the sharpness of image on the monitor.
ROM		Read Only Memory, storage inside the computer where information is held permanently and cannot be changed.
Root directory		The main directory – all other directories are contained in the root directory.
Site licence		Usually, the purchaser of a piece of software pays for the right to use that piece of software on a **particular** computer, or a **specified number** of computers. A **site licence** however, entitles the purchaser to use the software on **any** computer at a particular site.
Software		All computer programs associated with the computer, for example applications software. You use hardware to run software.
Spreadsheet		An application that enables you to make calculations, project figures for the future, carry out 'what if' calculations, supplies short cuts to quantities of calculations that would be time-consuming to do manually using a calculator, and create graphs of the information within a few seconds.
Subdirectory		A directory within a directory. A directory being a group of files.
Syntax		The grammatical rules you follow when you issue a DOS command or write a computer program.

Term	Pronunciation /usage	Definition
System software		The programs which provide the link between the applications software and the hardware. For example DOS (Disk Operating System) and Windows.
System unit		The box-like component of the PC that contains the CPU and other necessary cards inside, and one or more disc drives, possibly one or more CD-ROM drives.
Telecommunications		Technology enabling you to send data down telephone lines.
Telecottages		Business support services set up in rural areas to support home-based and rural industries and teleworkers.
Telephone switchboard		An electronic device which organizes incoming and outgoing telephone calls.
Telex service		Telex is a BT service that your organization can subscribe to. It involves hiring the line to the telex exchange and the rental of a teleprinter, plus the charge for each telex sent.
Utilities		Packages that enable you to manage data operations and storage. DOS is a collection of utilities and you can get other utilities to help you with specific tasks such as checking your disks for viruses.
VDU		A television-like terminal used to display the application screens, for example, showing text, tables or charts and available commands.

Term	Pronunciation /usage	Definition
Video conferencing		The ability to talk to people over long distances, by using video cameras and monitors connected telecommunication networks. This provides the ability to send and receive live images such as people, documents, flip charts and sales demonstrations.
Wide Area Network or WAN	wan to rhyme with 'tan'	A network of computers in which there can be several miles of land or sea between computers.
Wild card		A character used to represent other characters in a DOS command. The wildcard * = any characters. The wildcard ? = any one character. So for example if, at the DOS prompt you wished to list all the files in the root directory beginning with a the command would be dir c:a*.*.
Window		A rectangular area on the screen through which you view an application, or document.
Word processor		An application you can use to manipulate text – type letters, memos, brochures and so on – and print them.

Appendix I

ROMAN NUMERALS

1   Units: I (1)   X (10)   C (100)   M (1000)
      Fives: V (5)   L (50)   D (500)

2 The four **unit** symbols can be repeated to write two or three units of the **same** symbol. For example:

I	=	1	II	=	2	III	=	3
X	=	10	XX	=	20	XXX	=	30
C	=	100	CC	=	20	CCC	=	300
M	=	1000	MM	=	2000	MMM	=	3000

3 The symbol 'I' may be used or repeated (up to III) **after** any of the above units or fives, in which case it **adds** to the symbol it follows. For example:

I	=	1	VI	=	6	XI	=	11	LI	=	51
II	=	2	VII	=	7	XI	=	12	LII	=	52
III	=	3	VII	=	8	XIII	=	13	LIII	=	53

CI	=	101	DI	=	501	MI	=	1001
CII	=	102	DII	=	502	MII	=	1002
CIII	=	103	DIII	=	503	MIII	=	1003

4 To write 4, 9, 40, 400 and 900, take the symbol immediately **above** and put the appropriate unit symbol **in front**, which means that it is **subtracted** from the higher symbol. For example:

4	(5–1)	=	IV	9	(10–1)	=	IX
40	(50–10)	=	XL	90	(100–10)	=	XC
400	(500–100)	=	CD	900	(1000–100)	=	CM

Note:

> I can be placed **only** before V or X
>
> X can be placed **only** before L or C
>
> C can be placed **only** before D or M

5 To express numbers other than those in point 4, take the unit or five symbol immediately **below** and add it to the remaining symbols by putting these after the unit or five symbol. For example:

6	(5 + 1)	=	VI	14	(10 + 4)	=	XIV
7	(5 + 2)	=	VII	15	(10 + 5)	=	XV
8	(5 + 3)	=	VIII	16	(10 + 6)	=	XVI
				17	(10 + 7)	=	XVII
				18	(10 + 8)	=	XVIII

60	(50 + 10)	=	LX	600	(500 + 100)	=	DC
70	(50 + 20)	=	LXX	700	(500 + 200)	=	DCC
80	(50 + 30)	=	LXXX	800	(500 + 300)	=	DCCC

6 A horizontal line drawn over the unit symbol means that the unit is multiplied by 1000. For example:

$$\overline{M} \quad = \quad 1000 \quad x \quad 1000 \quad = \quad 1,000,000$$

7 To convert Arabic figures into Roman numerals, take each figure in turn. For example, to convert 467, proceed as follows:

400	=	500	−	100	=	CD;
60	=	50	+	10	=	LC
7	=	5	+	2	=	VII

Therefore, 467 = CDLXVII

This Appendix is reproduced by kind permission of Stanley Thorne (Publishers) Ltd, from *Applied Typing*, 6th ed, by A., Drummond & A., Coles-Mogford with I., Scattergood (1983)

Appendix II

CONVERSION TABLES

Length

1 mm	0.039 in	1/64 in	0.397 mm
2 mm	0.079 in	1/32 in	0.794 mm
3 mm	0.118 in	1/16 in	1.587 mm
4 mm	0.158 in	1/8 in	3.175 mm
5 mm	0.197 in	1/4 in	6.350 mm
6 mm	0.236 in	1/2 in	12.700 mm
7 mm	0.276 in	3/4 in	19.050 mm
8 mm	0.315 in	1 in	25.400 mm
9 mm	0.354 in	12 in (1 ft)	304.800 mm
10 mm (1 cm)	0.394 in	36 in (1 yd)	914.400 mm
1000 mm (1 m)	39.370 in	1 mile (1760 yds)	1.609 k

Area

1 sq cm	0.155 sq in
1 sq in	6.452 sq cm
1 sq m	1.196 sq yds
1 sq ft	929.030 sq cm
1 sq km	0.386 sq miles
1 sq yd	0.836 sq m
1 acre (4840 yd 2)	4046.86 sq m
1 sq mile	2.59 sq km

Volume

1 cu cm	0.061 cu in
1 cu in	16.387 cu cm
1 cu m	1.308 cu yds
1 cu ft	0.028 cu m
1 cu yd	0.765 cu m

Capacity

1 cl	0.352 fl oz
1 fl oz	2.841 cl
1 l	1.760 pints
1 pint	0.568 l
1 gallon	4.546 l

Weight

1 g	0.035 oz
1 oz	28.350 g
1 kg	2.205 lb.
1 lb.	0.454 kg
1 metric ton	0.984 tons
1 cwt	50.802 kg
1 ton	1.016 metric tons

Temperature

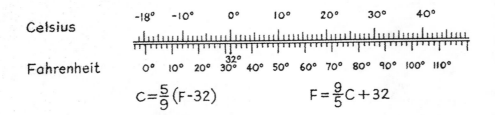

$$C = \frac{5}{9}(F-32) \qquad F = \frac{9}{5}C + 32$$

The above tables of both metric and imperial equivalents are correct to three places of decimals.

Appendix III

A TRAINING APPROACH FOR COMPUTER SKILLS

Six common computer training misconceptions

☒ *Training is a perk*

Wrong – Training is a necessity. Properly planned computer training relates directly to departmental needs which in turn should relate directly to the company's business plan. It is the intelligent and efficient way to ensure motivated, well-informed and effective users.

☒ *Any computer course will do*

Wrong – I have known Staff Development departments send staff on training for software that is not even used anywhere in the company! They think they are updating staff skills! The member of staff has an interesting day attending the training but of course never has the opportunity to apply these skills to the benefit of the company. It is vital to only send staff for training on the software currently in use by the company – not software that is currently being discussed, or software that may be useful some time in the future. See the next point.

☒ *We need to give the training in plenty of time so that staff are prepared when the computer or software arrives.*

Wrong – I have come across managers who think that they are very organized sending their staff on software training twelve weeks before the software will be available to use. Unfortunately, if there is a gap between user training and actually using the software, then it will be a miracle if they remember **any** of their newly learnt skills. The longer the gap, the worse the problem. More than a week, and they may not like to admit it, but they will not remember anything they have learnt. This is normal, but staff will feel it is their own fault and blame themselves for being bad or slow learners. Other staff will react angrily to the situation – either blaming the course – 'it was a dreadful course anyway'; or blaming the software – 'the software is too difficult'. In either case it is not the course participant that has failed, but whoever organized the training in the first place.

Ideally, each member of staff's training needs to be completed the day or two before the computer or software is ready to use. Any earlier and you risk skills learnt on the course being forgotten.

✖ It's the same as a typewriter so they don't really need any training

Wrong – Let's consider how someone uses a typewriter. There is only one type of interaction between the user and the typewriter – the user presses the control (this may be a character key or carriage return,, or the on-off switch) and the typewriter has one response to one switch. Now, consider how someone uses a computer. The user has a variety of commands available. With many of these commands more information is required from the user. There are several different ways the computer asks for information, or displays the options available to the user. This is its 'interface'. The user has to be trained to use this interface which offers thousands more options and possibilities than a typewriter ever could. Training is a must because the interface can be initially misleading and confusing to three groups of people:

- a new user;
- an experienced user confronted with a new application;
- an experienced user confronted with a new version of an
- application they have been using.

A lack of training is often the cause of frustration and disenchantment with computers – and any subsequent training may not be able to counteract these negative feelings.

✖ The software is 'intuitive' – so the staff do not need training. They'll pick it up as they go along.

Wrong – 'Intuitive' software, is software that had been cleverly designed to be as obvious to use as possible. With the introduction of graphical user interfaces this type of software design is the norm. However, the advantages are only really obvious to people who have experience of a fairly wide range of applications. If your staff are generally inexperienced, or there is a change of software, they will need training.

✖ Train the staff in the software they have to use for work – that's all the need.

Wrong – There are several aspects to computer training. You can see in the approach outlined below that the training is not just about how to use a specific application, but also more general information such as how to use a computer safely, and very importantly, how to organize files properly. In all these courses 65–70 per cent of the time should be spent **practising** the relevant skills. For most situations this approach would be ideal:

Training for computer skills

- **Starting off properly**: Covering how to switch the machine on, enter the required software, carry out simple but useful tasks on that software, save what has been done, exit the software, and switch the computer off. Health and safety at the computer should also be covered. The end result here should be a confident user, able to do a few specific things very well and safely.
- **Learning how to organize computer work**: Covering how to organize work on the computer, to include how file storage works, how to create directories, how to store files in specific directories, how to clear files that are no longer needed and how to make backups. Until you and your staff are able to do these things you run the risk of files being lost, and serious things going wrong. The end result here should be a confident user, able to organize directories and files on computer. You may want to include in the training the procedures and conventions you want to use across the office for things like backups, directory creation and naming files.
- **Learn more about the system software**: Covering how to use a graphical user interface (GUI). This training should include how to use features for opening and closing windows, switching between windows, working in more than one window at a time. Transferring items from one software package to another. Included in this demonstration should be how to use the Windows help facility. Particularly how to search for help, print out help and switch between the help window and the activity being carried out.
- **Learn more about the applications software**: In-depth training into the software and how it relates to processes and procedures at work.

It is important that users are not expected to do what they have not been trained to do. This will mean introducing your new processes slowly, in parallel with the relevant training.

Further Reading

In addition to the reading lists at the end of each chapter, the following general reading list covers the writing of some of the management gurus who have something to say on the subject of effective communication within organizations.

De Bono, E., *The Use of Lateral Thinking*, McGraw-Hill, 1967

De Bono, E., *Lateral Thinking for Management*, McGraw-Hill, 1971

De Bono, E., *Conflicts: A Better Way To Resolve Them*, Penguin, 1985

De Bono, E., *I Am Right, You Are Wrong*, Viking, 1990

Drucker, P.F., *The Practice of Management*, Harper & Row, 1954

Drucker, P.F., *Management: Tasks, Responsibilities, Practices*, Harper & Row, 1954

Drucker, P.F., *The New Realities*, Heinemann, 1989

Handy, C., *The Age of Unreason*, Arrow, 1989

Handy, C., *Inside Organizations: 21 Ideas for Managers*, BBC Books, 1990

Herzberg, F., *Managerial Choice: To Be Efficient And To Be Human*, Dow Jones, 1976

McGregor, D., *Leadership and Motivation*, MIT Press, 1966

McGregor, D., *The Professional Manager,* McGraw-Hill, 1967

Maslow, A.H., *Motivation and Personality*, Harper & Row, 1970

Pascale, R.T., *Managing On The Edge*, Viking, 1990

Peters, T., & Waterman Jr, R.H., *In Search Of Excellence*, Harper & Row, 1982

Que, Books published by Que are good in-depth guides to applications and system software

Vaughan, T., *Multimedia Making It Work*, 2nd edn, McGraw-Hill, 1994

Winder, D., *All You Need To Know About The Internet*, Future Publishing, 1995

Also available from Cassell

Index